DATE DUE

OC 24 '97			
FE 19 '98			
MY 27 '99			
OC 2 '03			
OC 2 '03			
OC 29 '03			
NO 24 '03			
JA 23 '04			

DEMCO 38-296

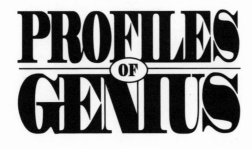

PROFILES OF GENIUS

Thirteen Creative Men Who Changed the World

TED TURNER
Turner Broadcasting

FRED SMITH
Federal Express

ARTHUR JONES
Nautilus

TOM MONAGHAN
Domino's Pizza

AKIO MORITA
Sony

WILLIAM LEAR
Lear Jet

MARCEL BICH
Bic Pens and Lighters

SOICHIRO HONDA
Honda Motors

HOWARD HEAD
Head Ski and Prince Tennis

NOLAN BUSHNELL
Atari and Pizza Time Theatre

STEVEN JOBS
Apple Computer and Next

SOLOMON PRICE
The Price Club

WILLIAM GATES III
Microsoft

GENE N. LANDRUM

Prometheus Books • *Buffalo, New York*

Published 1993 by Prometheus Books

97 96 95 94 93   5 4 3 2

Library of Congress Cataloging-in-Publication Data

Landrum, Gene N.
    Profiles of genius : thirteen creative men who changed the world / by Gene N. Landrum.
    Includes bibliographical references and index.
    ISBN 0-87975-832-5
    1. Businessmen—Biography. 2. Creative ability in business—Case studies. 3. Success in business—Case studies. I. Title.
HC29.L36   1993
338′.04′0922—dc20   93-18637
                                                                        CIP

Printed in the United States of America on acid-free paper.

To

my wife Diedra,

my editor, confidante, soul-mate, counselor,

and

consultant on the Promethean personality

Contents

8   CONTENTS

Preface

The selection process for the top innovative visionaries of the past forty years was destined to be controversial at best. There were certainly many entrepreneurs who achieved noteworthy creations who were not included in this study. However, some rational parameters were necessary, which led to an arbitrary set of criteria for the selection of these subjects. If the potential candidates did not meet these criteria they were discarded, regardless of their accomplishments.

Father of the industry. The individual must have created a new industry or major market segment within an industry. Sam Walton (Wal-Mart) and Lee Iacocca (Chrysler) did not meet this criterion.

Five-year market dominance. The product or service created must have been a dominant factor within the industry and have remained so for a period of at least five years. John DeLorean of Delorean Motor Company and Donald Burr of People's Express did not meet this criterion.

Technology or market created by the entrepreneur. The individual must have created the idea, designed the product or service, or have implemented the idea or design personally via a new firm or existing company. Al Neuharth of Gannett and Ross Perot of Electronic Data Services did not meet this criterion.

Mass-market appeal. The product or service must have been national or international in scope. Donald Trump's New York real estate empire did not meet this criterion.

Contemporary development. The product or service must have been created or made its initial impact since 1950. Thomas Edison, Henry Ford, David Packard, and Edwin Land (Polaroid) did not meet this criterion.

9

Entrepreneurs Considered but Not Selected

There were numerous individuals considered in arriving at the final list of pre-eminent innovative visionaries. Some of these went through a cursory evaluation due to their high visibility, such as Donald Trump and Lee Iacocca. Others have had dramatic financial success, such as Bill Hewlett, David Packard, Edwin Land, An Wang, and Sam Walton. They were potential candidates but did not quite fit the profile demanded based on the aforementioned criteria. The entrepreneurial spirit of Mary Kay and Judi Sheppard Misset (Jazzercise) are awe-inspiring. They were considered potential subjects to the point of reading their books and contacting their firms. The market dominance of the innovations of Ray Kroc, Rupert Murdoch, and Ross Perot certainly merited consideration, but these captains of industry also did not quite meet the necessary criteria.

Detailed research was done on Sandra Kurtzig (Ask Computers) and Gilbert Trigano (Club Med). Kemmons Wilson, the originator of Holiday Inns, was a prime candidate due to his breakthrough innovation of drive-in lodging in the 1950s. The same was true of Allen Neuharth of Gannett, who was instrumental in the *USA Today* innovation. Richard Branson was a candidate for his Virgin Atlantic empire in England. The founders of Jacuzzi, Baskin-Robbins, Calvin Klein, and Famous Amos were also looked at in detail, as were the founders of Computerland, Intel, Walden University, Lotus, Radio Shack, and Micron. These candidates were eliminated for functional or practical reasons at various stages of the research effort. After deliberation over vast amounts of research data thirteen candidates chosen for this book appear to best represent the ideal in terms of contemporary innovations of a multinational nature that have mass market appeal and have sustained their multinational influence over a long period time.

1

Creative Genius— What Makes the Difference?

I have no particular talent, I am merely extremely inquisitive.

—Albert Einstein

It takes a deaf man to hear.

—Thomas Edison

Art is not truth, art is a lie that makes us realize the truth.

—Pablo Picasso

What causes creative behavior? Is it an inborn trait or talent, as commonly believed? Is nature more important than nurture?—heredity more critical than environment? It would seem not—if you consider the histories of the great geniuses Edison, Picasso, Einstein, and the other thirteen individuals explored in this work. Freud hypothesized that our personalities become indelibly imprinted between the ages of five and eight. No doubt many of our behavioral idiosyncracies and traits have been formed due to imprinting and conditioning by this early age, but the evidence indicates that this infantile personality is set in putty, not concrete.

Albert Einstein was the acknowledged scientific genius of the nuclear age, Pablo Picasso the most revered and idolized painter of the twentieth century, and Thomas Edison the most prolific inventor in history. A comparative analysis of what made them tick, what made them so unbelievably creative and innovative, and how they accomplished such prodigious feats of creativity seems to be the correct methodology to home in on the critical factors of creative genius. The similarity of experiences and behavior characteristics is amazing for these three titans of creativity. Additionally, the thirteen contemporary visionaries in this work have behavior characteristics and experiences surprisingly similar

11

to the three older geniuses. This is a disparate group of individuals, yet they have many similarities and differences which are discussed and speculated on as follows.

Early Physical Moves Create Independence

Ironically many of the factors that appear to be predictive of creative behavior are internal patterns imprinted by our early experiences with the external world. Early physical moves was one of these imprintings. It was experienced by virtually every one of the subjects in this work. The family unit usually remained intact for these creative prodigies, but the whole family experienced numerous relocations to foreign environments. The early moving is a consistent finding with the longitudinal research done at Berkeley (Institute for Personality Assessment—MacKinnon, 1965), where they found successful architects had a similar history of childhood relocations to foreign environments.

The Edison family moved from Ohio to Michigan when Edison was four and then back to Ohio. As a teenager he lived in Cincinnati, Detroit, Louisville, New Orleans, Memphis, and Boston. Picasso moved from Malaga, Spain, to Carunna around the age of eight, and then on to Barcelona at the age of fifteen. Einstein was moved at the age of one from Ulm, Germany, to Munich and then as a teenager to Milan, Italy. He lived in Zurich, Switzerland, from the age of fifteen. He was relegated to a boarding house in Munich during one move, which was also a childhood experience of Ted Turner, Fred Smith, Arthur Jones, Marcel Bich, and Tom Monaghan.

Entrepreneurial Fathers

Edison's father engaged in lumber, grain, and other trades as an entrepreneur. Success and failure followed him constantly, causing the family to relocate. It also gave Thomas reason for embarking on an entrepreneurial career at the ripe old age of twelve. Picasso's father was a tutor, teacher, artist, and curator at various times during an up-and-down existence in nineteenth-century Spain. He was constantly reassigned or dismissed, causing a disruptive existence for the family. Einstein's father was an entrepreneur operating a technology shop in nineteenth-century Germany. He specialized in electrical engineering projects and failed at business at least three different times. He badgered Albert to become an electrical engineer, which Albert resisted.

First Born

Einstein and Picasso were first-born children, as were nine of the thirteen contemporary innovators in this work. In fact, twelve of the thirteen contemporary innovators were first-born males, which is a consistent finding in most research on creative superstars. Thomas Edison was not first born but seventh, but just as in the case of Freud, was born when the next youngest sibling at home was fourteen and no longer a threat to the attention and idolization of the newborn. Doting attention and expectations, demands for perfection, and assumed preeminence appear to be the critical factors at work among those raised as first-born or only children.

Unusual Female Influence in Upbringing

Picasso had five women in the household doting on him for his first five years. His mother told him, "If you become a soldier, you'll be a general. If you become a monk, you'll end up as Pope" (Huffington, 1988). A testimony to this inordinate feminine influence was Picasso taking his mother's name, "Picasso," instead of his father's name, "Ruiz." According to Picasso's biographer, he "had a lifelong ambivalence about women. Contempt was his way of exorcising his fear of women's power."

Thomas Edison said, "My mother was the making of me, she understood me; she let me follow my bent." He didn't start school until the age of eight and then his mother removed him from school after only three months. The schoolmaster had said her son was backward. She disagreed and embarked on his formal education herself. Einstein was byproduct of a Jewish mother and a sister who idolized him. He was in fact more devoted to his sister than to his wives throughout his life. His biographer Clark said, "He preferred to have women rather than men around him."

Rebellious Nonconformity

The Jewish Einstein family were so nontraditional and independent in their thinking that they sent Albert to a Catholic elementary school. Albert Einstein always had a "fundamental irreverence for authority," according to Ronald Clark (Einstein, 1988). He detested German authoritarianism, which culminated in his rejecting his German citizenship at the age of fifteen. Picasso, on the other hand, rejected all authority from any group. He had an "all-consuming urge to challenge, shock, to destroy and remake the world," according to Matisse. He said, "I too am against everything. I too believe that everything is unknown, that everything is an enemy" (Huffington, 1988). In elementary school he would purposely disobey the rules in order to be sent to a cell where he could do what he wished—draw. Edison was always his own person and marched to his own drummer. He was never accepted by the scientific establishment and he never accepted them. The media characterized him as "an eccentric and iconoclast." He delighted in statements that surprised, stunned or provoked his listeners.

Slow Learners as Children

Both Picasso and Einstein were classified as dyslexics. Edison never started attending school until he was eight years old and then dropped out after only three months of formal schooling. Later in life he said, "Do you think I would have amounted to anything if I went to school? University-trained scientists only saw that which they were taught to look for and thus missed the great secrets of nature" (Josephson, 1959). Picasso could not pass elementary school classwork and his father bribed the officials to allow him to continue his education. Reading and writing were mysteries he never comprehended. Einstein didn't talk until very late and at age nine was still less than fluent. He was expelled from the Munich Gymnasium for being disruptive and when his father asked the headmaster what profession Albert was suited for he responded, "It doesn't matter; he'll never make a success of anything" (Clark, 1988). All three hated school with a passion, as did most of the creative visionaries studied here. Many of these visionaries were asked to leave their institutions as being unduly disruptive (Turner and Monaghan).

Early Inquisitiveness

Edison had a laboratory at the age of ten and his own business selling food on the railroad at the age of twelve. As a teenager he traveled the country living by his wits as telegrapher, laborer, and mechanic. He began experimenting and inventing as a teenager with his own lab on a train and operated his own design business by the age of twenty. Picasso could draw before he could write or talk. His first words were "piz" for "pencil" or to "draw." He discovered the magic of the rewards of creation by drawing for his parents and relatives to receive ego strokes. He painted the Malaga port at the age of seven and a bullfight in oil at eight. He said later, "I never did any childish drawings. Never. Not even when I was a small boy." Einstein was purported to have deduced that something in space was the cause of his father's compass always pointing in the same direction. This was at the age of five. Albert became the master of his own education and destiny by the age of fifteen. He mastered the violin early.

A Work Ethic Beyond Economic Need

Edison worked eighteen-hour days most of his life and two shifts (sixteen-hour days) at the age of seventy-five. Most of his life and until the age of sixty-five his standard work day consisted of eighteen-hour days with catnaps and occasional breaks to eat. He would often sleep in the lab for days at a time. According to Josephson, "Edison could never understand the limitations of the strength of other men because his own mental and physical endurance seemed to be without limit . . . Edison worked with minimum rest periods of three or four hours a day, his enormous recuperative powers helping to sustain him." He once locked his employees and himself in a "laboratory prison" for sixty hours without food or water until they fixed a difficult problem. Work was the elixir of his life, as it is for most great creative geniuses, including Picasso and Einstein.

Picasso had an "inexhaustible vitality," according to Huffington. He produced prodigious amounts of work daily for most of his life. He painted eighteen hours a day virtually every day until his eighties and when asked why, he said, "I never get tired." Biographer Huffington said, "Picasso had inexhaustible passion and energy for work and sex." At the age of ninety he was still producing works of art and told a reporter, "I am overburdened with work. I don't have a single second to spare, and can't think of anything else."

Einstein felt that there was never enough time for work. He discarded socks as unnecessary complications of life that diverted one's energies from what was important. He was considered the absent-minded professor not because he was, but because he relegated social and other events to the category of useless wastes of his time and energy.

Resolute Optimism and Confidence

The great innovators of the world are so confident in their own ability that they often come across as arrogant. Einstein's talent was discounted by educators in his early life due to his arrogance. Professor Weber of Zurich Polytechnic told him, "But you have one fault: one can't tell you anything." Einstein had the self-confidence of one with vision who "knows." He believed in himself to such a degree that he was capable of defying Newtonian physics and all scientific doctrine of the time. His optimism was borne of inquisitiveness that transcended the dogma of the day.

Edison had an irrepressible enthusiasm for every one of his inventions. He said, "The trouble with other inventors is that they try a few things and quit. I never quit until I get what I want" (Josephson, 1959). Edison would call a press conference just after having had an insightful idea for a new concept. He would then rush back to the lab to validate his intuitive concept through experimentation. This was Edison's method of self-motivation and overachievement and also served to gain him financial support for his inventions.

Picasso said, "I do not seek, I find," a tribute to his irrepressible self-confidence. Picasso believed in Nietzsche's superman and honestly felt he was the personification of the superman in art. This omniscient belief system allowed him to defy all authority based on his "divine" right of creativity and exploration. At eighteen, he did a drawing of himself called "I the King," a testimony to an all-consuming self-confidence.

Voracious Readers as Children

Books are often the confidants, friends, and mistresses of the creative. Edison buried himself in literature from a very early age. He read Victor Hugo's *Les Miserables* at ten and Newton's *Principia* shortly after. At twelve he was quoted as saying, "My refuge was the Detroit Public Library. I started with the first book on the bottom shelf and went through the lot, one by one. I didn't read a few books, I read the library." Edison's method of investigating a new subject was in buying a book and reading on it. Einstein read Immanuel Kant's *Critique of Pure Reason* at the age of thirteen and understood it. He also read Darwin and other scientific textbooks for pleasure. Picasso read Nietzsche, especially his "will to power" thesis, and, like Hitler, was convinced that his iconoclastic behavior and creative destruction were philosophically apt. Voracious reading habits and fantasy heroes have been key to most innovative and creative genius. It imprints "larger than life" images on the psyches of the young and gives them positive role models to emulate later in life.

Charismatic Showman

The ability to charm and motivate followers is fundamental to becoming a great leader. Introverted personalities such as Edison, Picasso, and especially Einstein are not easily identified with charisma and showmanship. Einstein's biographer, Ronald Clark, says, "If Charisma has a modern meaning outside the public relations trade, Einstein had it." This is surprising when conjuring up the image of the introverted personality and absent-minded professor who fathered the theory of relativity.

Picasso's charismatic influence was legend. Gertrude Stein said, "His radiance, an inner fire one sensed in him, gave him a sort of magnetism which I was unable to resist." His long-term friend, poet Jean Cocteau, characterized him as having "a discharge of electricity . . . rigor, flair, showmanship and magnetic radiance. He radiated an almost cosmic and irresistible self-confidence." Coco Channel remarked, "I trembled when near him." This was a remarkable influence for a diminutive, five-foot-three Spaniard.

Edison had an irrepressible, infectious enthusiasm. He would use the press for instant credibility and communication for his projects. He was news and the media were responsible for immortalizing him as "the wizard of Menlo Park" and "the father of modern electronics." His ability to charm the world as the great technological problem-solver was truly charismatic. The public rushed to his labs for a glimpse of the "wizard" at work.

Living on the Edge

"Factories or Death" was Edison's slogan when the bankers and Wall Street were reticent to finance the production of his light bulb in 1880. He supplied 90 percent of the needed capital because "Wall Street could not see its way clear to finance a new and untried business . . . I was forced to go into the manufacturing business myself." The factories ultimately became the nucleus of the conglomerate General Electric. Edison's philosophy was, "You take the risk to build your product or you do not survive to see the product flourish." He risked his total fortune and was broke at the age of fifty-five after years of creative success based on his belief in his products. Ted Turner did the same in the launching of CNN. Turner used Edison's same logic in risking his $100 million fortune on the CNN launch. He was convinced it was "CNN or defeat"—by the networks. He has always maintained that the greater risk was "doing nothing."

Picasso believed that he could impact reality with his art. He never attempted to appease the establishment and therefore lived his life on the edge of acceptance. He joined the Communist Party after the war in absolute defiance of the establishment. He said, "Painting is freedom. . . . If you jump, you might fall on the wrong side of the rope. But if you're not willing to take the risk of breaking your neck, what good is it? You don't jump at all. You have to wake people up. To revolutionize their way of identifying things. You've got to create images they won't accept." Huffington said, "He had an exhibitionist's need to defy and shock" and he was "trapped in his anxiety and egocentricity."

Einstein biographer Clark said, "A good deal of his genius lay in the imagination which gave him courage to challenge accepted beliefs." Einstein was not afraid to risk upsetting the establishment and once did so by defying his mentor, Max Planck, causing Clark to say, "Only Einstein would have dared to do it." He was comfortable living on the edge and violating classical dogmatic attitudes.

Conclusions

The personality characteristics and other influences found to be dominant in the creative and entrepreneurial geniuses in this work are very consistent. The differences found between the nineteenth-century childhoods of Edison, Einstein, and Picasso and the late-twentieth-century childhoods of Turner, Gates, Smith, et al. are not that different. Their work ethic and risk-taking natures are the same. It shows that success is a matter of focusing energy in an intransigent drive towards goals using unassailable self-esteem to pursue dreams regardless of the obstacles. A Promethean spirit is important, as are other facets of the personality of the creator/entrepreneur. This personality type is not genetically preconditioned, as many of us have been taught. The Promethean personality is based on an individual's desire to create and innovate, not on some lucky draw of the cards at birth.

Thomas Edison, Pablo Picasso, and Albert Einstein were from completely disparate economic backgrounds, countries, and even spoke different languages. Edison, the great inventor/entrepreneur, Picasso, the artist who chronicled the twentieth century's unconscious, and Einstein, the quintessential intellect of our age, all had a Promethean temperament. Their very natures are synonymous with creativity and innovation. The thirteen contemporary innovators detailed in this book are more recent examples of this creative genius in action. The similarity of their personality characteristics is amazing. Every one of the thirteen contemporary innovators in this work are as different as were Edison, Einstein, and Picasso, but their differences are only reinforced by their similarities.

The Promethean temperament is without question the single most universal factor in large-scale innovative success and these individuals epitomize that behavior. The following biographical profiles give character to these geniuses. Change and creative destruction was their forte. This will be discussed in chapter 2.

2

Innovation, Change, and the Creative Personality

The future exists first in *imagination,* then in *will,* then in *reality.*
—R. A. Wilson, *Prometheus Rising,* 1983

Change and Creative Behavior

The story of creative and innovative behavior is about change. In this case it is about thirteen iconoclastic individuals who have demonstrated a unique ability to deal with change in the world and redefine it for their own purposes. These inno-visionary characters, not unlike Edison, Picasso, and Einstein, became consummate entrepreneurs, creators, and innovators because of a driven and focused desire to change the world. They used a personal vision as their tool to overcome the vagaries of change and did not allow change to rule their lives as many less-innovative personalities are wont to do. These visionaries never blindly accepted traditional dogmas as their roadmap for life. In fact, they defied most conventions and authority, and existing experts were used only to gather information from, as they became their own experts. They ignored the establishment and marched to their own drummer regardless of the price to be paid for their rebellion.

These individualists listened to their introspective drums, which beat tunes unheard by the establishment. They usually pursued their fantasies and dreams with the fervor of a sailor on short leave. Their style was to operate as if they were double-parked on the highway of life, and were not afraid of infuriating the fundamentalists who gave tickets for violating the rules of the industry.

Their unique vision of the world and inviolable belief in themselves gave

19

them an ability to create and innovate beyond the norm. Their exceptional personality traits and behavior methodologies (discussed in the next chapter) allowed them to redefine the way the world communicates, works, plays, eats, and entertains itself. What made them unique? Why were they able to achieve what great industrial conglomerates were unable to achieve? Because, as I will discuss later, they were creative and destructive often in a simultaneous burst of creative energy, disregarding and disrespectful of the established order of things. Picasso epitomized this phenomenon of being both creator and destroyer in virtually everything he did.

The innovative genius is almost always a qualitative mentality who is right-brain driven while living in a quantitatively driven left-brain world. He uses inductive logic to realize holistic solutions while the establishment world is striving for a deductive reality using mechanistic solutions to maintain the status quo. These visionaries are Promethean-spirited, driving them to tread where others are afraid and inspiring them to bet the farm on their personal visions of reality. This willingness to sacrifice the present order of things for a better future is seldom available to the traditionalist mentality and almost always available to the visionary personality.

Iconoclasts—Change Artists of the World

Change is personified in America by the Silicon Valley—an area in northern California bounded by Stanford University in Palo Alto to the north and the garlic fields of Gilroy to the south. This world of integrated circuits, alternative lifestyles, and the drug culture is the domain of iconoclast entrepreneurs and innovators. These individuals are not necessarily insane or psychotic (due to their maverick natures), as the traditionalists are often wont to say. They gain their unsavory reputations because they are willing to challenge the given way. They personify the Edisons, Picassos, and Einsteins who were never willing to accept the present and existing ways of the world as sacrosanct or inviolable. This renegade attitude makes them nonconformist and eccentric and therefore feared by the fundamentalist majority. Their creative talent is their strength, which is the very trait that makes them abhorrent to the traditionalists, who forever protect the status quo. Silicon Valley has become known as the spawning ground of the new and different due to the large population of creative geniuses living there who constantly defy the old and established.

Rebellion is one of the key fundamental traits found in Edison, Picasso, and Einstein and also in the thirteen contemporary visionaries studied here. It is essential to the truly inno-visionary personality and critical to all large-scale breakthrough innovation. A nonconforming attitude and rebellion against the status quo is integral to successful creativity and entrepreneurship. It is also available for anyone so inclined to pursue a career in creative endeavors. Normally thought to be inborn, it has recently been shown that anyone can master the traits and characteristics of the creative. Anyone willing to pay the price of being labeled eccentric and different can become a creative and innovative person. Changing lifelong imprints and conditioning is the only obstacle in the path of creativity and innovation for anyone with slightly above-average talent.

California—Creative and Crazy

Silicon Valley spawned countless new technological products between 1950 and 1990. These ranged from the creation of chemically induced birth control by Syntex to the invention of the microprocessor—computer on a chip—by Fairchild and Intel. The Valley was beset with entrepreneurial whiz kids who emulated the mid-nineteenth-century Gold Rushers. This Silicon Valley mentality of creative destruction was aimed at utilizing what George Gilder termed the "microcosm"—the evolution of all products to solid state, making them smaller, faster, and cheaper. Change was their god and no existing product or concept was safe from their inquisitiveness.

Why Silicon Valley?

Michael Hutchison in *The Anatomy of Sex and Power* suggests that as this country was settled the "Big T"—thrill-seeking and high testosterone—personalities continued their trek West, continually moving away from the more structured cities and societies that were not accepting of their eccentric and nonconformist styles of behavior. When they reached California they were met by the raging Pacific, could go no further, and therefore settled that state as the devil's advocate for America's unconscious. Hutchison's theory is that "Big T" personalities are found in greater abundance in California than in any other place in America. My twenty years' experience in Silicon Valley validates that observation, as does the fact that California has had more Nobel laureates than all other states combined.

Creativity and risk-taking behavior are highly correlated to high testosterone, according to Frank Farley of the University of Wisconsin. Three of the thirteen individuals in this work are from California and they typically took inordinate risks, lived by their wits, and meet the test of Farley's Big T personality type. The typical executive in Silicon Valley is far more inclined to risk-taking, libidinally driven lifestyles, and highly creative endeavors than those in other parts of the country where I have lived and worked. One of the reasons is the acceptance of nonconforming behavior in the Valley. When you are in a house with deviants, no one is considered deviant, and societally induced conformity is lessened if not eliminated. In other words, the executive who takes inordinate risks to hit the jackpot in Silicon Valley is not under the same pressure of compliance to corporate dogma as the executive in other, more traditionally based locales.

The Paradox of Silicon Valley

Silicon Valley entrepreneurs typically exhibit unique traits and qualities not found in other areas of the country. They scorn tradition, disregard personal self-preservation, dismiss nay-saying authorities, take inordinate risks, intuit new concepts, and persevere beyond the ordinary. These characteristics are diametrically opposed to those taught in management school and a dramatic contrast to those personality traits revered by big business and academia.

Were these entrepreneurs genetically different? No. Were they more intelligent? No. Were they educated differently? No. Their success was a self-fulfilling prophecy based on their inflated optimism and belief in their own dreams of reality. And it was all right to be different in Silicon Valley. These renegade entrepreneurs constantly violated most of the sacrosanct dogmas and policies considered gospel in more traditional organizations. In a high-risk environment it is more acceptable to take high risks. It is more acceptable to question the established way of things. It is also all right to dress, act, and manage a company in a different style from that considered acceptable in Boston, Chicago, or Cincinnati.

Personality can never be removed from its social setting, as Adler pointed out, and the Silicon Valley is a prime example of this process at work. Personality then becomes one of the dominant factors for predicting success or failure in all creative, innovative, and entrepreneurial endeavors. I also believe it is why the Japanese have been so eminently successful at the innovative process and why Detroit has not.

Silicon Chips and Entrepreneurship

Silicon Valley spawned the integrated circuit (Fairchild), the microprocessor (Intel), the first video games (Atari), and the first personal computer (Apple). Nolan Bushnell and Steve Jobs, two of the subjects in this book, were products of the Silicon Valley and two of the most bizarre and nonconforming of them. They were rebels beyond belief. Their management styles were considered eccentric or even psychotic by more traditional executives. Their unconventional business behavior was inspired by qualitative, intuitive, and inductive reasoning that contradicted all traditional disciplines taught by the business schools. However, they were eminently successful in spite of their bizarre business practices. Bushnell accumulated a personal net worth of some $80 million by age thirty-six. Steve Jobs amassed some $225 million by age twenty-four. It was not uncommon to attend a party of one hundred people in the early eighties where half of the individuals were multimillionaires. Such are the rewards of entrepreneurial risk in stratospheric levels. Great risk is always rewarded with great personal remuneration if the success is commensurate to the risk.

Personal Computers and the Creative Personality

If the personality is the panacea for successful creativity and innovation then we should look at the personality in some depth. Figure 1 shows the personal computer as a metaphor for the development of the human personality. Since personality is the basis for my conclusions on success in creative and innovative endeavors, I find it interesting to depict the evolutionary development of the computer and the personality as analogous.

Humans acquire their personality as a function of their peculiar genetic evolution. That is, anyone's height, eye color, and gender (at least for the present) are a function of their inherited genes. This is analogous to requiring an Apple or IBM-compatible personal computer, which is a fixed-logic type machine based on its manufacturing specifications. Various imprintings occur prenatally and determine the outcome of many personal traits such as a proclivity for right- or left-handedness. Jung and others (Reich's orgone) believe there is a collective unconscious that also affects all people in a collective and universal sense. The PC is likewise imprinted with an operating system such as MS-DOS in order to deal with the outside world in many respects similar to the human developmental process. The individual acquires many new evolutionary techniques to deal with its environment by various conditionings, especially during the infantile and growth stages of development. Various results occur such as extroverted and introverted behaviors based on these conditionings. The PC is then conditioned by another level of software such as Windows, which allows it to interact with the world in a distinct style that makes it different. The human computer learns to function and interact with its environment. Individuals likewise learn to take risk and avoid risk in order to appease inner drives for fulfillment or to avoid the fears of failure. The PC uses many application programs such as WordPerfect and Lotus 1-2-3 to function in the day-to-day world. The human learns similarly how to function and survive.

Figure 1

Personal Computer as Personality Metaphor

HUMAN	HUMAN PERSONALITY: EVOLUTIONARY STAGES OF CHANGE		COMPUTER
	Developmental	*Functional*	
Genetic Qualities (Male/Female)	RNA/DNA	Eye Color	IBM or Apple Macintosh Hardware
Collective Uncon- scious (Reich's Orgone)	Imprinting	Left/Right Handedness	Operating Soft- ware (MS-DOS)
Unconscious	Conditioning	Extroversion Introversion	Applications Soft- ware (Windows)
Conscious	Learning	Risk-taking	WordPerfect Lotus

This metaphor is just that, and is not meant to demean the human in any way nor to elevate the PC to any exalted level of eminence. The developmental stages, however, have meaning relative to anyone wanting to become creative and innovative and change the way the world functions. At each stage or level of development it becomes easier and easier to change and evolve from one program to another for either the PC or for any personality. The belief that a personality is extroverted or introverted and cannot be changed to meet the requirements of the individual is as antiquated as saying the computer can only function as a word processor and not for other functions required for the given situation. Imprinting, conditioning, and learning is what has created the individual personality and this work is aimed at showing how unique individuals with different personalities changed the world based on their unique personalities. Any of their behavior traits are available to anyone desirous of such behavior. It is only a matter of paying the price to change. The individual subjects in this work were not dealt the best hands, not the hands they would have preferred, but they invariably played the hands with elegance and passion to win at the game of creativity and innovation. Anyone desiring to accomplish the same can do so if they are willing to pay the price of entry to the game.

Change—The Inno-visionary's Bible

All great innovations or creative endeavors must deal with change. The Greeks were the first to deal with "change" as a philosophical concept. Heraclitus said, "Permanence is an illusion" and "I cannot step into the river twice" to describe how fleeting life is and that change is the only constant. Socrates introduced man into the equation by creating the word "psyche" and Aristotle refined the concept by creating the first psychology of behavior. Hippocrates defined four temperaments of man: sanguine, choleric, phlegmatic, and melancholic. Greek mythology then had Zeus commission four gods to represent the temperaments of man. Prometheus—the alter-ego of the consummate innovator—was commissioned as the god who gave man science and technology and saved him from ignorance. He did so by robbing fire from the sun and instilling it in man, thereby transforming him from clay to an enlightened state. Prometheus was sentenced to a terrible death by being "nailed hard and fast in the open sky" while vultures tore at his liver for his attempt to give man enlightenment. This precedent was to be reenacted over the next 2,500 years with virtually every innovator who dared to enlighten the masses with new concepts that violated traditional dogmas.

Innovators and Creators as Loners

Edison, Einstein, and Picasso were loners. They spent their youth reading and in an introspective search for happiness to overcome their feelings of rejection and solitude. They were unbelievably creative but also rejected by their peers and traditionalists. Their experience has precedents among the famous and infamous.

Galileo was ostracized by the Catholic Church for his telescope as was Guttenburg for creating type. Columbus was imprisoned, Newton and Pasteur ridiculed, and Darwin charged with heresy. Giordano Bruno was burned at the stake in 1600 for teaching that the earth moves. Professor John Henry Popper pronounced that Edison's electric light bulb invention had no future. And Edison himself refuted Tesla's alternating current generators in defense of his own direct current theories. J. P. Morgan told Alexander Bell that his invention had "no commercial value." *Scientific American* reported the Wright Brothers' flight as a hoax. The ultimate rejection would be humorous if not so sad. A top broadcast executive in the thirties sent a junior executive to the lobby to get rid of the kook who had a radio that would transmit pictures. This executive warned the young man to heed all caution and make sure the lunatic in the lobby did not have guns or knives. The kook in the lobby was Milo Farnsworth, who had created the first operating television. The fear of the unknown had once again created a self-proclaimed inquisition against anyone daring to change the existing way. The Promethean spirit was, as always, forced to circumvent the establishment in order to overcome ignorance and hostility against the new and different.

The above resistances to change are almost always traceable to organizations that are in control of industries, markets, or dogmas. Giordano Bruno's execution was due to the Catholic Church wanting to maintain total control over a changing society. So-called experts have long used ignorance to gain control in any society in any era. Experts have an investment in their present expertise and will kill anyone or anything attempting to usurp that expertise. Until the experts are out of power or die the new has a hard time gaining acceptance without terrible conflict. An example was Edison's refutation of Tesla's alternating current system, which was based on Edison's ego and self-serving desires to protect his direct current concepts. He went to his death believing that his DC system was the better way than AC to transmit electricity.

Simple Sells

Recent research verifies that all organizations are more effective in dealing with change if they are small and less complex. That is, small is beautiful in dynamic environments—small companies, small systems, small organizations. Dr. Illya Prigogine, a 1977 Nobel Prize winner, proved that, "The more complex the system, the greater is its instability." This theory gives credence to the point of this book, that almost all creative breakthroughs belong to neophyte and small organizations and are virtually never given birth by large, complex organizations. Prigogine proved mathematically that dealing with change demands less complexity and simpler organizations. That is exactly what a new start-up entrepreneurial organization is and why these organizations have been responsible for the majority of the growth in America for the past twenty years. Additionally, the simple and highly focused personality of the small entrepreneur is what has allowed him to overcome the awesome economic advantage of large industry leaders.

Risk—The Inno-visionary's Elixir for Success

The ability to take risks to achieve goals is fundamental to success in the innovative process. A strong risk-taking nature is probably the most overriding consistency found in the behaviors of the thirteen individuals in this book (see figure 2). No other trait was as universal in their characters or as pervasive through both their business and personal lives. The ability to bet the farm on one's belief is fundamental to successful entrepreneurship. Money is only one issue in assessing risk-taking behavior. A resilient psyche capable of absorbing attacks on reputation, intelligence, ego, competence, and families is also critical to successful innovation. Open hostility and ego attacks often accompany any attempt at "destroying the existing ways of things." In other words, risking reputation and psychological abuse is high on the list of positive risk-taking behavior necesary for creating change.

The money risk is often of secondary importance when the industry experts, your closest associates, the media, and even your family says "you're crazy." However, the great innovators and creators never considered the economics of any venture. Project success at whatever cost was always the underlying motivation behind all creative endeavor. Risk-takers seem to fall into the first of the three categories, detailed in figure 2.

The operating styles of the three management types can be explained in terms of a sporting event. Risk-takers play continual offense even when the situation calls for a more cautious approach. Care-takers play defense even when the situation calls for a more aggressive stance or approach. Under-takers have given up the game prior to starting, as they are not expecting to win and thus play neither offense nor defense but just show up and occasionally play the game "not to lose," in contrast to playing the game to win.

One of the findings in this research is that those individuals who attempt to take *all* of the risk out of any venture also take out *all* of the potential opportunity. Fear drives people to eliminate risk when they should be evaluating the nature of the risks and *not* attempting to eliminate it, as the risk is what makes all ventures both interesting and rewarding. If an opportunity does not have risk, it is usually not worth the effort. Do you know any CPAs lately who have ventured out into the unknown waters of "risk opportunity" and become billionaires? I have never heard of one.

Risk-Reward Curve

The risk-reward curve shown in figure 3 depicts the roles played by the mature organization, which is far more comfortable operating in a risk-averse manner, and the new start-up venture, which is classically prone to live on the edge with rampant risk-taking as its strategy. The entrepreneur sacrifices everything because he has little to lose. His motive is greed, in contrast to the mature organization, which is motivated by fear.

Research on large-scale innovative visionaries indicates that they tend to defy the above risk-reward principles. These visionaries (a Ted Turner or Fred Smith) tend to continue to risk long beyond the time when the business factors dictate the risk. Their risk-taking decisions remain in the start-up stage or

Figure 2

Management Types

RISK-TAKERS

Leaders who function best in entrepreneurial organizations
Have a right-brain/intuitive operating style
Have a long-term, qualitative perspective
Primarily motivated by greed
Personified by creators, entrepreneurs, innovators

CARE-TAKERS

Followers who function best in static organizations
Have a left-brain/sensor operating style
Have a short-term, quantitative perspective
Motivated by security
Personified by bureaucrats, experts, politicians

UNDER-TAKERS

Parasites who function best in declining organizations or those in chaos
Have a brain-dead operating style
Have a negative and past-oriented perspective
Motivated by fear of failure or being discovered
Personified by criminals, clerks, parasites

entrepreneurial area. The classic or traditional executive remains in the mature area of risk-taking as they are programmed to protect their asset base at all costs. When the Ted Turners and Bill Lears finally reached this lofty position, they continued in their entrepreneurial risk-taking ways.

There Are No Experts

Darwin and Einstein were loners when it came to their great breakthroughs. There were no experts to help them as the experts were the very ones who were being overturned—on the one hand, the Church's biblical interpretation of the origins of life and, on the other, Newton's principles. Einstein's theory of relativity was a nonexistent concept and any data would have prejudiced his intuitive belief systems on space and time. Market research cannot assist

Figure 3

Entrepreneurial Risk/Reward Curve

The Fear vs. Greed Syndrome

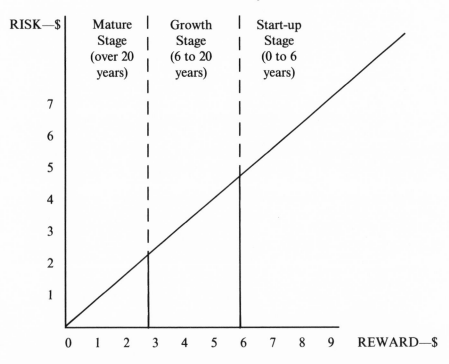

Innovative firms experience risks inversely related to their age and size. That is, during the first 6 months a firm will risk everything for a large potential opportunity since the firm's assets and revenues are virtually nonexistent. As an organization moves down the curve with higher assets and therefore much greater "risk of loss," their propensity to take risks drops in direct linear proportion to their size and age. They go from risk-taking to care-taking and finally to under-taking.

in the solution of nonexistent concepts. Peter Drucker said, "Market research does not work. One cannot do market research on something that does not exist" (Drucker, 1985). Darwin certainly didn't use his Bible training from Oxford to substantiate his theory of natural selection. And none of the inno-visionaries in this work did any focus group studies on their breakthrough concepts.

New concepts will always generate spurious responses that will prove counterproductive to the innovative process. Since experts virtually always use the

Figure 4

Organizational Risk/Reward Principles

Organizational Size. Risk is a function of the size of a business. The large firms are risk-averse and small firms take inordinate risk.

Velocity of Growth. Risk varies as a function of a company's growth. Speed creates errors, thus more risk, and slowness begets greater efficiency and less risk.

Maturity of Organization. Risk increases with the age of an organization. New firms explore the unknown and old firms protect the past.

Sacred Cows in Organizations Inhibit Risk-taking. As infrastructure is built icons—policies, procedures, etc.—become sacrosanct and are protected.

Smallness Enhances Large-scale Risk-taking. Reaction time in decision-making, product wars, and new opportunities are the forte of smallness.

External Pressures Influence Risk-taking. Soicietal, community, trade union, and government actions usually inhibit risk-taking.

Wall Street Paranoia. The quarterly report inhibits risk-taking as it places all emphasis on short-term rather than long-term opportunities—the self-preservation principle.

Cultural Inhibitors. Lifetime employment makes risk-taking less critical and far more objective. Insecurity in employment inhibits risk-taking more than any factor.

Theory X Management Inhibits Risk-taking. Hierarchical organizations inhibit risk-taking through administrative controls and procedures.

Visibility Influences Risk-taking. Low-profile firms tend to take greater risks than high-profile firms, which have the media, governments, and stockholders to placate.

Figure 5

Personal Risk-taking Propensity of Inno-visionaries
They risked far beyond the time needed for business survival!

Innovators	Personal Risk-taking Activities
Marcel Bich	Competed in the America's Cup three times. Likens business to competitive sports and runs his business like a sporting contest.
Nolan Bushnell	Competitive skier, gambler, with personal planes and boats. Competed in the Transpac Race twice and finished first once. Inveterate game player and risk-taker. Played videos for hours at $100 per game.
William Gates	Likes fast boats and sports cars. Many speeding tickets. At Harvard would stay up all night playing poker; called poker addict by Harvard classmates. Accused of "red mist" (race drivers' adrenalin hit) due to competitive nature.
Howard Head	Alpine skier, scuba diver, and competitor at tennis. Won $6,000 playing poker to finance Head Ski.
Soichiro Honda	Professional race car driver (almost killed at age 36). Helicopter pilot at age 55. Competitive golfer and gambler.
Steven Jobs	Owns personal jet and competitive in everything in business and private.
Arthur Jones	Bush pilot and wing-walker at 19. Wild game hunter (caught crocodiles by hand). Bitten by poisonous snakes hundreds of times. Crashed jeep into tree at 75 mph. Saved an associate from a wild lion and received broken neck.
Bill Lear	Pilot at 19, three plane crashes, flew in days of no instruments and designed his own plane. Flew the Lear as a test pilot. Fearless competitor and gambler. Placed a 10-year-old in the cockpit and hid in the back to irritate the FAA.
Tom Monaghan	Private pilot. Almost died flying his own small Cessna twice. Marathoner, racketball, planes, boats. Fearless.
Akio Morita	Pilot at 60. Competitive tennis, golf, and skiing.
Sol Price	Social consciousness, not only competitive drive. Fearless in business.
Fred Smith	Pilot at 15. Two Purple Hearts, Silver & Bronze Stars, and Vietnamese Cross of Gallantry. Two tours at front in Vietnam. Gambled and won $26,000 to make payroll at Federal Express in early 1970s. Very competitive at tennis.
Ted Turner	Competitive sailor. Won the America's Cup in 1977 and the Fastnet Death Race in 1979, in which 15 racers died. Inveterate gambler. Once won a bet by drinking bottle of Chivas Regal in ten minutes. 350 racing trophies. Risked TBS three times after he was enormously successful and wealthy. Did not need to take any risks, let alone the $100 million gamble for the whole company.

past in attempting to predict the future they are always at a severe disadvantage in creative endeavors to those using intuitive thinking and discarding the past in their interpretations of reality. Innovators use the "gut" in creating their concepts. Using a past model of reality will doom any new product to failure, as it will any new venture. It will create erroneous conclusions in justifying the existing way of things.

A major problem with expert opinion is the tendency of the expert to have a strong desire to preserve and validate the present way of things, since experts happen to have an ego investment in the very thing in which they are considered an expert. If they should invest in its destruction, they are in essence destroying some of their own credibility. The ego is injured, as is the very pedestal on which the expert stands, if he should ever admit to the new. Therefore the expert never capitulates. That is why Thomas Kuhn was able to show that it takes thirty years (*The Structure of Scientific Revolutions,* 1959) for any new concept to gain acceptance. Other research has shown that older scientists die (Wilson, 1990) before accepting new concepts that violate their own beliefs in reality.

Expert Myopia

In 1959, Haloid, a small research firm, offered IBM the sales rights for the 914 plain paper copier. Haloid was looking for someone with the human and financial resources to take this revolutionary new product to market. IBM, in doing its due diligence, hired a consulting group with supposed expertise in technological products—Arthur D. Little—to advise it on the market potential for this unknown product. The consultants spent three months on the project and estimated the worldwide market potential for the plain paper copier at five thousand total units. One of the justifications for their opinion was the cheap price of carbon paper! IBM used the consultants' "expert" advice to reject Haloid's offer. Ten years later (1969) Haloid, now known as Xerox, was generating sales revenues of $1 billion from the 914 copier every year. These so-called "experts" had predicted five thousand units, which even at the inflated price of $20,000 each would have amounted to $100 million in revenue. What insight! They had missed the market by a quantum amount, but more importantly had misled a client due to their own special expertise in the here and now.

IBM was also involved in another gigantic miscalculation in a market it helped create and dominate. During the mid-sixties, IBM estimated the worldwide potential for word processors at six thousand work stations based on their knowledge of existing technology and preordained beliefs. By 1973 (just eight years later) there were a hundred thousand units in operation, which was still only 4 percent of U.S. work stations. By 1990 there were over fifty million word-processing software programs in use on personal computers with monthly growth alone dwarfing IBM's original estimate. Recent estimates place the potential revenues at $100 million annually by the turn of the century.

Sony engineering executives and market researchers told Chairman Akio Morita that they could not sell ten thousand Walkmans in the mid-1970s. Morita, the consummate visionary and risk-taker, ignored their advice and actually offered to resign as chairman if the product was not as successful as he predicted. Within ten years Sony had sold over twenty million of these units, which the engineers and market researchers said could not be sold because it did not record music as well as play music.

Experts in the exercise equipment field told Arthur Jones that it would be impossible to ever sell a painted exercise machine. He ignored them and proceeded to sell hundreds of millions of dollars in machines that were painted and considered unsalable by the so-called experts. Expert opinion is not only impractical and nonproductive, it is often outright dangerous to the innovative process.

Creative Destruction

Picasso, the consummate creator and destroyer of whatever he touched, was convinced that all creativity was based on destroying the old way. He said, "The painter takes whatever it is and destroys it. At the same time he gives it another life. . . . He must destroy. He demolish the framework itself" (Huffington, 1988). Most innovations in history have had this same need for destruction, as the new is usually incompatible with the old, especially in the world of creativity.

Change creates fear in establishment organizations and paranoia in the minds of the executives hired to protect the status quo in these institutions. This mental set is understandable because Joseph Schumpeter's famous description of the innovative process—"creative destruction"—is fundamental to all change. The new can only be created by destroying the old. A new romance is always created at the expense of an old one. The new building demands the demolition of the old building. A new pizza formula always replaces someone's favorite recipe. A new automobile model always obsoletes its predecessor. The old dies hard but the new is always born at the expense of the old. This is not always a palatable concept, but it is the reality of life in a world of change.

If change requires destruction of the present system or product, then any student of human behavior can accurately predict the resistance to any change by the establishment in any system. The self-preservation principle so inculcated into the psyches of contemporary managers will automatically produce outright hostility to any individual or group suggesting obsolescence of "their" products or programs. The very charter of all corporate entities is "the protection of the assets, principles, and culture of the institution." This "preservation mentality" is obviously in conflict with the acceptance of the maverick (innovative) individuals in any organization. After all, these rebels will destroy the existing way of things. Therefore, resistance to change becomes standard operating procedure and self-preservation behavior becomes the way of life in establishment organizations. This behavior is both confirmed and reinforced by the boards of directors, who also buy into the desire to preserve the status quo. This top down (pyramidal) resistance to all change and innovation in the corporate hierarchy forces the creative and innovative employees to adapt or leave the organization, to engage in the "fight" or "flight" syndrome made famous in stress workshops. Most leave to avoid the conflict required to fight the organizational culture when their only desire is to help the organization through exercising their creativity.

Rebels Are the True Creators

Edison, Picasso, and Einstein were all rebels. They defied authority even as very young children. Einstein was expelled from his Munich high school with the admonition, "Your presence in the class is disruptive and affects the other students" (Clark, 1971). Huffington, Picasso's biographer, painted this picture of his personality: "He defied Law, morality, and convention . . . Rage and rebellion were his forte." Edison's biographer, Josephson, was even more graphic in describing Edison as "a queer fish and eccentric."

Virtually all great breakthrough innovations have emanated from this so-called "fringe" element of the labor force. Innovators are rebels and ostracized by the establishment and therefore have little to lose in defying the sacrosanct dogmas of their dissenters—the traditionalists and experts. The creators and innovators must either capitulate to the establishment and buy into the old ways or go it alone and become entrepreneurs and innovators. They usually pay the price of their nonconformity and become social outcasts, marginal employees, or, at times, great creative geniuses. Examples in history abound of those who worked in other than their fields in order to circumvent the establishment or in defiance of it.

Nicholaus Copernicus perfected his theory of planetary motions while he was a canon at the cathedral of Frauenburg, Poland. Galileo was trained in medicine—not astronomy or science. Luigi Galvani was also trained in medicine, not electricity. His research on how muscles and nerves conduct electricity became the basis for the invention of the electric battery. Gregor Mendel was a clergyman when he propounded the concepts for the foundation of genetics. Einstein created the theory of relativity working as a clerk at the Swiss Patent Office. Charles Darwin was an ordained minister awaiting assignment to a church when he took his historic trip on the *Beagle* and concocted the theory of evolution.

The thirteen inno-visionaries in this book created their concepts as entrepreneurs who had attempted to work with or through the establishment but were severely rejected, ostracized, ignored, or just sent away as pesky upstart kooks. They persevered due to a resilient psyche that allowed them to be ridiculed and rejected without personal devastation from the experience. They utilized powerful self-esteems and strong value systems to overcome their constant rejections. These paradoxes of the innovative process beg for an axiom on the subject:

The most likely to create new concepts tend to stagnate

The most unlikely to create new concepts tend to innovate

Industry leaders normally have all the resources and knowledge to create the new and different, but they and their directors are deeply mired in the preservation of the status quo. They protect their existing products and programs and allow fear to rob them of any chance to create or innovate. Anyone afraid of destroying the old to get the new will never be able to achieve a worthwhile breakthrough innovation. Ten reasons for this corporate ineptitude in the creative process are described in chapter 3.

3

Ten Reasons Why
Traditional Management Types
Are Inept at Innovation

> Large bureaucracies tend to stifle their own purposes. . . . Endemic in most
> industrial organizations, private and public, this problem becomes deadly in
> the microcosm. The pace of change creates too many decisions, too many
> nodes, to be managed effectively in a centralized system.
> —George Gilder, *Microcosm*

Gilder makes a very strong case for "small is beautiful" in the era of the microcosm
(his term for the world of microtechnology), where all things become faster
and smarter as they get smaller. He believes the entrepreneur/innovator is the
only salvation for high-technology organizations to compete in the global
markets. He says, "The balance of power in electronics is moving away from
large established companies toward nimble start-ups focused relentlessly on
innovation." Alvin Toffler agrees with this assessment, as he feels dynamic
change is beyond the ability of the bureaucratic organization to handle. In
his newest work, *Powershift* (1990), he says:

> As an old system cracks, the faceless bureaucrat-managers who run it are
> blown away by a guerilla army of risk-taking investors, promoters, organizers,
> and managers, many of them anti-bureaucratic individualists, all of them skilled
> at either acquiring knowledge or controlling its dissemination.

Toffler's assessment of the large bureaucratic institution is summed up in his
aphorism "Camelphant." He uses this name to define the large, immobile firm
because it has the IQ of the camel and the slow gait of the elephant. The
essence of these macroeconomic arguments is that a dynamic environment

36

demands dynamic organization and management to effectively compete in global markets. A conservative organization protecting its asset and market base is not well equipped to function in an environment that is dependent on quick decisions and insightful problem solving. The hierarchical organization is not comfortable opting for long-range opportunities at the expense of the near-term income statement. The small, quick, and technologically responsive organization with a high risk-taking propensity is far better suited to operate in the dynamic world of business than an industry-leading bureaucracy. Burton Klein of Harvard says that once a firm becomes static all new discoveries (innovations) will come from new firms. A quote from his *Dynamic Economics* (1977) confirms the magnitude of this fact:

> The advance will seldom come from major firms in the industry. In fact, of some fifty inventions. . . . I could find no case in which the advance in question came from a major firm in the industry.

Arrogance

An arrogant attitude is counterproductive to the innovative process. Toffler (1990) said, "Many of the world's largest corporations are as arthritic and arrogant as any Soviet ministry." When a person or organization thinks it knows all of the answers it seldom is capable of functioning in an innovative or creative manner. New opportunities are lost on the pseudo-omniscient since they have closed off all avenues for accepting new knowledge because they perceive they already know what is correct. This attitude is self-defeating in any dynamic environment, especially when the markets or products are evolving and changing as they are in the 1990s. Arrogance is a luxury that is exorbitantly expensive, as is explained by Drucker in *Innovation and Entrepreneurship* (1984):

> Innovations that exploit changes in industry structure are particularly effective if the industry and its markets are dominated by one very large manufacturer or supplier, or a very few . . . these large dominant producers and suppliers, having been successful and unchallenged for many years, tend to be *arrogant.*

Short-term Mentality

Mortgaging the present for the future is endemic to the large, bureaucratic organization. Decisionmaking that always opts for the safe way is not consistent with the necessities of breaking new ground and innovating. All innovation and risk-taking are long-term processes of betting present investment dollars for potential future returns. All of the great innovations in history have had this perspective.

Norman Lear was responsible for breaking down many barriers in network television. He created "All in The Family" and other innovative programs that were visionary. He said,

> Everywhere one looks, it seems to me that short-term thinking in business is the greatest impact on our culture. . . . Short-term thinking is the societal disease of our time.

If a business organization takes care of the long run and treats their customers, suppliers, and employees in that way, the short run will take care of itself. The Japanese have demonstrated this, to the chagrin of many large Western enterprises. The great innovators of the world have done likewise.

Expert Syndrome

The expert mentality of large firms has lost more business opportunities for them than any other factor. An example discussed earlier was IBM's rejection of the Haloid 914 plain paper copier in 1959. Sony would have foregone the twenty-five million Walkman sales had Chairman Akio Morita listened to his experts. The market research at Sony predicted that no one would buy a tape player that would not record as well as play. Morita did not have any insight into consumer preferences, but he was willing to bet his job on his intuitive belief in what he considered a good product idea. Bill Hewlett saved the HP-35 calculator from a similar fate in 1971. The market research department at Hewlett Packard gave the same "expert" opinions on the market acceptance of the first electronic slide rule calculator. The experts predicted that slide rules at $19 would never be replaced by an expensive and sophisticated electronic calculator. Bill Hewlett said, "I don't give a damn if no one else wants one, I do. Build it!" The marketplace predicted to reject his product then made the HP-35 the hottest electronic product in the world for three years.

Bill Lear was told by expert aeronautical engineers that his jet would never fly. Lear, the irascible ninth-grade dropout, built it and flew it himself, to the dismay and chagrin of the experts. IBM, Intel, HP, Atari, and countless others predicted the personal computer business was a hobbyist fad. They said the Apple computer would never sell. Steve Jobs didn't listen. The networks told Ted Turner he was crazy to attempt a global, twenty-four-hour news network. Just ten years later President Bush, Mikhail Gorbachev, and Saddam Hussein were watching CNN News during the Gulf War instead of the experts' stations (the networks). British economist Ely Devons (1954) describes the uncanny immortality of experts who insist on quantifying a qualitative world:

> Like the primitive magicians, all kinds of experts are encouraged to engage in their mysterious calculations and are allowed to preserve their credibility even when events prove them wrong.

It's not what you don't know that hurts you, it's what you think you know that can be devastating. The executives that are not smart enough to know they should not be in a market are the ones best suited to dominate that market, because they do not know they cannot. Bernie Siegel, the famous cancer surgeon turned psychological healer, has shown that doctors have a predisposition for dying in accordance with mortality statistics due to their conditioning in school on the cancer mortality rates. Siegel's research has shown that the little old lady who doesn't know her statistical mortality tends to live far longer than the "expert" doctors who have been conditioned by their quantitative reality.

The expert mentality of the large organization constantly derails its ability to innovate. Conversely, the neophyte nature of the entrepreneur is conducive to the latter's ability to create breakthrough innovations. Mark Sheppard, president of Texas Instruments during the 1970s, commented on why TI was able to outstrip the giants of the electronics industry when it was so inexperienced and small. His insight is prophetic and instructive to those who think they are experts: "Those companies all *knew* the things that weren't possible. We didn't. We were stupid."

MBA Syndrome—The Quantitative Mentality

The left-brained, deductive, quantitative-oriented "numbers crunchers" who have been trained to use "control" and "budgets" and "stringent policies" as their operating style are a serious threat to any new concept. Their "analysis-paralysis" management style is what kills new projects if they cannot be reduced to numerical justification. Most new innovations, cannot, by definition, be reduced to financial justification, especially prior to market acceptance. The "adaptor" personalities who dominate the staffs of traditional organizations are trained to utilize quantitative modeling techniques as taught in academia as a means of approving or denying new product concepts. This methodology is destined to destroy all creativity and innovation.

Any new concept can be rejected through financial analysis. Most large organizations operate in the belief that middle-management numbers crunchers are operating in the best interest of the firm when they "prove" the new project is "unprofitable" and should be cancelled. Ironically, this approach is just as ludicrous for approving projects as it is for killing them. You cannot justify any new product or concept with numbers. Qualitative and intuitive belief in the market opportunity is the most reliable form of product justification.

Left-brained, quantitatively driven staff personnel should never be allowed the opportunity to kill a new project. The innovative process is a function of intuitive and inductive thinking of the highest qualitative nature and only those individuals with the long-range responsibility for the organization should be allowed to shelve a new product. The budgetary mentality of the large organization often violates this principle since it has been groomed to worship the "management by the numbers" game. This mentality fits the model of preservation of assets and existing systems but is totally counter to effective innovation.

Burton Klein said, "Highly structured organizations are inefficient when dealing with changes in their environments." He believed a firm could not remain dynamic if it did not continue to face new challenges and take risks. The pyramidal and hierarchical firms cannot innovate effectively as long as they allow the MBA bean counters to intercede on new product and market opportunities. The lack of the pyramidal structure that encourages quantitative management by the numbers is one of the greatest assets of entrepreneurial firms. It allows them to effectively compete in the areas of creativity and innovation. The Copernican period is past and it is time that business and educational leaders recognize Einstein's gift to us: the world is *qualitative* not *quantitative!*

Cultural Dysfunction

The operating culture of any organization is a factor in its ability to innovate. The larger and older the firm the more it is intolerant of individuality and risk-taking. The protection of assets becomes the paramount objective and this is communicated overtly and covertly through policy actions to management and ultimately to all employees. These cultural influences tend to inhibit creativity in the innovative employee and proves counterproductive to innovation and new product development.

Lifetime employment or lack of job continuity is culturally induced. The threat of job loss is a stressful factor to employees in Western cultures, whereas the employees in Eastern cultures are not so intimidated by such threats. In a culture that promotes lifetime job security (as in Japan), the risk-taking behavior of individuals is not a function of the personal implications of the outcome of the decision as it is in the United States. The American manager will make decisions based on how the decision affects his personal well being.

This virtually never happens in Japan. Personal gains and losses become a major element in every Western decision. In Japan, the personal implications are never a factor.

Entrepreneurs will risk the farm, because it is their farm and they are the recipients of all the rewards and losses. They may lose the company but they will not lose their job. In any large organization, the manager's job is being risked and no manager will risk the loss of his job for a potential organizational gain, even if the risk is small and the gain is potentially large. The only risk that will be taken is one that does not threaten the job of the decision maker. It is this operating culture that is counterproductive to the large firm's ability to innovate. Warren Bennis makes this point in his 1989 leadership book, *On Becoming a Leader:*

> The leader may discover that the culture of his own corporation is an obstacle to the changes he wants to introduce, because as currently constituted, it is more devoted to preserving *itself* than to meeting new challenges.

Organizations Are Intolerant of the Maverick

Truly creative innovative geniuses are rebels, unique, psychopathic, and at times everything in between. They are normally more concerned about a project's future than conforming to bureaucratic idealogies or dogmas. They have a long-term, goal-oriented mentality that is counter to the short-term, now-oriented mentality of the organization. Most organizations have a pyramidal approach that is dedicated to the creation of "me too" employees who follow orders myopically based on a top-down hierarchical management philosophy. This has motivated bureaucracies to control their organizations by keeping employees immature and subservient. This allows for optimum control. Winslow, writing on the creative and innovative process in 1989, said:

> In organizations with defensive climates, tight hierarchies, and autocratic controls, the [innovative] behavior will be seen as disruptive, "kooky," downright immoral and certainly deviant. The truth is that little growth is accomplished by those who have adjusted to the conservative policies of the past.

Risk Aversity

Thomas Edison, the quintessential innovative genius, was notorious for saying that, "Genius is 99 percent perspiration and 1 percent inspiration." This was based on his trial-and-error technique for inventing. This same trial-and-error strategy is the Bible for all entrepreneurs and innovators and should be encouraged by the large organizations who desire to become more innovative. Risk-taking must be tolerated if any innovation is to be successful. Most large organizations do not tolerate risk-taking or trial-and-error creation. Most employees are on board for long-term job benefits and not as part of an entrepreneurial experience and equity opportunity. The emloyee attracted to a bureaucracy is looking for the "womb" relationship offered by such an organization and innovative risk-taking is not their forte.

Due to its nature and organization the large firm will not be inclined to take the same degree of risk as the start-up since it has more to risk. The reason that large firms do not typically take the risks necessary for creating large-scale innovations is the management mentality. The management and employees have no incentive to take risks. Their only incentives are based on taking no risks. In other words, the self-preservation principle will dominate all risk-taking decision-making in any large organization. Therefore, all risk taking will be consistent with the employees' perceived personal gains and not any corporate gains accruing to the organization. The risk objectives of the firm can only be met by meeting the risk objectives of the personnel. Until this concept is understood and rectified, an American organization will not successfully innovate to the same degree as a Japanese firm, whose employees do not face loss of employment due to long-term or high-risk decision-making.

Executive compensation is tied to return on assets or return on sales in the preponderance of corporate organizations in the Western world. This creates a sense of near-term expediency in the minds and actions of the management that is counter to risk-taking and long-range opportunities. Peter Drucker confirms the severity of this in his 1985 work *Innovation and Entrepreneurship:*

> The compensation scheme that is most popular in "large" businesses, one based on return on assets or on investment, is a near-complete bar to innovation.

Micro Versus Macro Vision

The large firm tends to think small and near term in its attempt to innovate. Ironically, the small firms typically think big and long term. What a dichotomy! The large firms establish research and development budgets and are satisfied not to go over the budget. They do not evaluate the revenues generated from the R & D activities because R & D is a staff function and not responsible for creating revenues. They receive their rewards and kudos by obtaining patents and receiving design awards. They receive no recognition or rewards if one of their products generates millions in revenue. But if they are the recipients of a Nobel Prize, they are exuberant even if the firm is in chapter 11. The corporate incentives to innovate are misdirected and counter to the long-term innovative process.

Creativity should not be an end in itself but should only exist as a means to accomplish innovation. The success of any creativity should be marketplace acceptance, not the invention itself. "It ain't creative if it doesn't sell." The only true creativity from the lab is when a product is shipped and paid for, which allows for future research and creativity. Peters and Waterman confirm this in their 1982 book *In Search of Excellence:*

> Big companies seem to foster huge laboratory operations that produce papers and patents by the ton, but rarely new products.

The Xerox Parc research lab in Palo Alto during the 1970s was an example of what should not occur. State-of-the-art products and concepts were created but never implemented due to a political organization that inhibited the commercialization of the products. The Parc Altos personal computer (Macintosh equivalent) was designed, built, programmed, and tested in 1975, far in advance of any other competitive personal computers. This was an absolute breakthrough product that preceded the release of the Apple Macintosh by over eight years. The Altos was never marketed due to Xerox's microvision by their top management. Xerox's concentration on the micro-oriented issues and corporate politics lost a monumental lead for a product they pioneered and should have cashed in on in the marketplace. They had creative vision but not innovative vision. They had the macrovision to create it and the insecurity and microvision to kill it.

Dupont created its New Venture Development group in the 1960s chartered to implement new product developments. But the product innovations fell to nearly zero after early successes like nylon. The company spent over $16 billion on R & D during the 1960s, which by 1969 had contributed exactly nothing to the bottom line. These examples are all too common in the large, microvision organizations.

NIH Syndrome

The not-invented-here syndrome is prevalent in most high-technology firms. The ego orientation and self-preservation principle are what allows this concept to gain foothold in the large organization. The ego must be eliminated from all creative decisions in order to allow the large firm to effectively innovate. The Japanese have operated this way to a much greater degree than American firms. They have far less "ego" involved in their decisionmaking.

One example was Sony's acquisition of the transistor license in 1953. Sony immediately proceeded to use this American-created technology to out-innovate the people who created the concept. Japan is estimated to have paid some $9 billion for U.S. technology during the period between 1956 and 1978. This technology cost the United States an estimated $500 billion to $1 trillion to develop and it was sold to Japan for a piddling $9 billion. One example of this was Sony's acquisition of the Ampex VCR designs. Sony took the Ampex and RCA creations, made vast improvements, and together with JVC came to dominate the worldwide market for video recording.

A quote from the head of the MIT office for technological licensing suggests the degree to which the NIH factor is at work in our larger organizations:

> The biggest surprise to me is that we do most of our licensing to small companies; it's not because we don't offer it to large companies but because large companies aren't designed to successfully integrate embryonic technologies. The structures aren't in place. (Schrage, 1991)

The large firm that allows its creative personnel to protect their egos at the expense of the organization is destined to lose out in the competitive world of changing technologies. Innovation is not just creative product technology. It is the ability to package, market, price, distribute, and merchandise better than others. The single most innovative factor in the Bic lighter success was the "Flick Your BIC" ad. It caught the imagination of the consumer. The single most successful innovation by Honda when he came to America with his revolutionary motorcycles was the ad "You Meet the Nicest People on a Honda." He was creating an image that countered the "black leather jacket" image of his competition and his innovatiion was rewarded with market domination for motorcycles designed for the middle class. There is no room for the NIH factor in the large or small firm, but the concept is far more prevalent in the large firm.

Wall Street Mentality

The worship of the quarterly earnings-per-share (EPS) statement by most large organizations is the single most detrimental factor for innovation. The fear of a lower stock price or loss of employment due to not meeting the quarterly projections, drives the management of public firms to sacrifice the unknown future for the secure present. The Wall Street influence makes this mentality the most overriding factor in long-range decision-making in the organization. Akio Morita of Sony and Soichiro Honda have both been very vocal on how the quarterly earnings pressure is a detriment to America's ability to maintaining global parity. The American executive spends more time looking over his shoulder than peering into the future. The Japanese spend more time projecting the future than covering their tails since they do not have to contend with the quarterly earnings report. This fear over stock price and earnings per share is counterproductive to all long-term decisionmaking and innovation. Long-term projects are too often rejected due to the desire for near-term profits.

The Wall Street influence is not a factor in new start-up firms. The venture capitalists or other investors tend to exercise some influence but nothing like the influence of Wall Street on a large public firm. The entrepreneur fights for survival on a daily basis but this fight tends to toughen them relative to their mortality. The management of the large public firm has no such daily threats and tends to succumb to the Wall Street influences to a much greater degree than the entrepreneur has with his financial threats. Entrepreneurs have permanent job security and the mortality is more with the firm than with their jobs. The reverse is what is operating in all large public firms.

Summary

Between 1977 and 1990 small businesses created most of the twenty million new jobs in the United States. They have been responsible for nearly all new concepts and breakthrough products that were previously nonexistent. The era of the dominant large enterprise that is invincible and omnipotent is over—witness IBM's crisis during 1993 when their losses were in the billions, and the Sears Catalogue, an American institution, which went the way of the horse and buggy in 1993. The inflexible and arrogant monoliths of yesteryear will need to learn to adapt and change in the context of the changing world around them. If they do not, their competitors will engulf them. The economies of scale of the past are history. Speed, technology, intelligent risk-taking, and competitive drive are the ingredients of operating in a dynamic, high-technology global society.

4

The Paradox of Innovation

The man who produces an idea in any field of rational endeavor—the man
who discovers new knowledge—is the permanent benefactor of humanity.
—John Galt in Ayn Rand's *Atlas Shrugged*

One of the ultimate paradoxes in the world of business exists in the area of
innovation and creativity. Ironically, those most likely to create and innovate
tend to stagnate; and those least likely to innovate become the consummate
innovators of the world. Experts in most industries never create the breakthroughs while the less trained personalities break the new ground.

Many real-life examples of this "paradox of business innovation" are found
in the annals of history. Ironically, Edison built the first phonograph and the
first sound movie projector, although he had been deaf since the age of twelve.
Should an individual who never made it to high school have developed the
first engine to meet the emission control standards of the United States while
this individual was not even American? Or how could a nineteen-year-old college
dropout have created the PC computer industry when he had no formal education,
no money, no business acumen, no computer experience? And consider a ninth-
grade dropout developing the most successful business jet in history when the
aeronautical engineers of the time said it wouldn't fly. Why was Sony able
to develop and dominate the worldwide consumer electronics market when the
transistor and solid state electronics industries were created in the United States?
Numerous other paradoxes exist that are just as absurd as the above. These
will be explored later relative to the personal behaviors that were so instrumental
in allowing these innovators to overcome enormous odds.

Industry leaders like IBM, General Motors, Cessna, and Texas Instruments
are only a few of the firms that should have wiped out the above upstarts.
But they didn't. Xerox had developed a Macintosh-type personal computer
called the Altos and had successfully tested it two years prior to the formation

of Apple Computer. This was eight years prior to Apple's release of the Mac-intosh. What happens to these industry leaders once they reach the top? Why do neophyte entrepreneurs "out-innovate" the multinational behemoths who spend billions to lead their industries? This book analyzes thirteen such stories of consummate innovative geniuses who were not only *not* deterred by the giants but actually enjoyed fighting them. Their insights, resilience, unique behaviors and traits, and risk-taking mentality allowed them to overcome the advantages of the industry leaders. The personality characteristics and accom-plishments of these creative geniuses, shown in figure 6, will be explored in great detail in the following chapters.

A Historical Perspective: Darwin to Holiday Inns

Paradoxes in the fields of innovation and creativity have existed for many centuries. During this time change has accelerated at an ever-increasing rate. This interrelationship between innovation and the acceleration of change has been partially responsible for the major breakthroughs seen by the entrepreneurs in this work. The faster the growth rate of any society, the less stable is the establishment (see Prigogine's theory of "dissipative structures") and the greater the chance of change occurring. Advances by the most unlikely of candidates gives credence to Prigogine's theory that change occurs after a system reaches the breaking point and is more likely the more mature the system. The innovations in this work were created in the face of some of the oldest and most mature organizations and by the most unlikely of candidates.

Should Charles Darwin have created the theory of evolution? No way! He was an ordained minister awaiting his assignment within the church and only by accident was he given the opportunity to spend two years on the *Beagle* seeing the world. His trip aroused his natural curiosity on the various species of animals and his intuitive mind drew conclusions diametrically op-posed to everything he had been taught about life and its origins. Here was a man educated to preach the word of God and ironically created the theory of evolution, which overturned the teachings he was trained to spread. His Oxford education and distinguished family background probably saved his books from being burned.

Darwin wrote *On the Origin of Species* due to a naturally inquisitive nature and because of his problem-solving ability. He was not searching for a solution to man's destiny. His elegant theories on biological evolution and natural selection were an accident of fate, common traits found in most creative and innovative people. Darwin's revolutionary theories should have emanated from the research scientists of the day, not from an ordained minister awaiting an assignment within the church.

Figure 6

Inno-visionary Accomplishments

Innovator	Achievement	Firm
Created an Industry		
1. Steve Jobs	First personal computer	Apple—1976
2. Fred Smith	First overnight delivery service	Federal Express—1972
3. Nolan Bushnell	Father of video games—Pong	Atari—1972
4. Bill Gates	Creator of first PC software	Microsoft—1978
Revolutionalized Fitness		
5. Arthur Jones	Created automated exercising	Nautilus—1970
Changed the Way the World Works		
6. Ted Turner	Created 24-hour cable news	CNN—1980
7. Marcel Bich	Created "throwaway" culture	BIC—1953
Changed the Way We Play		
8. Howard Head	Developed first metal ski and first oversized tennis rackets	Head Ski—1950 Prince—1970
Perfected Transportation		
9. Soichiro Honda	Created motorbikes & first pollution-free auto engines. Best-selling auto in world	Honda—1947
10. Bill Lear	Developed first business jets	Lear Jet—1963
Created New Markets		
11. Tom Monaghan	Innovated home-delivered pizza	Domino's—1960
12. Akio Morita	Father of transistor radio, which spawned consumer electronics revolution, Walkman, Trinitron, etc.	Sony—1946
13. Sol Price	Created first warehouse club	Price Club—1977

Six centuries earlier the Englishman Roger Bacon, a Franciscan monk, came up with a revolutionary idea that refraction defects of the eye could be corrected with eyeglasses. He accomplished this extraordinary feat in the face of the incontrovertible evidence of the time that it could not be done. He proceeded to put glasses on the monks mainly because he did not know he could not do it. The renowned scientists of the day had preordained his failure. Roger Bacon's resolute nature and self-determination allowed him to solve a major societal problem and in solving the problem he outwitted the so-called experts of the day.

At the turn of the century the Victorian influence on women caused them to stay in isolation during their pregnancy. There were no maternity clothes made at this time, as the idea of a woman cavorting around in such a state was abhorrent to society. Socializing was *verboten* at the time and there were no maternity clothes available for women to wear to any social event outside the home. The major New York garment manufacturers were afraid to defy the establishment. This myopic mentality left the maternity clothing market open for exploitation by a widowed Lithuanian immigrant with no business acumen or skills.

Lane Bryant, a young widow, took up sewing in Manhattan in order to support her infant son. She did not hesitate to create maternity clothes for pregnant women from New York's high society. By ignoring tradition and the societal ban on women being seen while pregnant she unwittingly liberated women from cloistered pregnancies. She not only transformed society but simultaneously built an empire around a niche market ignored by the industry leaders.

Lane Bryant was not deterred by the social mores of the 1906 Victorian era, as were the industry leaders. The establishment garment manufacturers were more concerned with protecting their existing markets and therefore allowed this immigrant widow to walk off with a major innovative coup. Lane Bryant pioneered in waters where others were afraid to tread. She didn't know she shouldn't have created the Lane Bryant chain of clothing stores, so she followed her intuitive impulses and built the dominant chain in the industry. Lane Bryant now dominates both maternity wear and oversized clothing in the United States, a remarkable achievement for an immigrant widow with zero resources. She shocked the establishment and destroyed a bastion of societal dogma. This is the standard operating forte of the inno-visionary personality.

In 1894, King Gillette was a bottle cap salesman with a penchant for creating a new world order. He wrote a book, *The Human Drift,* due to his aspirations of becoming a political philosopher and building a utopia for all mankind. King Gillette was a failure at creating a new world order and instead diverted his energies to inventing the first razor with replaceable blades in 1901.

Gillette's revolutionary concept—replacing blades not razors—was enhanced by an even more innovative achievement—selling the razor shaft at below cost and marking up the blades to offset the losses on the razor. Having a monopoly on the sale of the highly profitable blades gave him a dominant business that has flourished for the past ninety years.

Gillette's ingenuity created a vast consumable market for replaceable blades and eliminated his competition for razors. His removable blade invention revolutionized shaving during the early 1900s (until that time, shaving was accomplished with a straight razor that required sharpening prior to every shave). King Gillette created a product that should have been created by the existing razor firms of the day. He should not have been the one to have changed the world of shaving, but he did. King Gillette never achieved his dream of becoming a world-renowned political philosopher, but achieved immortality and worldwide acclaim as a preeminent entrepreneur.

Ray Kroc, an uneducated paper cup and milkshake mixer salesman, had entrepreneurial vision. He had the vision to spot a unique market opportunity for an emerging fast-food generation. His intuitive insight into a future market demand was coupled with an obsessive operating style that created the world's largest fast-food operation—McDonald's. Ray Kroc was one of the least likely candidates to become a visionary genius. He had no formal education, no money, and no experience in the fast-food industry. Yet he out-performed all of the corporate fast-food operations in the world. Why? Mostly due to a resolute belief system, vision, a gambling mentality, and a Promethean temperament that pushed him to pursue his dreams.

The Jacuzzi whirlpool was not originally developed as the product for which it has gained international recognition and acclaim. The backyard spa, health club muscle relaxer, and recreational pleasure tub has become the primary market for the jacuzzi. However, it was invented by Candido Jacuzzi in the early 1950s as a therapeutic device to help his son's severe rheumatoid arthritis. In other words, it was created to solve a different problem and fill a different product niche than the one that has made it a commercial success. This is not an isolated case. Problems solved elegantly usually reward those that solve the problems regardless of their original intent.

Richard Carlson, a New York City patent attorney, wanted better copies than his mimeograph could provide. He could not motivate the 1950 business equipment manufacturers to build a plain paper copy machine. So he took the task into his own hands and developed the Xerox 914 plain paper copier in order to solve his problem. Once again, problem resolution was the prime mover behind the innovative effort, and Carlson's elegant solution paid enormous dividends to the innovator—Xerox.

The motel industry was spawned in the early 1950s as a byproduct of an irascible contractor who saw the need for a more practical solution for family housing for the weary traveler. Kemmons Wilson, a small contractor in Memphis, Tennessee, wanted a hotel near the highway, with parking for his car, and without the sophisticated lobby and dining operation associated with hotels of the time. He decided the world needed something he called a "motel." This high school dropout created the Holiday Inn chain to fill his dream of reality and this chain became the largest motel chain in the world within a few years, surpassing Sheraton, Hilton, and the other giants of the industry.

Wilson's motel idea was based on an innovative solution to a problem that he found important. Wilson told reporters that his mother instilled in him a strong feeling that he was the master of his fate, and that he was capable of accomplishing anything he wanted. The hospitality industry giants of the time were Hilton and Sheraton Hotels, who should have been listening to the advice of Wilson's mother. They would have been the choice to revolutionalize the travel and lodging business. Wilson was an uneducated Memphis contractor who had a dream he innovated into reality. He accomplished this in spite of the significant resource disadvantage he had relative to the Hilton and Sheraton chains. He shouldn't have been the creator of the motel industry, but he was and the industry leaders have never caught up.

Inno-visionaries—Modern Paradoxes

Paradoxes have become increasingly prevalent since 1950. The thirteen individual subjects in this work represent the modern version of creative visionaries who should not have become the fathers of their industries. They had talent, energy, and unusual vision but these factors should not have allowed them to achieve such awesome success. They were assisted by the myopic and self-preservation mentality of the industry leaders, who walked away from the obvious and unwittingly became the creative foil for these innovators.

Many factors enter into the equation for success. Personality traits and behavior characteristics are a recurring element in successful individuals and these personal factors can tell us a great deal about the creative and innovative personality. Figure 7, a chart of the thirteen innovative visionaries, lists their most noteworthy accomplishments coupled with their most visible traits. Virtually every one of the innovator subjects has one or more of these traits in greater or lesser degrees. The trait tied to each individual is for emphasis and in most cases was the factor that the media or the individual himself considered the critical variable in his success.

Summary

Why has virtually every breakthrough concept been the child of a neophyte innovative entrepreneur and *not* the industry leaders? Research confirms this to be the case in virtually every industry or profession. Why did the carriage makers at the turn of the century not see the potential in the horseless variety— automobiles? How did Kodak, with its total monopoly in the photographic industry, not see the demand for instant photography? Burton Klein of Harvard studied this phenomenon and in his study of fifty of the top twentieth-century breakthrough inventions (*Dynamic Economics,* 1977), he said, "I could

Figure 7

Inno-visionaries—
Successes and Predominant Behavior Patterns

Innovator	Creation	Dominant Traits and Behaviors
They Created an Industry		
Steve Jobs	First personal computer	Autocratic—He would be king
Fred Smith	First overnight package delivery	Charismatic—Inspirational leader
Nolan Bushnell	Father of video games—Pong	Confident—An awesome self-esteem
Bill Gates	Creator of MS-DOS software	Driven—Type "A" behavior and habits
Revolutionalized Fitness		
Arthur Jones	Automated exercise equipment	Rebellious—Maverick defies tradition
Changed the Way the World Works		
Ted Turner	First 24-hour cable news	Risk-taker—A gambler mentality
Marcel Bich	Created "throwaway" culture	Focused—Goal-oriented to a fault
Changed the Way We Play		
Howard Head	First metal ski, oversized tennis rackets	Intuitive—Right-brain mentality
Perfected Transportation		
Soichiro Honda	Revolutionized motorcycles, first catalytic engine	Persistence—Persevering prevails
Bill Lear	Revolutionized business jets	Passionate—Psychic and libidinal energy
Created New Markets		
Tom Monaghan	Innovated home-delivered pizza	Competitive—Winning is everything
Akio Morita	Father of mass-market VCR, Walkman, etc.	Persuasive—Preeminent salesperson
Sol Price	Created wholesale club industry	Impatient—Intolerant of mediocrity

find no case in which the advance in question came from a major firm in the industry." Klein's findings, the thirteen visionaries in this work, in addition to the hundreds of others researched by this author, have uncovered an almost universal truth, that industry leaders and experts never lead the way in large-scale innovative products or concepts.

The thirteen inno-visionaries in this work have had a profound impact on how the world functions. Others have made more money—Sam Walton, Ray Kroc, Ross Perot, and Rupert Murdoch (the most noteworthy exception is Bill Gates, whose fortune at this writing is $7 billion). Lee Iacocca and Tom Watson, Jr., have received more press for their management expertise. John Sculley (Steven Jobs's replacement at Apple), Al Neuharth, and David Packard have received more accolades from academia for their business acumen. Edwin Land and An Wang had more tributes for their inventiveness. And Hugh Hefner, of *Playboy* fame, has been far more visible.

These inno-visionaries have accomplished something far more important than recognition and money. They changed the way the world works, which is the acknowledged lifeblood of the future for any economic system. They created something that was not there before by breaking new ground and pioneering in virgin territory. They took outlandish risks to prove their ideas had merit and left the world with more than they took from it. This is not to say their breakthrough concepts may not have been created by someone else, but they were not. These inno-visionaries exceeded the limits that society dictates for greatness. Their international acclaim and personal fortunes are small reward relative to the indelible marks each left on how we live, eat, work and play. Not many individuals have made such enormous contributions in local or regional markets let alone in the global society of today's "future shock" world. These quintessential visionaries have made the world more efficient and were the consummate change agents in their given fields of endeavor.

Ayn Rand said, "The man who discovers new knowledge is the permanent benefactor of humanity." An example is Steve Jobs's Apple Computer innovation, which resulted in the creation of over three hundred new millionaires in just over four years of operation. George Gilder gives further credit to the enormous contribution of these innovative visionaries: "Society is always in deep debt to the entrepreneurs who sustain it and [who] rarely consume by themselves more than the smallest share of what they give society."

5

The Inno-visionary Personality

The Big T's seek power: the power of dominating others through aggression and the strength of the individual will; the power of affirming the self through acts of creativity, energy, spontaneity; and the power to transcend ordinary reality through high-risk life lived without rules, beyond the boundaries. Little t's also seek power: the power of being part of a network of relationships or of an ideological structure that can give order to reality.
—Frank Farley, University of Wisconsin researcher on personality

Can Anyone Be Creative?

Creative people and innovative visionaries are divergent thinkers who dance to their own tunes and are oblivious of the established ways of thinking and operating. One cannot expect to become creative or innovative without questioning tradition. Order and creativity are at opposite ends of the spectrum. They are incompatible in the laboratory or in life. The only way to create unique concepts is to be a unique personality and to be ready and willing to be different, even to destroy the present order of things. Nothing less will work for elegant creativity.

Frank Farley, a University of Wisconsin researcher, has found that creative personalities have much higher levels of testosterone than noncreative types. He has labeled these individuals Big T personalities—for testosterone and thrill-seeking—since both factors are found in abundance in the creative personality and are a causal factor in both creativity and sexual drive. The Big T personality can be destructive (Hitler, Bonnie and Clyde) or constructive (Evel Kneivel, Thomas Edison), and in some instances both (Picasso). The Big T personality types are highly stimulated by action and change. They have a talent for disorder and nonconforming behavior and are consummate rebels.

Figure 8

Preferences

Big T	Little t
For Arousal	

Big T	Little t
Uncertainty	Certainty
High risk	Low risk
Novelty	Familiarity
Complexity	Simplicity
Low structure	High structure
High conflict	Low conflict

For Learning

Big T	Little t
Open space	Self-contained classrooms
High variety	Low variety
Bright colors	Soft colors
High activity	Low activity
Noisy	Quiet
Dramatic	Undramatic

Research has shown that creative individuals transmute childhood frustrations into adult actions that result in overachieveing and success. This confirms Freud's thesis that creative behavior is simply redirected psychic or sexual energy. Farley says creative individuals are physiologically aroused due to inordinate levels of testosterone. Farley's research has found that these Big T and little t personalities have different tendencies for learning and arousal preferences, as shown in figure 8.

Psychological History of the Creative Personality

Various theories dot the landscape of the creative personality. Freud theorized that the driven and creative personality was a function of Eros (he used Leonardo da Vinci as an example of how sublimated energy was redirected into creative drives). Freud also made a most astute observation on mankind's ability to create. He said that any individual who was able to fulfill all his unconscious desires for pleasure would be totally incapable of achieving anything worthwhile in life. There is certainly much precedent in history to substantiate this (Roman Empire, sons of the rich, etc.).

Adler saw the creative personality as a function of striving for power or superiority, which he labeled the "will to power." Carl Jung created a system of functional or psychological types of behavior (personality types) and labeled them: sensors, intuitors, thinkers, and feelers. He believed that everyone interacts with the world in one of these four dimensions of behavior. All thirteen of the subjects in this book were evaluated using the Jungian analysis and all were labeled with the Promethean type (intuitive-thinking) personality (see figure 11). These Jungian (Myers-Briggs) personality archetypes have since been correlated to the Innovator personality styles developed by Michael Kirton (see figure 13). These personalities are dominant in how they perceive the world—intuitively—and how they make decisions—thinking rationally.

David Keirsey later refined the Myers-Briggs Type Indicator intuitive/thinking personality types into what he labeled the Promethean personality type. According to Keirsey, this personality type seeks new opportunities as opposed to order and structure. My research has led to the conclusion that the Keirsey Promethean temperament is totally consistent with the inno-visionary personality, which includes Edison, Picasso, Einstein, and the thirteen innovator subjects presented here. They all had Promethean-spirited, right-brain innovator-style personalities, with a passionately and compulsively driven nature, and took risks with the flair of an Evel Knievel.

Brain Preferences in Decision-making

The creative and innovative personalities in this work were much more holistically inclined than the normal population of business executives. In fact, their decision-making and operating styles were virtually the opposite found in traditional organizations. Great creative minds are holistic but operate inversely to the normal population! Innovators tend to *plan* (create their products and concepts) using their left brain in a very quantitative manner, and tend to *implement* (operate their businesses and perform most decision-making functions) in a qualitative, right-brain manner. They are holistic in their brain functioning, which is in total contrast to the "normal" business executive, who operates and makes decisions in the reverse manner. Our schools tend to educate business majors in the traditional fashion of budgeting, modeling, and quantitative analysis, which is not the way the great entrepreneurs appear to operate. This dichotomy leaves some doubt as to the viability of our educational approach to training executives to compete in global markets.

Research on the thirteen innovative visionary personality types presented here found that they tended to think and plan in a left-brain orientation and to operate and manage intuitively with a right-brain orientation. They favored

Figure 9

Inno-Visionary Styles of Brain Use

Creators (Innovators)   **Traditionalist (Adaptors)**

Long-term, Product-planning

Utilize left-brain functions
*quantitative, digital, deductive,
rational, micro, short-term, objective,
verbal*

Utilize right-brain functions
*qualitative, analogue, inductive, intui-
tive, macro, long-term, subjective,
visual*

Short-term, Business-operating

Utilize right-brain functions
*qualitative, analogue, inductive, intui-
tive, macro, long-term, subjective,
visual*

Utilize left-brain functions
*quantitative, digital, deductive,
rational, micro, short-term, objective,
verbal*

a qualitative/intuitive style of management rather than a quantitative/rational operating style found in the typical corporate executive. Turner and Lear never bothered to produce a plan for any of their multimillion-dollar enterprises, which risked their total fortunes. Conversely, they tended to plan and create their original concepts by thinking through the problems in a very left-brain, technically oriented way (many were educated in engineering or the sciences). In other words, they would think out their solutions very rationally, by using their left brains; however, when it came to administering their business operations, they would switch to a right-brain orientation. They were intolerant of rational structure and detail. They ran their business operations qualitatively yet insisted on quantitative detail in their products and concepts (just the opposite of what is taught in management school). Their product decisions were rational decisions and their business decisions were gut decisions. They deplored formal research, referring to it as "analysis-paralysis." They always processed information holistically (right-brain dominant), in contrast to left-brain managers, who tend to process sequentially. Edison, Picasso, and Einstein were similar in their right/left brain predilections. Einstein always agreed that he was more like an artist than a scientist in his use of intuition in his creative methodology. He said, "When I examine myself and my methods of thought I come to the conclusion that the gift of fantasy has meant more to me than my talent for absorbing positive knowledge" (Clark, 1971).

Myers-Briggs Type Indicator

The Myers-Briggs Type Indicator was used to classify each of the innovator subjects into one of sixteen distinct categories. There was universal consistency on two of the eight categories. All subjects were intuitors on the sensing/intuiting scale. This bipolar preference determines how people gather information and therefore perceive the world (forest or trees view of the world). These individuals saw opportunities in a qualitative sense rather than the detail preferred by sensors. Edison, Einstein, and Picasso had the same preference for intuiting over sensing.

On the decision-making scale of thinking versus feeling, all of the subjects were strong "thinkers." They made impersonally based decisions in contrast to decisions based on personal feelings. This is not surprising since 75 percent of the male population in America are thinkers and 75 percent of the female population are feelers. When combining the intuitive-thinking dimensions the relative proportion of the population shrinks dramatically, as these types only represent 12 percent of the general population. As seen in figure 11, most were judgers (closers) instead of the more spontaneous (open-ended) perceivers. There was an even split among extroversion and introversion among the subjects, but in general intuitive thinkers represent a very small percent of the general population.

Edison was an INTJ—introverted intuitive thinking judger, although he was on the cusp of the spontaneous perceiver type and the more structured judging type. Einstein and Picasso were INTPs—introverted intuitive thinking perceivers. They were energized internally and lived their lives in an open-ended way. Figure 10 shows the Myers-Briggs bipolar dimensions and the classifications for each of the innovator subjects.

Keirsey's Personality Temperaments

Psychological researcher David Keirsey refined the MBTI system of personality typology and drew conclusions on self-actualized behaviors. He has described the Promethean temperament as the quintessential innovator and visionary and labeled them the Promethean temperament. His classifications and psychological profiles are exacting descriptions of the creators and innovators in this work. Keirsey's leadership chart shows his various temperaments and their representation in the American population (1 to 2 percent). Keirsey describes the Promethean temperament as unique in the general population but very pervasive within the creative and entrepreneurial community. His analysis of the Promethean type personality relative to various management barometers is described in figure 12.

Figure 10

Myers-Briggs Personality Types

Personality-Type Poles	Code	Operating Characteristics
Introvert or extrovert	I or E	Internal versus external energy
Sensing or intuition	S or N	Micro versus macro processing
Feeling or thinking	F or T	Emotional versus rational decisions
Perceiving or judging	P or J	Open-ended versus closure

Figure 11

Creative Geniuses and Their Myers-Briggs Types

Entrepreneurs	M-B Type	Preferences	Percent of the Population
Marcel Bich	INTJ	Introverted intuitive thinking judger	1
Nolan Bushnell	ENTP	Extroverted intuitive thinking perceiver	5
Bill Gates	INTP	Introverted intuitive thinking perceiver	1
Howard Head	ENTJ	Extroverted intuitive thinking judger	5
Soichiro Honda	ENTJ	Extroverted intuitive thinking judger	5
Steve Jobs	INTJ	Introverted intuitive thinking judger	1
Arthur Jones	INTJ	Introverted intuitive thinking judger	1
Bill Lear	ENTJ	Extroverted intuitive thinking judger	5
Tom Monaghan	INTP	Introverted intuitive thinking perceiver	1
Akio Morita	ENTJ	Extroverted intuitive thinking judger	5
Sol Price	INTJ	Introverted intuitive thinking judger	1
Fred Smith	ENTJ	Extroverted intuitive thinking judger	5
Ted Turner	INTJ	Introverted intuitive thinking judger	1

Michael Kirton's Styles

Another barometer of the innovator visionary personality is the style of their behavior. One of the researchers in this area was Michael Kirton, who came up with two styles, which he labeled "adaptor" and "innovator." The "innovator style," according to Kirton, is more inclined to doing things differently, and the "adaptor style" prefers doing things excellently. Kirton's styles show the

Figure 12

David Keirsey's Leadership Temperaments
(*Portraits of Temperament,* 1987)

Promethean—Intuitive/Thinking (NT)

These personality types are the architects of change. They see life as a process of acquiring knowledge and competence for its own sake. They tend to focus on patterns that appear in all things and excel at deriving new laws and principles. They value competence and quality, seek to solve problems and enigmas and admire power and genius. Intellectual stimulation is their forte and they are a culture's foremost visionaries and pioneers. They are insensitive to authority, as competence is their only criterion for success.

Managerial Strengths

The NT visionary manager is intolerant of error and inefficiency, and demands a great deal of himself and others. He can envision the organization ten years hence and draw a blueprint for the ten-year goals. He never says things twice. He sees the forest, not the trees. His focus is on the possibility and he is often intellectually ingenious and pioneers in technical and administrative areas. NTs have a long-range, sweeping view of things and are very innovative, creative, and entrepreneurial in their perspective.

Managerial Weaknesses

When the visionary manager is involved in the creative process, he has enormous drive; but once the castle is designed, he is more than willing to allow someone else to take over execution and construction. He is often insensitive to the feelings of others. His intellectual problem resolution sets high standards and he often loses patience with those not as interested in the impersonal solutions.

Ways of Dealing with Colleagues

The NT manager works well with idea and new concept managers. Communication skills are sometimes lacking, as he tends to be nonconforming and ahead of the crowd. He tends to be on the growing edge of change and seldom looks back. He is an excellent decision-maker, works well under pressure and honors commitments. He is an innovator who focuses on results, not procedures, to meet objectives.

Contributions to a Management Team

If an organization does not have a visionary/architect/builder on the management team, planned change may be minimal, and sooner or later deterioration will occur. The status quo will continue, perhaps to obsolescence. The NT manager can contribute theoretical structure to the management team.

unique differences in the behaviors of the inno-visionaries researched in this study and the adaptor-style executives normally found in the large, bureaucratic-type organizations. Creative personalities are almost universally found in the innovator behavior column of figure 13, while the traditionalists are to be found in the adaptor column. Kirton's styles of behavior have been correlated with Keirsey's Promethean temperaments and Myers-Briggs's MBTI personality types.

Key Traits and Behaviors

The key traits found in the research on these subjects were listed in figure 7. These individuals are creative, innovative, and entrepreneurial and often succinctly described as: powerful, energetic, visionary, compulsive, and persevering. They prospered on change with a risk-taking propensity second only to sky divers and mountain climbers. Their ability to work hard, to fail, to sacrifice, and to risk everything seems to differentiate them from others who have not made it. Large-scale innovations of the magnitude created by these intuitive visionaries are available to anyone willing to pay the price. It appears that anyone can successfully adapt and mimic creative and innovative behavior and become the personality type necessary. It is not easy to achieve, but, contrary to early psychological theorists, it is certainly within the realm of any introspective thinking person who knows the road to his or her dream.

Notice that one key or pertinent trait was assigned to each of the innovators, but that does not mean that this trait is the only one possessed by that individual, or that a reader not possessing that trait is predestined to fail at the innovative process. All of the innovators have some of each of these behavior patterns and characteristics, as do all of the readers of this text. Some possess more or less of each of the components of these behaviors, and not possessing one of them does not prohibit anyone from achieving the ultimate success desired.

Order of Birth

Einstein and Picasso were first-borns, which seems to fit the profile of the creative geniuses of the world. Edison was the seventh born but like Freud was born when the nearest sibling was much older and therefore the excessive nurturing and doting was there to influence the child to greatness. First children seem to gain an edge in omnipotent self-esteem and resolute psyches necessary for great renown in the world of creativity. The thirteen inno-visionaries were predominantly first-borns, which gives further credence to this hypothesis.

Figure 13

Michael Kirton's Adaptors and Innovators

Adaptor	**Innovator**
Is essential to the functioning of the institution all the time, but occasionally needs to be "dug out" of his systems	In the institution is ideal in unscheduled crises, or better still, to help avoid them, if he can be controlled
Characterized by precision, reliability, efficiency, methodicalness, prudence, discipline, conformity	Seen as undisciplined, thinking tangentially, approaching tasks from unsuspected angles
Seen as sound, conforming, safe, dependable	Seen as unsound, impractical; often shocks his opposite
Is an authority within given structures	Tends to take control in unstructured situations
Challenges rules rarely, cautiously when assured of strong support	Often challenges rules, has little respect for past custom
Tends to high self-doubt; reacts to criticism by closer outward conformity	Appears to have low self-doubt when generating ideas, not needing consensus to maintain certitude in the face of opposition
Provides a safe base for the innovator's riskier operations	Provides the dynamics to bring about periodic radical change, without which institutions tend to ossify
Efficient	Unique ideas
Predictable and stable	Flexible and ingenious
Good manager of time and money	Unconstrained by limited resources
Organized	Spontaneous
Thorough, comprehensive planner	Enthusiastic; insightful
Applies structure to ideas or innovations	Breaks new ground
Creative in productive ways	Productive in creative ways
Cautious risk-taker; seems close-minded	Capricious risk-taker; seems arrogant
Avoids "rocking the boat"	May seek change for the sake of change

Twelve of the thirteen were first-born males and nine of the thirteen were the first born regardless of gender. Bushnell, Gates, and Head had older sisters and Price had one older brother. The others were the first born in their family. Adler and his disciples have shown that leadership qualities and the desire for perfection, superiority, and organization are the province of the first born. Twenty-one of the first twenty-three astronauts were first-borns. Fifty-two percent of all presidents of the United States have been first-borns. First-borns have higher IQs and are overrepresented among Rhodes scholars, Ivy League students and those with high SAT scores. Being first born is not the only element in being creative and innovative, but it appears to be a big help.

Six of the thirteen subjects in this work spent much of their early years in academies, foster homes, or orphanages. Steve Jobs was an orphan. Fred Smith's father died when he was four, as did Tom Monaghan's father, and both spent time in boarding schools or worse. Bill Lear was raised by a dominant mother who created a love/hate relationship with him during his formative years. Arthur Jones was sent to live with a German family just after his birth since his mother had decided to attend medical school. Ted Turner was "interred" (his phrase) in a boarding school at the age of four and was in various military or boarding schools most of the time. Marcel Bich attended academies in Spain and France. Monaghan spent his whole childhood and adolescence in foster homes or orphanages.

The isolation and need to assume adult responsibility at an early age seem to have had a material impact on the psyches of these subjects. It made them self-reliant beyond their years. It also instilled in them an individuality and self-sufficiency that became their salvation when the going got rough. Recent findings have shown that the order of birth isn't nearly as important as the position in the family in which you are raised. If an older brother or sister exists but is no longer in the family (Freud's case), then the behavior effects are dramatically different. Arthur Jones was not the only child but he was sent away at birth to be raised by a German family as an only child. That is more pertinent and impinges on the conditioning of the child more than the order of birth.

The family setting and environment appears to have been the most important factor in the belief systems for these thirteen subjects. Self-confidence, overachieving, striving for superiority, and compulsive perfection are all highly correlated to upbringing as an only child. The "only child" environment forces these individuals to fend for themselves at a very early age and ultimately teaches them to be captains of their own ships. Figure 14 outlines the sibling and birth-order status of the individuals studied in this volume.

Figure 14

Inno-visionary Sibling and Birth-Order Status

Only Child

Steve Jobs	Adopted by intact family as baby
Bill Lear	Raised alone by dominant mother
Fred Smith	Father died at four, raised by mother

First Born

Bill Gates	One younger sister—prominent intact family
Soichiro Honda	Five of eight siblings died due to poor environment
Arthur Jones	Younger sister, raised by German family and others
Akio Morita	Two younger brothers and one sister, family intact
Tom Monaghan	Father died at four. One younger brother. Foster homes, orphanages, seminary, and institution
Marcel Bich	Two younger brothers—family intact but transient

Second Born

Nolan Bushnell	One older sister and two younger sisters, family intact
Howard Head	One older sister, family intact
Sol Price	One older brother, younger sister

Early Family Life

Innovative and creative individuals appear to live their lives fulfilling their childhood self-images. Research indicates that both male and female creative geniuses are preprogrammed (imprinted and conditioned) during their formative years. These individuals then spend their lives living out their early dreams of reality and fulfilling the labels given them and which they have bought into. In other words, their identities become self-fulfilling prophecies due to their desire to appease guilt, insecurities, and inadequacies of the past or not to disappoint their mothers.

Kemmons Wilson, founder of Holiday Inns, spent his life proving his mother was correct in saying he was wonderful. Thomas Edison did the same, as did Picasso and Bill Lear. Their mothers had programmed them to believe in themselves to such a degree they never questioned the validity of the fact— they merely actualized their self-images and became overachievers to meet their mothers' perception of them. In contrast, Ted Turner spent his life proving his father was wrong in saying that he was *not* good enough to compete. He became so competitive that his desire for racing trophies exceeded all common sense and care for his personal safety. His maniacal risk-taking behavior appeared to be a driven act in order to exorcise these past ghosts of his father's taunting and intimidating goal orientation.

Self-Employed Fathers

All thirteen subjects had fathers who were self-employed for the greater part of their lives. This was also the case for Edison, Picasso, and Einstein. These creative geniuses learned from early on that it was not necessary to "buy into" the corporate womb in order to achieve success or security in the world of business. They all spent a lot of time alone, as is common with only children. Most were voracious readers and often fantasized about great world leaders and conquerors who were larger-than-life characters. (Turner idolized Alexander the Great, Monaghan—Frank Lloyd Wright, Lear—Horatio Alger, Bushnell—Walt Disney, Price—Ghandi, Jones—Attila the Hun, Head—Plato, etc.).

Permissive Parental Guidance

As teenagers the inno-visionaries were encouraged to work and operate their own small-scale businesses. Edison is the crowning example of this with his own business at the age of twelve. Bill Gates and Fred Smith had sizable businesses as teenagers while still in school. A constant in the early lives of these creative geniuses was that they were given the freedom to take risks, to create, to build ham radios, to travel, and to make decisions like an adult. Morita was groomed from a very young child to take over the family sake business (which he declined in order to start Sony).

   This freedom to make adult decisions was pervasive in the families of these visionaries. Three of the subjects gained such a strong belief system in their own self-sufficiency that they ran away from home as teenagers and started their ways in life (Jones, Lear, and Monaghan). Most were told they were the greatest and had this omniscient belief drummed into their psyches on a continuing basis. Ted Turner and Bill Lear were the classic examples of this positive brainwashing technique. Turner's father actually admitted to grooming Ted to be insecure, as he felt insecurity was the basis for overachieving and ultimate greatness. Frequent moving and a transient lifestyle at a very early age seem to have been other factors in making these individuals feel like they were subjects of the world and not predestined to operate in some

Figure 15

Age of Innovation by Whiz Kids

Under 20	Age	Innovation
Bill Gates	19	Microsoft
Steve Jobs	19	Apple Computer
Under 30		
Nolan Bushnell	29	Atari
Soichiro Honda	22	Machine shop in Japan
Bill Lear	22	Repair shop/first car radio
Tom Monaghan	23	Domino's Pizza
Akio Morita	24	Sony
Fred Smith	25	Federal Express
Ted Turner	24	Turner Billboards
Under 40		
Howard Head	35	Head Ski Company
Sol Price	37	Fed Mart discount chain
Over 40		
Marcel Bich	42	Bic pens
Arthur Jones	47	Nautilus (barnstorming and flying service at 25 years old)

small hamlet. They were challenged by the new and different and not afraid of it due to these early experiences. None of them had overprotective mothers, which appears to be counterproductive to the innovative process. They were allowed to explore new territory and err without loss of love or self-image.

Age and Creative Endeavors

These entrepreneurs were very young when they created their first breakthrough innovations. Two were in their teens and nine of the thirteen were under thirty when they started their businesses. Frank Farley's research on testosterone (1986) indicates that the highest levels are seen between the ages of sixteen and twenty-four, which gives credence to these data. Eleven of the thirteen were under forty and the two who were over forty (Jones and Bich) were very successful in other enterprises prior to their great breakthrough innovations. A vital youth seems to have been a positive factor in their accomplishments. Einstein was only twenty-six when he concocted the special theory of relativity, and Picasso painted before he talked.

Sex Drive

The passionate drives of these innovative and creative visionaries was not just spent in the toils of entrepreneurship. The inno-visionaries were very potent progenitors indeed, as they had three times the national average of children (4.8 average) and seven of the more prolific ones averaged six children each. They also exceeded the American averages for marriage with an average of 2.5 marriages each. Seven of the thirteen averaged three marriages each. Arthur Jones was married five times, all of them to women under the age of nineteen whom he divorced by age thirty. Bill Lear had four marriages but was also a notorious philanderer who kept mistresses in several towns in the United States and Switzerland. Many of the others were playboys and partiers. Some had numerous mistresses (Bich, Lear), others had liaisons within the confines of their businesses (Bushnell, Turner, Lear, Smith), some were into less controversial one-night stands (Honda, Head, Jobs). Two had children outside of marriage (Jobs and Bich). Their fathering propensity seems a throwback to older, agrarian times. Marcel Bich had ten children, Fred Smith seven, Nolan Bushnell seven, and Bill Lear six. Edison fathered six by two women, Picasso four by three women, and Einstein three by two women.

Research on great leaders and their sexual prowess has been well documented by Napoleon Hill, *Think & Grow Rich;* Michael Hutchison, *The Anatomy of Sex & Power;* and Frank Farley, *The World of Type T Personality.* The subjects of this work seem to fit that same mold, although there were exceptions. It appears that high sex drive is definitely correlated to innovation, entrepreneurship, and creativity.

Renaissance Men

The inno-visionaries are compulsive creators and entrepreneurs who allow their fertile minds to lead them into many diverse markets and industries. All but three studied here had multiple start-up businesses in different industries and even the three who did not (Gates, Smith, and Monaghan) had entrepreneurial experiences in different businesses as teenagers. Smith founded Ardent Record

Company and recorded two hits, "Big Satin Mama" and "Rock House," while in high school. Gates had two successful enterprises, one of which earned him $20,000 at the age of fifteen and the second, with TRW, earned him $30,000 while in high school. Monaghan owned a paper stand and route. All the rest have had short attention spans and continued to create and innovate in new industries and products.

Bill Lear was the most prolific innovator. He emulates the true renaissance spirit of da Vinci and Edison. He developed the first operating car radio (Motorola), invented numerous breakthrough aeronautical instruments, created the Lear jet, designed and perfected the first eight-track stereo system, and patented the first steam-driven car. His corporate heritage lives on through Lear-Siegler and Gates-Lear Jet. Arthur Jones filmed the first African television series by *National Geographic,* "Wild Cargo." He produced and starred in these for a five-year period. This experience ultimately evolved into his Nautilus exercise equipment innovation. Bushnell first created the Pong video games in his twenties. He then moved on to family entertainment with a chain of 250 Pizza Time Theatres. Lesser known were his many enterprises in robotics, microwaves, computer schools, talking toys, video buying terminals, and satellite mapping systems.

Howard Head developed both the first metal ski and then the first oversized tennis rackets. Sol Price moved from the legal trade to discount merchandising. Steve Jobs has moved from the PC to computer work stations. The irrepressible Ted Turner has evolved from a family-owned billboard business to radio, cable television, big league baseball, NBA basketball, and promotion of the Goodwill Games. He has recently adopted social consciousness and various ecological projects. These were Renaissance men whose fertile minds were always on the lookout for a bigger problem to solve and were not afraid of looking for unique solutions not yet considered.

Formal Education

These innovative visionaries were well-read but for the most part self-educated in the likeness of Lincoln. Three never got past the ninth grade and ironically these three made their marks in fields normally reserved for highly educated technologists. Lear competed in the high-technology arena of aeronautical engineers, Honda competed with technologists in automotive engineering in both the automobile and motorcycle industries, and Jones competed in the highly technical biophysics world of muscle-building via automated exercise machines. Yet none of them made it to high school. Edison, with only three months of formal schooling, is of course the quintessential success story of technological creativity without formal education.

Two of the thirteen innovators received graduate degrees. Bich and Price both had law degrees but neither used these advanced degrees in their innovative creations. The education and knowledge certainly must have proved beneficial to their effectiveness in business but the actual degrees were found unnecessary to their creations.

Steve Jobs, the acknowledged father of the personal computer, Bill Gates, the developer of first PC software systems, and Soichiro Honda, the creator of the motorbike, had less than four years of college among the three of them. Arthur Jones, Honda, and Bill Lear not only had significant breakthrough products, they had hundreds of patents to their credit and none of these three ever attended a college. Soichiro Honda, with over a hundred patents and little formal education, has been characterized by economist George Gilder as "the world's most brilliant and successful entrepreneur of mechanical engineering since Henry Ford."

The lack of formal education apparently has little or no bearing on competence and knowledge in creativity and innovation. These visionaries were convinced that "too much formal education is not conducive to successful entrepreneurship and innovation." Edison said, "I can hire mathematicians, but they can't hire me." He maintained that, "University-trained scientists only saw that which they were taught to look for and thus missed the great secrets of nature" (Josephson, 1959).

One of the reasons for the inverse relationship found between formal education and great breakthrough creativity is that you cannot capture an industry from the top. You must live it, create it, and become it. Only in this way can you be at the top and the bottom from the start. You will have started at the bottom, where it is necessary to toil to understand the roots of the enterprise. Those individuals starting out with masters degrees are reticent to start at the bottom or too far from the top, therefore they are never going to be in the position demanded of large-scale innovative success.

The consummate innovators of the world are classically immersed in problem resolution and not in demonstrating competence to a boss through educational prowess. The creative individual refuses to be put in the box of mediocrity—the aim of our formal educational system. Great creative geniuses refuse to accept useless conformity and dogmas dictated by the educational system. Those who accept the traditional dogmas are destined to live within the constraints of those dogmas. Those who rebel against the system are able to achieve a great deal since they were not trained as to what was possible or impossible. Einstein gave credence to this philosophy with the observation, "It is nothing short of a miracle that the modern methods of instruction have not entirely strangled the holy curiosity of inquiry." George Gilder further acknowledged this premise with his caustic comment on Ivy League schools: "Nothing has been so rare in recent years as an Ivy League graduate who has made a significant innovation in American enterprise."

Figure 16

Formal Education of Inno-visionaries

Less than High School

Soichiro Honda	Eighth grade
Bill Lear	Eighth grade
Arthur Jones	Ninth grade

High School with Some College

Steve Jobs	Reed College, less than a semester
Bill Gates	Harvard dropout at nineteen
Tom Monaghan	Less than a semester of college
Ted Turner	Kicked out of Brown in his senior year

College Educated

Marcel Bich	Lycee Carnot law, 1939
Nolan Bushnell	University of Utah, engineering, 1968—graduated last in class
Howard Head	Harvard, engineering—honors, 1936
Akio Morita	Osaka Imperial University, physics, 1945
Sol Price	University of Southern California, law degree, 1938
Fred Smith	Yale University, economics, 1966

Intelligence and Innovation

Research has shown that successful innovation and creativity requires high intelligence. However, too much intelligence (an IQ above 150 [genius]) has proven counterproductive to innovation according to Herzberg and others. These inno-visionaries were all bright—probably in the 120–150 IQ range. Gates and Jones may have had genius IQs based on the available knowledge on these two exceptional characters. Steve Jobs was valedictorian of his high school class. Bill Gates scored a perfect 800 on the math SAT while in the seventh grade. Ted Turner was a respected student at Brown, Akio Morita taught physics briefly prior to turning entrepreneur, and Arthur Jones was considered a genius by many of his employees. It appears intelligence can be of some help, but it is in no way correlated to successful creativity or innovation.

Figure 17

Socio-Economic Class of Inno-visionaries

Innovator	Father's Profession	Economic Status
Lower Socio-Economic Upbringing		
Soichiro Honda	Blacksmith/bicycle repair	Poor agrarian family—malnutrition killed five of nine siblings
Bill Lear	Carpenter	Mother cleaned houses
Tom Monaghan	Truck driver (died when Tom was 4)	Raised in various homes and orphanages
Middle-Class Upbringing		
Marcel Bich	Surveyor	Moved constantly as child, spent much time in boarding schools
Nolan Bushnell	Brickmason	Blue-collar Mormon work ethic
Howard Head	Dentist	Upper middle class
Sol Price	Garment salesman	New York City youth in garment industry
Privileged Upbringing		
Bill Gates	Prominent lawyer	Socially prominent
Arthur Jones	Both parents doctors	Economically advantaged but emotionally deprived
Akio Morita	Wealthy sake family	The wealthiest of all subjects
Fred Smith	Entrepreneur	Trust fund of $8.5 million
Ted Turner	Entrepreneur	Raised in boarding schools

Socio-Economic and Family Status

There is no pattern for early socio-economic status as a factor in the success of these thirteen subjects. Akio Morita and Soichiro Honda were raised within a few miles of each other. Morita grew up in palatial splendor with tennis courts, servants, and all of the trappings of money and power. Honda was a few miles away, trapped in agrarian poverty to the point that five of his siblings died of malnutrition before reaching adulthood. In fact, Honda himself was color blind due to his lack of nutrition as a youth.

The data indicates that three were members of the lower socio-economic classes, four were raised in middle-class families, and five were from clearly advantaged environments. Money and cultural advantages or disadvantages do not appear to have had any bearing on the creative ability of any of these thirteen subjects. The list of their early family status in shown in figure 17.

Summary

The innovative visionary personality probably is high in testosterone with a right-brain predilection, a Promethean temperament who demonstrates a proclivity for ignoring tradition and enjoys being different. Introversion/extroversion or structured/nonstructured lifestyles have no bearing on creative success. Some, if not all, of the following personality traits are critical to becoming a world-renowned creative genius: autocratic, charismatic, confident, driven, rebellious, risky, focused, intuitive, persistent, passionate, competitive, persuasive, and impatient.

Their order of birth is important relative to their upbringing in a protected and doting environment. They seem to flourish on the impetuousness of youth, have an inordinately high sex drive, are Renaissance men in terms of their prodigious output, have had little formal education, normal IQs and were from no distinct socio-economic group. Most were not religious, as they were driven by their own internal dreams of reality and did not appear to need spiritual support from anyone.

Most of them constantly lived "on the edge" both personally and in business. There is some evidence that they exhibit obsessive-compulsive styles of behavior and (as in Turner's case) have been treated for manic-depressive tendencies (Picasso was obviously afflicted with a similar problem but never treated). They almost never got sick in spite of a work ethic that would kill lesser individuals.

Their creative genius appears to have been largely serendipitous. They were not dealt a better hand of cards than other people. They played the hand of cards they were dealt with consummate elegance and won. Anyone willing to pay the price paid by these characters can master the game of innovation, creativity, and entrepreneurship to the same degree as these individuals. Nothing can stop creative and innovative success except a person's internal belief system.

6

Steven Jobs—Autocratic

Innovators operate as omnipotent potentates. They use an authoritarian attitude with their peers and employees to achieve their personal and business goals. They take power, whether they have it or not, in the Nietzschian "will to power" tradition of the "Superman Mentality." Their power typically emanates from the sheer force of their wills. They act as though they have been imbued with the power of divine right over their subjects and at times over their competitors. With Steve Jobs it was "my way or the highway" with most relationships in or out of the business environment. Jobs epitomized this autocratic management style of behavior, which caused many Apple employees to refer to him as "your Majesty." Jeff Raskin, an Apple executive during the early 1980s, characterized Jobs as the ultimate autocrat. He told reporters, "Steve would make a great king of France."

Inno-visionaries typically operate their businesses with total disregard for line and staff organization charts. They assume the autocrat's right to give direction to any employee regardless of intermediate authority levels. This eccentric management approach is prevalent in great innovators. Howard Hughes, Donald Trump, Walt Disney, Henry Ford, and many other famous entrepreneurs were guilty of this omnipotent management style. They autocratically assumed all of the responsibility, took all of the authority, and ignored the hierarchical structure of the organization. They did this, not with any sense of disruption, but with an an internal belief that it was their divine right, especially since they believed they had the "right" answers.

Napoleon and Hitler were political leaders who operated in this fashion. Most of the inno-visionaries featured in this work utilized this autocratic approach to operating a business. Power accedes to those who take it and these innovative geniuses were not shy in taking all the power at their disposal. It seems the meek are not destined to inherit the spoils of creativity, entrepreneurship, and innovation. Those who succeed are the aggressive—

73

sometimes arrogant/obnoxious—innovators who take all the power and authority they can muster and use it push their dreams to reality. They are willing to take all of the responsibility in order to gain all of the power, which appears to be the difference between them and those more traditional executives not willing to bet the farm on their own abilities.

> [Charismatic leaders] are known to be excessively impulsive and *autocratic* in their management style.
>
> —Jay Conger, *The Charismatic Leader*

Steve Jobs did not invent the first Apple personal computer, Steve Wozniak did. However, Steve Jobs was the surrogate father who nurtured the PC concept to fruition. Without Steve Jobs's insatiable energy and dedication to commercializing the Apple I, the PC would have had a different genesis. Regis McKenna, Apple Computer's press agent in the early days, gives testimony to Jobs's critical role in the development of the PC:

> I don't deny that Woz designed a good machine. But that machine would be sitting in hobby shops today were it not for Steven Jobs. Woz was fortunate to hook up with an evangelist.

The Apple I was released in 1976 but was not the first available programmable computer. That distinction went to the Altair 8800, which was a hobbyist unit marketed through mail-order catalogues in 1974. The Altair did not technically qualify as a personal computer in that it was not capable of user programming for storage and recall. Therefore, the Altair does not qualify as the first PC, since it did not create an end-user market. The Apple I resolved the user programming need and is universally considered the product that created the personal computer revolution. The Apple II was the first PC that was functionally equivalent to today's standards for the personal computer. It was released in 1977 equipped with a keyboard, external programming, and color monitor.

Steve Jobs created the personal computer out of the pure force of his will. The experts had labeled the personal computer as a niche hobbyist product only. These experts—with IBM leading the charge—proclaimed the PC would only appeal to a market consisting of long-haired radical hippies with a flair for technological innovation. The computer industry leaders—IBM and the seven dwarfs—were claiming that the only potential market was to those user types who were creating these new products. Jobs and Wozniak both qualified on all of these charges. But they refused to listen to the experts. They blazed the trail of uncertainty, with Jobs convinced there was a mass-market potential, even if the experts did not.

The enormity of Jobs's contribution is seen in a retrospective of the Jobs/

Wozniak relationship. Jobs had sold his Volkswagen bus and Wozniak sold his HP calculator for $1,300 to raise the money to build the first units of the Apple I. Steve Wozniak had decided to sell the designs for the Apple I for royalties. No one believed in it so they could not sell it and Jobs refused to allow Wozniak to give it away, which he had decided to do. In Jobs's inimical "autocratic style"—even though he was just nineteen at the time—he insisted on taking the product to market. Wozniak had actually given away plans to the Homebrew Club. Wozniak wanted to see his baby born in any way possible, even if he had to give it away.

Commercialization was beyond Wozniak's comprehension. He was a dedicated scientist/engineer, not an innovator. Jobs was the innovator who used his will power to persuade Wozniak to sell his treasured calculator for the seed money. He then went out and sold twenty-five units to a local hobbyist retail store. Jobs then turned his garage into a staging area, his bedroom into a board stuffing room, and his living room into a shipping and receiving department. And it wasn't even his house! It was his parents' house. He took over the house in his autocratic style and made it into a minifactory. Jobs gave life to the personal computer by forcing his will on Wozniak to sell his precious calculator, built the product by confiscating his parents' house without asking to set up an assembly operation, and commercialized the product by persuading a retailer to pay cash for an unknown product.

Experts and the First Personal Computer

Jobs and Wozniak faced immense pressure during the mid-1970s. IBM, the media, and some of the most eminent scientists of the electronic era had predicted they would fail. They had to live with these prophesies hanging over their heads while they attempted to raise money, launch a new product, and develop a new market for the product. These industry experts maintained there was *no* mass market for the Apple I or II, or for any personal computers for that matter. These authorities were no less than Robert Noyce, inventor of the integrated circuit and founder of Intel; Nolan Bushnell, founder of the video game industry and chairman of Atari; and Bill Hewlett, founder of Hewlett-Packard and innovator of the first electronic slide rule (Wozniak was employed at HP).

Ironically, Intel's 1971 revolutionary innovation—the microprocessor—was the technological device responsible for the creation of the personal computer industry. Noyce publically said the personal computer would be relegated to a hobbyist product only and there would be no mass market for the product. Hewlett-Packard executives agreed with Noyce and turned Wozniak down when he offered them the Apple product for royalties or better compensation. Nolan

Bushnell, the visionary father of video games and Jobs's former employer, rejected the Apple I, Apple II, and ultimately an opportunity to acquire Apple. He was convinced the product lacked mass-market potential.

IBM executives were guilty of the same marketing myopia demonstrated by the Silicon Valley experts. They had long studied the market potential for the personal computer, and, in a classic case of self-delusion and self-preservation, predicted that all desktop computing in the future would be the province of mainframes tied to remote desktop terminals. Steve Jobs was not deterred by this naysaying. He proceeded with the determination and vision of Columbus seeking a new world to the east while the experts preached the gospel of a flat world.

Power and Personal Belief Systems

In the classical style and resolve of innovative geniuses, Jobs and Wozniak persevered in the face of imminent failure. Great innovators are successful because they are *not* aware of their limitations. They *do not know* what the experts know, so they go where the experts don't go and are pleasantly shocked by what they learn. These two Steves were neophytes in business and in marketing and therefore did not know enough about markets to know that sophisticated computers *must* be sold by a direct sales force. They were not aware of the massive distribution organization required and thus were not constrained by not having one. The "experts" knew it was a bad risk, the Steves did not, so they proceeded anyway. A more knowledgeable pair would probably have capitulated to the great minds of Silicon Valley. These youthful innovators didn't know their enormous limitations and they succeeded in spite of them. They went on to create what Alvin Toffler and George Gilder have called "the most important innovation since the industrial revolution."

Jobs and Wozniak had no credible technological credentials. They didn't have the equivalent of a college education between them. They had the gall to ignore the exalted gurus of Silicon Valley—the Ph.D.s and business executives—and proceeded to create a new market for a new product category. The traditional executives advised them to get legitimate jobs and to stop fantasizing about a fictional market. Jobs didn't listen and continued to follow his intuition and belief in his own personal value systems.

Their vision, belief, will, and risk-taking propensity created a market that was to reach $30 billion within five years. This made the personal computer market as large as the revered mainframe business, an astonishing feat. The mainframe market had taken thirty years to reach $30 billion and the personal computer did it in under five years. IBM executives had been aggressively protecting mainframes by bad-mouthing the PC market and ignoring it. By

1980 IBM got interested and became a major player with the introduction of its own, now ubiquitous PC, but only after Apple had paved the way. The will of Steve Jobs had created a new market and forever changed the way the world works, writes, and computes.

Personal History

Steven Paul Jobs was born in February 1956 in Mountain View, California, the area destined to become the very heart of Silicon Valley and the micro-computer industry. Mountain View was the headquarters of Fairchild, where Robert Noyce gave life to the first integrated circuit a couple of years after Jobs's birth. Steve was an orphan who was doted on by his adoptive parents, Paul and Clara Jobs. He grew up a child of the 1960s. He courted rebellion and the nonconformity that symbolized the area and the era. His behavior and personality are a reflection of his early environment and it is quite likely that a Steve Jobs raised in Omaha would not have been the Steve Jobs of Apple Computer fame.

The rebellion of Haight-Ashbury, Esalen, Santa Cruz, and Berkeley were part of the Silicon Valley mystique. Long hair, marijuana, and sandals were part of the business and social scene in the Valley during Steve's formative years. He became a byproduct of this era, which was reflected in his days at Homestead High, where he was considered a rebel. Bucher's biography (1990) describes him as a loner in school and an iconoclast. Counterculture attitudes and lifestyles predominated in the area and Steve Jobs symbolizes the time and behavior. He rejected the opinions of the establishment, which became an asset later and contributed to his innovation and success. He was an oddball—even bizarre—and didn't get along with the other kids. He was spoiled and wanted his own way, a personality trait that followed him to Apple Computer.

Bucher describes Jobs as different. He hung out with older kids while in high school. One of them was Steve Wozniak, four years his senior. He was enamoured of electronics and was ecstatic when he and Wozniak put together a "blue box" to beat the phone company out of long distance calls. Wozniak built them while at Berkeley and Jobs sold them while still in high school. This was a precursor to their future as they played the same role three years later when Jobs (age twenty) and Wozniak (age twenty-four) founded Apple. Jobs graduated valedictorian of his high school class in 1972 and entered Reed College in Oregon. He dropped out after one semester to work for Atari and search for enlightenment.

Business and Personal Survival

Apple Computer was formed on April 1, 1976, and was incorporated and funded in early 1977. In 1978 Apple received enough venture capital money to sustain operations until a public offering in December 1980. By 1980 over 130,000 Apple II's had been sold. By 1982 14,000 software programs had been written for the Apple II and Apple ruled the world of the personal computer. In fact, most industry experts believe that IBM would have been forced to introduce their PC as an Apple compatible had Apple not made some grievous errors in hardware/software strategy. Jobs's ego and autocratic style would not allow any clones or plug-compatible units to violate the Apple operating structure. Apple even created its own incompatiblities by creating a Lisa, Macintosh, and Apple III without bothering to standardize the operating software. They finally learned of their gigantic mistake by the mid-1980s, but it was then too late. If not for that major blunder Apple would probably have owned the personal computer market.

Apple went public in December 1980, just four-and-a-half years after it began operations. The initial stock offering was at $22 per share, which made it the most successful public offering since Ford had gone public in the 1950s. Apple made the Fortune 500 list faster than any company in history. It became known as the user-friendly computer company based on dedication to simple customer operation and applications programs. The Apple user-friendly machines dominated the graphics and desktop publishing markets from the beginning. By 1992 sales had reached $7 billion in revenues. This staggering growth still represented only 10 percent of the worldwide personal computer market, giving some indication of the magnitude of the market that Steve Jobs has spawned. The personal computer became the ubiquitous tool of business and household computing, with over 100 million units installed worldwide by 1993.

As previously noted, Steve Jobs did not create any of the circuitry that drove the microprocessor-based personal computers. He did not assist in systems designs or in integrating the software to make them operational. In fact, Jobs had nothing to do with the technical design of the Apple I or II. Steve Wozniak created all of the technology behind the Apple I and II personal computers. Jobs functioned as the catalyst, the maven, the creator of the market, the father of the business risk. Wozniak wanted to sell his creation but instead Jobs convinced him to sell his Hewlett-Packard calculator and take an innovative risk.

Steve Wozniak was a Berkeley engineering student and dropped out in the early 1970s to start a family and work for Hewlett-Packard. His father was a Lockheed engineer and he had been steeped in the engineering genre. He was employed in 1975 as an engineer for HP and was quite adept at creative hardware and software designs. Steve Jobs, on the other hand, had one semester of formal education at Reed College in Oregon; other than his garage shop tinkering he was an electronics neophyte. So in 1975 Jobs had no technical expertise or experience except for a six-month game design position at Atari. Neither Jobs nor Wozniak had any experience in business or as managers when they started Apple Computer in 1976.

The lack of business experience, financing, and market acceptance made the early years at Apple a daily fight for survival. Bankruptcy was a constant fact of life until the company went public in December 1980. Two different sets of management brought in venture monies and increasing credibility. Mike Markkula became chairman and Mike Scott president in 1977 in order to bring the needed capital to the firm. They also added the first semblance of professional management. They generated business plans, marketing plans, and attracted venture capital. Even so, the company was nearly bankrupt for much of 1977, 1978, and 1979.

Mike Scott divisionalized the company in the early 1980s and in doing so gave Steve Jobs no responsiblities. Jobs was furious and asked why. He was told he lacked experience and was too volatile to be an effective manager. This move ultimately created the internal dissension and turmoil that led to Mike Scott's resignation and Jobs's elevation to chairman. Jobs had gone from no management responsibility or authority to total authority in one massive political move—all due to his autocratic iron will. The board of directors was convinced it was promoting Jobs to a position with a title but no operating involvement. The autocratic Jobs was to prove the board wrong in short order.

Personal Behavior Characteristics

Jobs had an internal drive for self-discovery. He spent much of his youth searching for enlightenment, first in a commune in Oregon and then on a trip to India, where he searched out the Maharishi Yogi. He was a child of the 1960s, with its alternative lifestyle and hallucinogenic drugs. He had lived his life searching for meaning (a sublimated desire to know his real parents). He experimented with primal scream therapy, marijuana, LSD, various diets, fastings, and was a vegetarian. Jobs was searching for an identity and was looking for it within the establishment culture. When Regis McKenna sent venture capitalist Don Valentine to meet the long-haired and sandaled Jobs, Valentine called McKenna and said, "Why did you send me to this renegade from the human race?" Jobs was rebellious and searching for acceptance whether through mystics, lifestyle, or a new business opportunity. It turned out to be a business opportunity.

Steve Jobs was compulsively driven to achieve power. He was a perfectionist and strove for excellence in all things. He relentlessly drove himself and others to achieve his goals and his personal dreams of reality. With Jobs, the only way was his way. During much of his time at Apple he had no title or position of authority bestowed on him by the board of directors. He assumed whatever power he had, which was substantial. Jobs gave direction, changed plans, created new products, and dictated policy without any authority to do so. He made and broke rules and was oblivious to the feelings of others while doing so, according to Bucher. Goals and objectives were always key to Jobs, regardless of the cost to the individuals or to the firm. He operated in this fashion and was not tolerant of any other behavior by his associates or employees.

Without Steve Jobs's passionate, driving personality, Apple Computer may never have happened. George Gilder, in the *Spirit of Enterprise* (1984), says of Jobs:

> In the repeated pattern of entrepreneurs, the anxieties of his early years became the energies of upward mobility. All the emotional turmoil and restless energy of his youth—the rebellion, the failure, the guilt, the betrayals, the identity maw—suddenly fused into an irrepressible force of creation.

Even Jobs admits that his role in the creation of the personal computer was somewhat an accident of timing and fate, saying "I'm just a guy who should have been a semi-talented poet on the Left Bank. I got sidetracked here."

Crisis is often the "mother of innovation." There has never been a more poignant example of this than with the creation of Apple Computer by Steve Jobs and Steve Wozniak. Wozniak was the electronics genius (Steve Jobs couldn't carry his oscilloscope), but Wozniak had a job, a career, and a family. Woz had a secure identity, knew exactly what he wanted, and was not striving for anything beyond creating new engineering concepts. Steve Jobs did not have an identity. He was an orphan, which was indelibly ingrained in his psyche. Jobs had no job, no career, no family, no friends. He was in constant search of his Nirvana. Jobs needed an identity. Wozniak did not. Jobs needed something greater in his life to live for, and that something became his passion— Apple Computer. It was his indefatigable energy, willpower, drive, and market focus that satiated his needs for identity. He had nothing else. Apple was his family, his work, his passion. It was his identity, his only identity.

Jobs is an introvert, which causes his energies to emanate from his own internal belief systems. This personality trait tends to create territorial inter- actions with others and give direction to his autocratic behavior. He is also an intuitor who operates with the possibilites in life. He always sees the forest, not the trees, and is intolerant of those who do not see things his way. His decisions are made rationally, through thought processes, in constrast to those who make decisions based on their feelings. Jobs is structured in his orientation to the outside world. He likes to finalize things and not leave them hanging.

The above profile makes Steve a Promethean temperament, as was pointed out in chapter 2. He is a perfectionist who strives for excellence in all things. He seeks knowledge for knowledge's sake and is open to new opportunities. Vision and risk-taking are key to the Promethean temperament and Jobs personifies these traits. His temperament causes Steve to be autocratic in managment as well as in his interpersonal relationships. Steve assumed control in most things and would have made an ideal role model for Adler's "striving for superiority" and "drive for perfection." Adler felt the insecurities and inadequacies of early life were reenacted in strong drives for achievement. Jobs certainly gives credence to those theories.

Lee Bucher's biographical sketch of Jobs in *Accidental Millionaire* paints a picture of him as arrogant, mercurial, tyrannical, and a combative perfectionist. His dictatorial managment style made him many enemies, even though it may have contributed to his ability to innovate. This autocratic and dictatorial style is not conducive to pyramidal or hierarchical organization structures. It will not be tolerated in bureaucratic organizations. This behavior made Jobs extremely controversial as an executive and ultimately cost him his job at Apple. You love him or hate him—not necessarily bad, but certainly disruptive in anything other than a start-up organization.

Risk-taking Proclivity

To launch Apple, Jobs went out and begged for money for an unknown concept. He sold the first twenty-five units of Apple I to the Byte Shop in Mountain View and didn't know if they would work. He used his family's two bedrooms and garage as the manufacturing facility for the first year. His sister assembled printed circuit boards. He called vendors and pleaded for credit for their parts. These are the sacrifices required of an entrepreneur. It is why Apple is a success story and the also-rans who didn't make it are not in this book. Apple made more millionaires than IBM, HP, and Digital Equipment Corporation put together. These visionaries took inordinate risks, which is the essence of the innovative process. It is what creates new concepts and industries.

Large-scale innovations are never spawned by people in a secure setting. They are created by people in search of their own niche in life. Steve Jobs fit this profile inordinately well. The Hollywood script that depicts the hero swashbuckling through life on his sailboat sells movie tickets but it does not create breakthroughs. It does not accurately depict the real-life struggle that takes place. Jobs, through sheer perseverence and determination, made it happen.

Apple almost folded in 1975, 1976, and 1977. The firm did not have the human and financial resources of IBM, HP, Intel, DEC, or myriad other firms that should have led the way in creating the personal computer industry. The two Steves had a dream and though they often lost faith, they never gave up, they always persevered. They came very close to getting out in 1976 when they tried to sell to Commodore, Atari, and HP. These three turned down a $100,000 price and salaries of $36,000 for the three principals for the ownership of Apple Computer. What luck for the founders. Exactly four years later Jobs's stock holdings alone were worth $256 million.

Jobs became chairman of Apple in 1981 and had a very volatile and rocky corporate career as an executive. When John Sculley arrived in 1983 it was the beginning of the end for the irascible and arrogant Jobs, who was finally removed from management in 1985. The culmination of the personal computer success story was when *Time* magazine changed its "Man of the Year" award in 1982 and declared "The Personal Computer" as the winner. Jobs's stock at the time was valued at $486 million.

Another Innovation and an Identity

Steve Jobs did not take his dismissal from Apple personally. He immediately embarked on a new innovation aimed at changing the world of education through the newest microprocessor technology. He created a new workstation product aimed at advancing the state of the art in distributed processing for education and business. His charismatic personality and enthusiasm attracted many followers from Apple. However, his biggest accomplishment was the massive backing he was able to attract from the investment community. He motivated the investors through his personal investment of $15 million into his new company—NeXT.

Jobs astounded the business world with a series of coups starting with a stock deal from Ross Perot to the tune of $20 million. He followed this with a capital infusion of $100 million from the Japanese conglomerate Canon. The *coup de grace* was a marriage with IBM that included a contract calling for tens of millions in sales revenues and other capital investments. His arch rival at Apple was now on his team. Jobs then insured both financial and academic credibility with investments from two prestigious universities, Stanford and Carnegie-Mellon. He followed these with a monumental sales deal with Businessland Computer stores for $100 million in orders for his yet-to-be-produced NeXT work station.

Steve Jobs made the above deals between 1985 and 1988, culminating with the October 1988 announcement of his new computer at a super-hyped show at the Davies Symphony Hall in San Francisco. The NeXT computer work station was received with critical acclaim. The sales never achieved the levels predicted by Jobs, and the media was writing his NeXT work stations off as a dismal failure in 1990. But by mid-1991, the work station market gained momentum and Jobs had released a second generation product that was much faster and more competitive. Jobs was projecting sales of $200 million for his new enterprise by late 1991. Jobs announced the sale of the NeXT hardward division to Canon in February 1993. He will concentrate on software only, thus competing in Bill Gates's turf. The industry analysis is that NeXT never made it.

Steve Jobs made the covers of both *Newsweek* and *Business Week* in October 1988. *Newsweek* gave Jobs the nickname "Mr. Chips." Its cover story said that he had put the wow back into computers. *Inc.* magazine honored him as the "Entrepreneur of the Decade" in its tenth-anniversary issue in 1989. Steve Jobs had become the consummate innovator and had achieved an identity. He was only thirty-four, single, and on his way to a second major innovative success. Steve was married to Laurene Powell, an MBA Stanford student, in Yosemite Park, on March 20, 1991.

Autocratic Success

Steve Jobs was successful because he believed. He believed in his way of doing things, to the chagrin of others. The Jobs philosophy was "my way or the highway." This philosophy is never possible in any endeavor without tremendous self-confidence, which is often motivated by self-doubt. He used his belief or "gut" insights to feel his way through the tough times. When a decision was dependent on following his intuitive belief or some other expert opinion, he always opted for his gut response. This is classic in innovator personalities, probably due to their having become so disenchanted with the pessimistic mentality of the experts. The experts bring an adversarial mentality to creativity. They are protecting the status quo. The innovator therefore becomes jaded relative to all expert opinion. Steve Jobs was more jaded than most and he marched to his own drum in an autocratic and even hostile way, daring the establishment to object. He exercised an autocratic willpower and achieved beyond the ordinary. His persuasiveness was legendary. One reporter described talking to Jobs as "entering a reality distortion field."

Steve Jobs was instrumental to the personal computer revolution. The present position of the PC as the pivotal instrument for the information age is due to the perseverance of Steve Jobs. The PC has been predicted to become one of the great technological innovations of the latter part of the twentieth century. Steve Jobs will go down in history as one of the innovators responsible for its development. His combative will made it happen. His desire to find an identity and become "king of the hill" was a critical factor in his success.

Steve Jobs was a pioneer. He was unquestionably "at the right place, at the right time, with the right product, and came equipped with the right temperament." He came prepared to pay the price that had to be paid at the time and paid it unequivocally. His autocratic and dictatorial management style may not be the greatest way to win friends and influence people but it certainly enhanced this great innovation. He used his "will to power" to an extent not often witnessed in the annals of business. Jobs's will was an iron will that persevered in the face of all adversity. That is what success is made of.

Steve Jobs has been called very lucky. He was. But remember that he was not dealt the best hand of cards ever dealt. In fact, it was probably a very mediocre hand in contrast to those held by others in the same era. He played his cards with panache and flamboyance. When the game is over history will show that he played his hand as well as it probably could have been played.

Steven Jobs
born February 1955
Mountain View, California

Dominant Behavior Characteristic: Autocratic
Motto: "Don't listen to the market researchers." Bell didn't with the phone!
Nickname: Mr. Chips
Firm Name: Apple Computer and NeXT
Location: Cupertino, California
First Innovation/Date: Apple Computer, 1975
Products: Apple I, Apple II, Lisa, Macintosh, NeXT work stations, NeXT Step
Initial Investment: $1,200 from sale of a Volkswagon and HP calculator
Second Innovation/Date: NeXT, 1986. Put $15 million of his own in this venture

---

Sibling Status: An orphan. An adopted younger sister to Paul and Clara Jobs
Personality Profile: Introverted intuitive thinking judger (INTJ)
Parents' Occupation: Stepfather a machinist, salesman
Childhood Data: An unhappy youth, loner, rebellious, disliked in school. Father
    often unemployed
Family Socio-Economic Status: Middle class
Formal Education: Homestead High and one semester at Reed College in Oregon
Age, First Business Venture: Blue Box venture at age 17
Age, Big Hit: 20
Hobbies/Activities: Hiking, oriental mysticism

Marital Status: Married March 20, 1991, at Yosemite to a Standford student
Children: One daughter, Lisa
Religion: I Ching. Oriental mysticism. Agnostic
Public Offering Date: December 1980, Apple at $22 per share, a $1.3 billion
    offering
Revenues or Units of Big Hit: Apple I, 600 units, Apple II, 700,000 units,
    1982
Revenues of Firm: 1992 revenues of Apple = $7 billion; 12,000 employees
Estimated Net Worth: $350 million, 1991 *Forbes* 400
Age Became Millionaire: 25 at public offering—$250 million
Heroes: None
Honors: "Entrepreneur of Decade" by *Inc.,* 1989. *Time* cover as one of America's
    top risk-takers, 1982. *Business Week* and *Newsweek* covers on October
    24, 1988. Apple fastest to hit *Fortune* 500 in history.

7

Fred Smith—Charismatic

*Charisma comes from the Greek meaning "gift of god" or "gift of divine grace."
German sociologist Max Weber defined charisma as an endowment that sets
leaders apart from ordinary men. He said these leaders became supernatural,
superhuman, and exceptional with "powers not accessible to the ordinary
person." Jay Conger, in* The Charismatic Leader, *insists that charisma is critical
to entrepreneurship, management of change, strategic vision, and motivation.*

*Most charismatics have an "aura" or "magnetism" that inspires others to
follow them blindly towards their visions of reality. Charismatic scholars say
this magical behavior is one of the world's most powerful forms of leadership.
They also agree that the charismatic inspires an intense passion in people that
drives them to action (e.g., the Jim Jones Kool-Aid debacle). Charismatics
have an almost magical, contagious, and religious appeal bordering on the
occult. Jesus, Napoleon, Roosevelt, Hitler, Ghandi, Kennedy, and the innovators
in this book are examples of the charismatic personality. Fred Smith especially
personifies an individual who inspired many followers to buy into his vision
of reality.*

*Research has shown that charismatic leaders are critical to the innovative
process. Subordinates have been shown to be more self-assured, work longer
hours, find their work more meaningful, experience greater trust in their leaders,
and have higher performance ratings than followers of noncharismatic but
effective leaders (Avolio and Bass, 1987). Large-scale innovation is dependent
on a Herculean effort by the total organization. A driven and charismatic
leader like Fred Smith is imperative for success in most high-risk new start-
up ventures.*

*Laura Rose, an Atlanta consultant, specializes in charismatic behavior of
executives. She insists that charisma is innate in everyone and can be developed
and learned. Leaders must work at being charismatic, not unlike working at
other management skills. Empowerment is easy if the "top dog" believes in*

the dream. The lack of charisma is precisely the problem with bureaucratic organizations, where there are no dreams.

The charismatic knows where he or she is going and is able to empower others to buy into the dream. The optimism from the charismatic personality is contagious and motivates followers. The charismatic's visions become the visions of the employees. Inno-visionaries like Steve Jobs and Fred Smith had such self-confidence (belief systems) that they looked infallible to their employees. Jay Conger said, "Because of their creativity, inspiration, unconventionality, and vision, charismatic leaders are potential sources of enormous transformation for organizations. . . . Many of the famous entreprenuers of this decade have been charismatic leaders . . . like Fred Smith." In Smith's case his employees worshipped him because he cared, he believed, and he was willing to risk everything for the dream.

> If Fred Smith lined up all 13,000 Federal Express employees on the Hernando de Soto Bridge in Memphis and said, "Jump!" 99.9 percent of them would leap into the swift Mississippi River below. That's how much faith they've got in this guy.
> —Heinz Adam, customer service manager, Federal Express

Fred Smith, the charismatic innovator who created overnight delivery, told *Inc.* magazine in 1986, "You absolutely, positively have to innovate—if only to survive." Fred Smith should know, since he risked his total inheritance for his Federal Express dream in the early 1970s. He refined an idea originally created for a college term paper and made it one of the greatest entrepreneurial success stories of our era.

The irony is that Smith started the company to perform a different service than overnight package delivery. Federal Express was started to fly Federal Reserve cash from region to region, which would have saved the government $3 million a day in financial float, according to Smith's estimates. The name Federal Express evolved out of that concept.

The contract Smith negotiated with the Federal Reserve system never materialized, but the overzealous entrepreneur had already made major commitments for airplanes—two jets from Pan American World Airways. He had personally invested $250,000, had guaranteed a $3.6 million bank loan, acquired passenger aircraft to be modified for package delivery, and had incorporated the new firm on June 28, 1971. Young Fred—twenty-six at the time—had a business and planes but no contracts. He was forced to innovate in his prophetic words "if only to survive." In fact, Smith himself said much later, "If the Federal Reserve contract had materialized, Federal Express probably would not have become what it is today" (Sigafoos, 1983).

The overnight package delivery business should have been created by the

United States Postal Service or United Parcel Service, who had been in business for some eighty years prior to Fred Smith's innovation. These organizations not only did not participate in the creation of the concept but actually predicted Smith's demise. Smith was not deterred by these dissenters. He followed his dream, which had originally been documented in a Yale term paper. He received an ignominious "C" for his efforts. The professor gave Fred all the standard reasons why his idea was not valid: federal airline regulations, the vast amounts of capital required, and competition from the large airlines, who already had package deliveries on their passenger routes. Fred Smith was a man on a mission and was undaunted by the professor's analysis. He designed an innovative breakthrough concept, a "hub and spokes" system of delivery (using Memphis as the hub), that has since become an industry standard for such delivery systems.

Fred started his first business venture after returning from Vietnam. It was a jet aircraft sales company named Arkansas Aviation. Smith says that his poor experience with parts deliveries is what originally motivated him to finally start Federal Express. "I became infuriated that I could not receive on any timely and reliable basis air freight shipments from places around the United States."

Federal Express began operations in April 1973. Profitability didn't arrive until 1976. The first years were fraught with much pain and suffering with bankruptcy a haunting possibility every quarter. During this period Smith's charismatic magnetism was at its greatest. He once convinced his employees to pawn their watches to cover a short-term bridge loan. Ex-president Art Bass gave testimony to Fred Smith's resilience and charismatic leadership during these hard times:

> This company should have died five or six times in its first three or four years but Fred refused to give up. Boy, was he tenacious. With sheer bull and courage, he pulled off a miracle. (Sigafoos, 1983)

Fred had risked his total inheritance—$8.5 million—on the Federal Express venture. He was told that he was crazy by friends, competitors, and the media. Waitley and Tucker describe his lack of support from the establishment in their book *Winning the Innovation Game:*

> Everyone told Fred Smith he was crazy to start an overnight package express. "There's no market for such a service," they said. "The Civil Aeronatics Board will never approve it. You won't be able to find reliable couriers. Besides, if there were a market for such a service, the major airlines would already be offering it."

Fred Smith, in the time-honored style of the true innovative visionary, listened to his own counsel. History has vindicated his decision: in 1983 Federal Express became the fastest company in history to achieve a billion dollars in revenues. Federal Express is the world's largest express transportation company and will top $10 billion in revenues by the mid-1990s. Venture capitalist David Silver says, "Federal Express Corporation is a miracle." Biographers Moskowitz, Levering, and Katz (1990) say Federal Express is "one of the great entrepreneurial sagas of the second half of the twentieth century."

Personal History

Smith was born on August 11, 1944, in Marks, Mississippi, a suburb of Memphis. Fred's father died when he was four years old. His father had been a Horatio Alger figure who made his fortune through hard work, vision, and mental fortitude. He had been the founder of Dixie Greyhound Bus Lines and a chain of restaurants called the Toddle House. Smith grew up knowing he would inherit millions on his twenty-first birthday, but he never let the money deter his drive for personal success.

Smith was born with a congenital bone disease called Calvé/Perthes disease. The disease affected his hip movement and caused him to wear braces and walk with the aid of crutches for most of his youth. His mother worked diligently at making Fred feel normal. She built up his self-esteem, kept him in constant therapy, and encouraged his participation in sports. He eventually outgrew the major effects of the childhood disease and its infirmity. He played both basketball and football in prep school and was voted the "Best All Around Student" at Memphis University School. Fred became enamored of Civil War history during this stage of his life and his heroes were the great military generals and leaders of the South. This early influence is quite reminiscent of Ted Turner, who was being raised in a private academy in Tennessee around the same time.

One of the lifelong influences in Smith's life was a letter from his father just prior to his death. This letter implored the boy to put his inheritance to work and not become part of the idle rich. This admonition from his father evidently motivated Fred to use the money as risk capital and also to take risks. He was also evidently driven to overachieve at a very early age. He learned to fly at the age of fifteen and took up cropdusting as a part-time hobby. At the age of sixteen he and two school friends formed a recording studio, Ardent Record Company, which is still in business. These teenagers operated the firm profitably and had a number of hits including "Big Satin Mama" and "Rock House." This early flirtation with entrepreneurial activity has been found consistently in the innovators in this study. They all worked hard or operated successful businesses while still in their teens.

Smith withdrew from the record business when he left for Yale. There he became known as a hard-partying guy. He was the one with the twin-engined Piper to ferry his Delta Kappa Epsilon buddies to the women's colleges in the area. Smith admits to being a "crummy student." However, his charisma and work ethic were apparent at this early age, as he was the campus disc jockey, helped organize the Yale Flying Club, and became a member of the prestigious senior secret honorary society known as Skull and Bones.

Business and Personal Survival

Smith graduated from Yale with a degree in economics in 1966 and immediately enlisted in the Marine Corps. He spent two tours of duty as a reconaissance pilot, where he flew two hundred missions in forward control planes. David Silver interviewed Fred for *Entrepreneurial Megabucks* and described his war years as responsible for his bigger-than-life innovative effort. "Experiences in Vietnam enabled Smith to intuit deprivation and perhaps desperation." These Vietnam experiences also seem to have driven Smith to exorcise a lot of ghosts from the past and motivated him to become a dynamic risk-taker.

Federal Express is a company only because of the tenacity and charisma of Fred Smith. He spent years developing market studies—he invested $150,000 in professional research—to convince the financial community that the concept was a potential business opportunity. He spent years coercing and romancing the venture capital community to partake in his overnight delivery concept. The Herculean technological, administrative, and financial variables of the package delivery business were mind-boggling. These are exemplified by these staggering numbers:

Federal Express integrates their customers with suppliers through a fleet of 395 airplanes, 29,000 trucks and vans, 25,000 delivery and pickup locations, and 297,000 calls per day in a massive communications linkup with trucks, customers, and suppliers. This system must contend with over a million pick-ups and deliveries daily in 119 countries.

Such an adminstrative feat should have been attempted by the better-financed major airlines, freight forwarding companies, or the United States Postal Service. The major airlines were strategically placed for this new business opportunity but were frightened by the risk to their own profitability. They had a huge stake in the air freight trade, while controlling the vehicles (airplanes) with which to make the deliveries. Emery, Airborne, and Flying Tiger were the major freight firms who should have taken on the overnight concept. These groups were all too afraid of the unknowns but Fred Smith bet the farm (his inheritance) on the concept. He also risked his reputation on his dream. His description of the trauma and terrible experiences of those years is illustrated by his testimony in a 1976 Memphis deposition:

> No man on this Earth will ever know what I went through during that year [1973], and I am lucky I remember my name much less the details that you are trying to ask me. With the trauma of that year, the pressure was so great on me, and there were so many events that went on, and so much travel and so many meetings with investment bankers, General Dynamics, and a hundred different people who came down to Memphis, I just don't recall specifics of virtually anything during that period of time, in addition to trying to run a company at the same time. (Sigafoos, 1983)

Fred Smith is the consummate risk-taker who has survived due to his magnetic charm and charisma. One of the stories of his flamboyant style in those early days was his making a payroll at the blackjack table. It was on one of those dark days of the early 1970s when Fred was struggling for a cash infusion from any source. Jessica Savitch of "NBC News" reported this story on July 19, 1973, after she ran into him at an airport. He reported that he had just been turned down by General Dynamics and was depressed. He looked at a flight to Memphis and another to Las Vegas and impulsively jumped on the Vegas flight. According to Savitch, Smith said,

> I was in Chicago when I was turned down for the umpteenth time from a source that I was sure would come through. I went to the airport to go back to Memphis, and saw on the TWA schedule a flight to Las Vegas. I won $27,000 starting with just a couple of hundred and sent it back to Memphis. The $27,000 wasn't decisive, but it was an omen that things would get better. (Sigafoos, 1983)

Smith is an intense competitor whether playing tennis, managing Federal Express, or flying. On one of the early flights between Little Rock and Memphis Fred was purported to have flown half the distance upside down in a jet. This knack for the dramatic is what attracts a dedicated following. Fred's employees idolize him, which is apparent from the quotes in the press or in comments from any of the Federal Express drivers. Jay Conger found the charismatic trait from his research and featured Smith in his scholarly work, *The Charismatic Leader.*

A February 1989 *Business Week* article quoted Federal Express director Roger Frock on Smith's ability as a leader, "We needed his charisma, his leadership." Other employees have characterized Smith as a master motivator with great sensitivity to his personnel. He has an almost matriarchal attitude toward his people. One illustration of his loyal, protective, and almost Japanese mentality for his employees is the fact that Federal Express has never had a layoff in its twenty years of operation. Part of this success is due to Fred's corporate philosophy, which he has labeled "People-Service-Profit." It isn't an accident that "people" is listed first; that is how charismatic leaders think.

Personal Behavior Characteristics

Fred Smith is a very private person and a voracious reader. He reads four hours a day on the subjects of history, politics, and economics. He is externally energized, which makes him an extrovert on the Myers-Briggs scale of personality type. He believes strongly in the use of intuition for any innovative effort. This philosophy is documented in 1986 quotes he gave to *Inc.* magazine: "If you want to innovate, you have to be capable of making intuitive judgments," and "in terms of large-scale innovation, you have to rely more heavily on your vision, your intuition."

Smith is a rational or "thinking" type when making decisions and his preference for living is planned and organized. In other words, he prefers a rational and structured or closed-end approach to business. The above analysis of Smith's preferences types him as an ENTJ on the Myers-Briggs Type Indicator, as shown in chapter 2. His Promethean intuitive-thinking temperament makes him a student of the opportunities and possibilities in the world. He is challenged by the future more than the past and the quality of life more than the quantity of life. He has a macro perspective with a holistic brain orientation that has a right-brain proclivity whenever planning the future. This characterization is substantiated by this description of Smith by Robert Sigafoos (1983):

> [He is] blessed with flair, strong intellectual curiosity, leadership ability, and seemingly boundless energy. He could not have a grander dream than the one he carried from Yale to Vietnam to Little Rock, then to Memphis. . . . He has the desire for power and achievement found in all great corporate leaders. And he sees himself as a leader in the forefront of exploiting the hot, new high technologies. . . . The reputation of this man is that of a hard hitting, determined executive who knows what he wants and is willing to pay the price—no matter how big.

Risk-taking Proclivity

Fred is an ardent risk-taker. He risked his entire fortune on an unknown concept when everyone told him that it was folly and that he was crazy. He proceeded anyway and then, after beating the devil from the door for years, jumped right back into the ultimate risk/reward game during the 1980s. Federal Express had finally made it and no longer had to worry about its mortality. But Smith was not content. He created another major innovation—ZapMail—that cost Federal $350 million in losses during the mid-1980s. He then shocked the world once more in 1989 with his purchase of Flying Tiger Airlines for $880 million and $1.4 billion in debt.

Smith's entrepreneurial and innovative talents are well documented but he admits the price for large-scale risk-taking and ultimate innovative success is enormous. He told *Inc.* magazine in October 1986,

> In terms of building an organization that is big and successful, you are going to have to pay a big price, personally. And you won't realize that until you are far enough along and have already paid that price—so you'd better be willing to live with it.

Smith's fertile and restless mind conjured up the acquisition of Flying Tiger Airlines in the late 1980s. This was possibly his largest risk to date. He believes this latest innovative concept will make Federal Express the preeminent worldwide package delivery firm, making the risk worthwhile. On February 13, 1989, *Business Week* described his new acquisition as "his grandest gamble yet." The Wall Street nonbelievers had a field day with this $880 million acquisition because it increased Federal Express's debt to $1.4 billion. The industry analysts have questioned Smith's sanity for risking the existing operations for a new, difficult, and questionable undertaking.

One argument they pose is that Tiger International is highly unionized and traditional while Federal Express is still quite entrepreneurial in spirit due to Fred Smith's leadership. They say Federal has a gung-ho and a "take no prisoners" attitude, in contrast to the more conservative Tiger International "adaptor" type personality. They argue that the merger cannot work because of these and other personnel differences operating within the two firms. Most of Smith's dissenters are saying he has a "Tiger by the tail." But Smith firmly believes that the international routes built by Tiger over the past forty years will make Federal Express the preeminent transportation company in the world. The past has vindicated Smith when everyone said he was crazy. This newest global innovation will probably do the same sometime around the millennium.

Charismatic Success

Fred Smith's persona and charisma are fundamental to Federal Express's success. Sigafoos, in *Absolutely Positively Overnight,* confirms the Smith influence with a characterization of Federal Express as "the Fred Smith Federal Express company." He believes the founder/leader and the organization have become "one and the same." This is not unusual, as many of the great world leaders have demonstrated with their charismatically built empires. Napoleon, Hitler, and Ghandi *were* their countries. The charismatic leadership style tends to create a following that sublimates their identity to that of the leader. Sigafoos dedicated one complete chapter to describing this happening at Federal Express.

> Fred Smith is only the most recent incarnation of that ancient tradition of the "King's Two Bodies." Smith is both the man and the company in the same way that the old European kings were both the person and the office, both the man and the land.

Federal Express was one of the largest venture capital start-ups in American business history, which makes it an entrepreneurial phenomenon. *Fortune* in December 1979 labeled it "one of the top ten business triumphs of the seventies." Dunn's named it "among the five best managed companies in 1981." Federal Express was acclaimed one of the "100 best companies to work for in America— 1985." And it won the prestigious Malcolm Baldridge Award for product quality in 1990. Federal Express was the first service-oriented company to win this very prestigious award.

Smith's overnight delivery service innovation has changed the way the world does business. It has changed and influenced global business operations to the same degree that Ted Turner's innovations have influenced the world of communication. The expanded European Common Market will now be accessible to many businesses previously isolated due to the cost of entry. These new businesses can now operate in a remote region without the need to invest in vast warehousing and parts inventories. This was not possible just a few years ago. These widespread business changes and opportunities have been made possible by the new mentality of Fred Smith's "absolutely positively overnight"—anywhere in the world. These new global changes and business opportunities have changed the world of business and will ultimately impact the balance of economic power in the world. The charismatic Fred Smith has been a key factor in these global changes and will be remembered for having changed the world of business for the better.

Frederick W. Smith
born April 11, 1944
Marks, Mississippi

Dominant Behavior Characteristic: Charismatic
Motto: "People—Service—Profit"
Nickname: None
Firm Name: Federal Express
Location: Memphis, Tennessee
First Innovation Date: Federal Express, 1973
Products: Overnight delivery service: unique hub and spokes system
Initial Investment: Inheritance of $8.5 million
Second Innovation/Date: ZapMail, 1984; Flying Tiger acquisition, 1989

Sibling Status: Only child from father's second marriage; stepsisters
Personality Profile: Extroverted intuitive thinking judger (ENTJ)
Parents' Occupation: Owner of Dixie Greyhound and Toddle House
Childhood Data: Born with birth defect—Calvé/Perthes disease. Braces and crutches through grade school. Father died when he was four.
Family Socio-Economic Status: Upper class, prep schools
Formal Education: Yale, economics, 1966
Age, First Business Venture: Organized Ardent Records at 16—recorded "Big Satin Mama" and "Rock House"
Hobbies/Activities: Pilot's license at 15. Competitive tennis player

---

Marital Status: Married twice
Children: Seven children
Religion: Unknown
Public Offering Date: April 12, 1978. Raised $80 million venture capital
Revenues or Units of Big Hit: First firm to hit $1 billion in 10 years
Revenues of Firm: 1992—$8 billion in revenues on 46 percent market share
Estimated Net Worth: $250 million, *Forbes* 1990
Age Became Millionaire: $8.5 million at 21 from inheritance
Heroes: Generals Lee and Grant
Honors: Voted one of best managed companies, 1981. *Fortune's* "Top 10 Business Triumphs of the 1970s." Two Purple Hearts, Silver and Bronze Stars, and the Vietnamese Cross of Gallantry

8

Tom Monaghan—Competitive

"I am determined to win, to outstrip our company's best performance and beat the competition." This is a quote from Tom Monaghan's 1986 biography, Pizza Tiger. This same attitude is pervasive among the top leaders and over-achievers of the world. Research by Psychological Motivations (Noyes, 1984) found that entrepreneurs were almost universally competitive to a fault. They were found to possess a "killer instinct" that was energized when competing at work or at play. A quote from the study shows the level of intensity typical for most entrepreneurial personalities, "It doesn't matter whom I play with. I always win. I play to win, and when the game's over it's kind of a letdown to give back the paper money." The study found that top entrepreneurial executives were competitive at both work and play and observers could not differentiate their behavior in either activity.

A friend described Bill Gates as having the competitive mentality of a race car driver who gets red mist in his eyes due to the adrenalin hit. Ted Turner's biographer described him as "an indefatigable competitor." Akio Morita said, "Despite some of its darker aspects, competition, in my opinion, is the key to the development of industry and its technology." Tom Monaghan is the consummate competitor. He used competition to describe his childhood in Pizza Tiger, "I was the best jigsaw puzzle solver, the best ping-pong player, the best marble shooter. I stood out in every team sport." When Monaghan was unable to sell Domino's in 1989-90 he returned to run the operation. He told the media he was "returning to the pizza wars." Ted Turner constantly describes business as winning the "fight," "game," "struggle," or "war."

Competitive energy is generated by adrenalin rushing to rescue us when we are presented with a "fight or flight" decision. Competitive individuals see business as a fight and their bodies automatically respond with a faster heart beat, oxygen and sugar release to the muscles, dilation of pupils, deepening of respiration, rise in supply of red blood cells for repairing damage, and contraction of the spleen. This all happens within seconds of any threat and the highly competitive entrepreneur tends to view the market and the opposition as mortal enemies. The entrepreneurial personality has been shown to have a natural inclination to "fight." Selye has shown that some individuals have a greater propensity for this "alarm reaction" than others. These individuals tend to be high on the stress scale and tend to use their nervous energy to overachieve and succeed.

Monaghan believes competition is extremely good for Domino's. Steve Jobs espoused the same philosophy when he was chairman of Apple Computer. Burton Klein's 1977 book Dynamic Economics showed how competition had a positive impact on success in business risk-taking. He pointed out that, "When a firm no longer faces genuine challenges it has a very small chance of remaining dynamic." He demonstrated that the most successful firms were those facing the greatest amount of competition and the least successful were those that did not face severe competition. Companies and people evidently become significantly sharper and better because they are pushed to a higher level of performance because of competition. Monaghan confirms this with his description of how Domino's stays on top: "Competition makes us sharper, keeps us looking for new answers and prevents us from getting complacent and thinking we know it all."

> If there were 500 Tom Monaghans to run the Fortune 500, America's *competitive* woes would be over.
>
> —Tom Peters, *In Search of Excellence*

The Innovation of Home-Delivered Pizza

Tom Mohaghan believes in competing but competing fairly. He says, "The real substance of life and work is in a constant battle to excel . . . but to my mind winning in business is nothing unless you do it strictly acccording to the rules." His idol, Ray Kroc, believed in the Machiavellian philosophy of "kill or be killed." Monaghan rejects that as not being the Christian way, but he will try to beat you if it is legal and moral.

Tom Monaghan believes. He believes in himself, in other people, in God, and in hot, fast, tasty home-delivered pizza. The success of the Domino's chain is a testimony to Monaghan's intransigent belief in these values, and it is this unrelenting pursuit of his dreams that has made him the consummate entrepreneur and innovative visionary.

Monaghan suffered more than his share of tragedy in both his business and personal life. He is a surviver who has continually risen from the ashes of defeat and each time reached even greater heights than before. During the first twenty years of Domino's struggle for survival, Tom persevered through a devastating fire that destroyed his records and store, three near bankruptcies (the worst of which spanned over a hundred lawsuits and fifteen hundred creditors with debt in excess of $1.5 million), a five-year lawsuit by Amstar that attempted to keep him from using the name Domino's, three partners who conspired to drive him from the business, and three near-fatal private plane crashes, two with him at the controls.

Monaghan overcame these obstacles and achieved the pinnacle of success as the king of the thirty-minute home-delivered pizza. He accomplished this despite a troubled childhood, no financial resources, and virtually no formal education. He had every reason to fail, yet overachieved as the consummate entrepreneur in the spirit of Horatio Alger. Tom still owns 97 percent of Domino's, which is now the largest home-delivery pizza chain in the world (500,000 pizzas delivered daily). He succeeded because of his dream and vision of excellence in product, service, and consumer satisfaction. He bet his career on an intransigent belief in home delivery of hot, tasty pizzas even though his competitors said the concept was neither sound nor economically feasible.

Tom Monaghan was ill-prepared to have created the largest home delivery pizza chain in the world. In 1973, after thirteen years in business, he had seventy-five stores. Pizza Hut had over three thousand; Pizza Inn, Little Caesar's, and Shakey's were national chains with significant brand recognition and financial resources to beat him at home delivery. These firms were all in a better position to have spotted the enormous demand for home-delivered pizzas. Society was evolving into a fast-food-oriented fiefdom due to the "instant" lifestyles of the "me generation" during the 1970s. The established industry leaders were pre-occupied with protecting their own market niches and not prepared to take the same risks as Monaghan in an unknown market. They were older and larger firms whose management had a self-preservation mentality dedicated to following the safe road. They were reticent to create a national chain requiring fleets of delivery vehicles, a solution for keeping pizzas warm during delivery, and meeting an impossible prep, cook, and delivery schedule. Tom Monaghan was not deterred by these monumental obstacles. He envisioned the opportunities and was competitive enough to overcome every problem.

Tom Monaghan's passion was a "guaranteed thirty-minute pizza delivery." He promoted this with a guarantee to deliver on time or the customer would get a cut in the price. He came up with the idea in the early 1960s but didn't attempt to implement it nationally until the early 1970s. He preached thirty-minute pizza delivery everywhere he went. His other innovative ideas included dough trays, corrugated pizza boxes, insulated bags, pizza screens, and conveyor ovens. The Domino's franchise system is very unique and also a Monaghan innovation. It is highly leveraged, which caused Monaghan's cash flow problems throughout the growth period of Domino's. His bouts with bankruptcy were caused by the franchising leverage. Leverage—the two-edged sword of the entrepreneur—caused Monaghan's many crises but also made him a billionaire.

Personal History

Tom Monaghan was born on March 25, 1937, in Ann Arbor, Michigan. Four years later, his father's death led to a childhood of foster homes and orphanages. He lived with a number of different families prior to entering the first grade. One was a very strict German family. (This experience is much the same as that of Arthur Jones of Nautilus.) Tom baled hay, milked cows, drove tractors, and delivered newspapers.

An unhappy and unsettled youth was responsible for Tom's many hours spent reading and dreaming of better days. He lived for six and a half years in a Catholic orphanage—St. Joseph's Home for Boys in Michigan. The time at St. Joseph's was one of the most influential on Tom's life, future business career, and success. It probably was the most unpleasant as well.

In his biography, Monaghan referred to St. Joseph's as a prison and his classmates as inmates. It appeared he made these references unconsciously, which tends to give some credence to their immense impact on his adult compulsions and drives. His mentor at the school was a Catholic nun, Sister Berada, whom he speaks of with reverence, referring to her as his surrogate mother.

As a child, Tom fantasized about larger-than-life world leaders discovered during his many hours in the library. He was raised as an only child, which gave him a great deal of time alone with his books. His heroes were P. T. Barnum, Frank Lloyd Wright, and great world leaders like Lincoln. He became enamored with their rise from poor beginnings to prominence and decided to emulate them. Striving to achieve this "rags to riches" dream kept him very competitive. He aspired to excellence from the insecurity bequeathed to him. Competing was his path and energy and drive were his vehicle. Tom became excellent at games and was driven to win at most childhood games he entered. It became his identity and solace. He also became a top student in the second grade, which he says was the first and last time education was important to him.

While in the sixth grade his mother brought his younger brother home to live with her and left Tom in the boarding school. This was a devastating experience for the eleven-year-old. She ultimately brought Tom home to live but the family interaction proved disasterous. She soon placed Tom in a state foster home. The constant moving and instability created an adversarial relationship between Tom and his mother. This instability continued unabated until the ninth grade, when Tom had enough of the insecurity and decided to become a priest. His decision appears to have been a lonely kid's search for the security and identity provided by the priesthood. It was also a flight from an unhappy home environment. He was accepted at Grand Rapids Seminary but was asked to leave after six months. He was told he lacked the "vocation" for the priesthood.

Monaghan moved in with his mother as a teenager and after he borrowed her car without telling her, she had him arrested. He refused to apologize to her and she had him put in jail. On his release she placed him in a detention home. In a 1989 interview with *GQ* magazine he said, "[I] have forgiven her everything but this." He barely graduated from St. Thomas High School in Ann Arbor in 1955, entered Ferris College and dropped out after one semester.

Tom enlisted in the Marine Corps in 1956, which proved to be a memorable learning experience for him. He thought he had joined the Army but found himself in the Marines. Tom spent his service time in the Orient dreaming of great accomplishments and reading Dale Carnegie, Frank Lloyd Wright, P. T. Barnum, and other biographies of famous and successful men (this has also been the pattern in the early lives of Turner, Lear, Smith, and Jones). The Marine Corps taught him discipline and fitness, which are the two traits he credits for the success of Domino's. He says the Marine Corps drilled these important characteristics into him.

Business and Personal Survival

Tom Monaghan was twenty-three in 1960 when he and his brother purchased DomiNicks in Ypsilanti, Michigan, with a loan of $900. He bought his brother's interest within the year for a used Volkswagen Beetle. By 1965 he had renamed the business Domino's and began operating three stores near college campuses. Tom struggled through two different partnerships during this period, which almost cost him the business. It ingrained in him the tenacity to never give in to adversity. He flirted with bankruptcy in 1966 and was bailed out at the eleventh hour after one of his nefarious partners went bankrupt and left him with the bills.

Tom opened his first franchise store in Ypsilanti in April 1967. A near disastrous fire almost wiped him out in 1968, the beginning of a period beset by crisis after crisis that would have defeated a lesser individual. Monaghan began 1969 on a roll and expanded to thirty-two company-owned stores that were built on credit through a highly leveraged franchise program. The expansion nearly bankrupted him as he ran out of cash and faced over one hundred lawsuits arising from a $1.5 million debt owed to fifteen hundred creditors. Monaghan never lost his sense of humor, referring to the debacle by commenting, "I've become a reverse millionaire." He calls to this time as "the crash period."

He says it occurred due to his lack of business acumen necessary to operate a chain of franchised and company stores.

Administration, financing, budgeting, and organization were not his forte, and Tom ended up $1.5 million in debt within eighteen months. This debacle actually cost him control of Domino's. On May 1, 1970, the bank that was financing Domino's took over the company and ran the finances with Tom as president but without authority. He would have been thrown out altogether except for the fact that he was the only person they could find who would work fifteen-hour days, seven days a week for $200 per week. Plus the company was technically insolvent and no aspiring executive would have touched the job.

On March 22, 1971, the bank decided there was no future in Domino's; it was convinced the firm was destined for the bankruptcy courts. The bank gave Tom back his stock in the company in exchange for a Domino's store operation. To Tom Monaghan's lasting credit and moral integrity he made a vow to pay off all creditors in total no matter how long it took. He made good on that promise by taking all the creditors' bills and amortizing them over long periods—payments of 2 percent per month for those over $1,000 and 4 percent for those under $1,000. He diligently paid every bill to every creditor. It took until September 10, 1977, nine long years, to pay off the last of the creditors. This is a tribute to Tom Monaghan's ethical integrity.

In 1975, Amstar (Domino Sugar) sued for trademark infringement for the rights to the Domino's name. Amstar won in the lower court and once again Domino's Pizza had a very dubious future. Tom Monaghan was a fighter. He appealed the judgment, and, after a five-year battle, a federal judge overturned the judgment on April 10, 1980. This represented the beginning of Domino's emergence as a dominant force in the pizza industry.

Monaghan says his success is due to his entrepreneurial spirit and idealism. He also feels religion (he attends mass daily) and the Golden Rule have helped him overcome much adversity. *People* magazine described him as a fitness freak because of his compulsion for exercise. He told reporters he couldn't understand their assessment, since his fitness program was just his method of putting order in his life. This statement gives us some insight into this compulsively driven man whose obsessive regimen defies logic for the average weekend athlete. Monaghan's exercise program is consistent with his desire to overachieve at anything he does. Monaghan's workout program is carried out in *all* weather conditions with the following orderly plan, which he feels is very normal:

> Six days a week, I do forty-five minutes of floor exercises, including 150 consecutive pushups, followed by a six-and-a-third mile run. Twice a week, I end my run in the fitness center at our new headquarters, Domino's Farms,

and work out for an hour. I do repetitions on the progressive resistance [Nautilus] weight machines as fast as possible and have a trainer help me work each muscle group to exhaustion. (Monaghan, 1986)

It's not the typical daily walk-about-the-park for the average executive. Tom confirms his obsessive behavior with, "I dislike moderation," which is clearly evident in the above exercise program as well as in his daily work habits. In *Pizza Tiger,* Tom admits to having worked for the first twenty years with only three days off a year, Thanksgiving, Christmas, and Easter. For the first ten years he worked seven days a week from 10:00 a.m. until 4:00 a.m. the following morning. He did this for $125 a week and a dream. By 1970 he had raised himself to $200 a week.

Personal Behavior Characteristics

Tom Monaghan is an introvert who is internally driven. He has a Promethean temperament based on an intuitive or right-brained approach to perceiving opportunities. A psychologist told him he thinks in patterns—qualitatively instead of quantitatively. He "leaps before he looks," which is quite evident by most of his business decisions and his airplane escapades. He makes decisions based on a rational or logical evaluation, in contrast to how he feels. He prefers open-ended decision-making and allowing things to work their way to fruition. His friend Eugene Power (founder of University Microfilms International) said of him:

I have watched you at board meetings, Tom, and you think intuitively. You do not go step by step through a logical consideration of facts, you go from problem to solution in a single leap. (Monaghan, 1986)

Monaghan describes himself at Domino's in the early years, "I was shy but had a lot of self-confidence." He told his wife on their engagement, "I am going to be a millionaire by the time I am thirty," and meant it. David Hanks, a designer who now works with him, says, "He wants things done quickly. He's always looking to the future, always dreaming." Hanks says that Monaghan is "pursuing a toyless boyhood" with his monumental acquisitions (*GQ,* July 1989). In addition to the Detroit Tigers—a mere $53 million investment—he has three planes, five boats, an island, two homes, and 250 classic cars. One of the cars, a 1931 Bugatti Royale, cost a trifling $8.5 million. In addition, he has accumulated $30 million in Frank Lloyd Wright artifacts. Monaghan is now in the process of disposing of most of these adult toys to devote more of his life to a spiritual existence.

Risk-taking Proclivity

Tom Monaghan has the risk-taking disposition of most innovative visionaries. He ventures into the unknown with the passion of a seasoned veteran regardless of the consequences. An example of this personal risk-taking mentality was an early experience with his Cessna 172 during the late 1960s. He decided not to waste time traveling between stores (a classic innovator trait), purchased the Cessna for fast, reliable transportation to visit franchisees, and took flying lessons.

After earning a student pilot permit and soloing in the plane he decided to fly from Detroit to Vermont over the Appalachian mountains. Tom took off with no flight plan and his navigation strategy consisted of a road map he had bought at a local gas station on his way to the airport. Tom rationalized that he could follow the road in case he got lost (the thought process of an unbelievable optimist or raving idiot). Bad weather came in over Buffalo and he found himself in serious trouble with zero visibility. He radioed for help and the "operator gasped in disbelief." Air traffic control talked Monaghan down through the cloud cover and into an emergency landing. Monaghan says, "I rolled to a stop near an ambulance and fire truck that were waiting to pick up the pieces." He traveled to Burlington on a bus.

On another trip to Indiana in April 1969 Monaghan landed with ice covering the whole plane and had to cut his way out. His most death-defying experience occurred on a summer flight to Pontiac, Michigan, when clouds closed in on him. His description of the experience:

> I lost control of the plane. It stalled and I found myself in a spin. I pulled back on the control yoke with all my might but I couldn't budge it. Plowed fields were whirling up towards me, and I realized there was nothing left to do but pray. I released the controls, closed my eyes, and folded my hands under my chin. . . . "Father in heaven please help me." The spinning stopped and suddenly the plane was flying level again. (Monaghan, 1986)

The instructor tried to convince Monaghan that he had used the correct tactic for correcting a spin in a Cessna 172. He was not convinced. The very religious Monaghan still believes a higher power intervened.

Competitive Success

Tom Monaghan created the world's largest pizza delivery firm based on a system of simplicity and efficiency. He refused to offer sandwiches or any other product that would distract his store managers from the main objective of delivering the best pizza in the fastest time. Take-out pizza was his business and his only business. The strategy worked and in 1989 Domino's claims to have delivered more than half of all the pizzas in America. His thirty-minute guaranteed delivery became the promotion that set him on his way to preeminence in the home delivery pizza business. Monaghan began the 1980s with five hundred stores and ended the decade with over five thousand. His innovative spirit entrenched him as the king of home-delivered pizza.

The indomitable Tom Monaghan persevered and won the pizza wars. His company dominates the home delivery pizza market in the United States and has a growing presence in most international markets. Domino's had over 6,000 stores going into 1993, generating over $3 billion in systemwide revenues. Tom Monaghan decided to sell Domino's in 1989 and retire to a life of philanthropy and leisure. He received no offers for the firm and announced to the media in mid-1991 that he was returning to the "pizza wars."

In 1984 Tom Monaghan realized a childhood dream and acquired the Detroit Tigers for $53 million. One of the highlights of his life was winning the pennant in his first year of ownership. He has been given six honorary doctorate degrees and was given the Harvard Business School Entrepreneur of the Year Award in 1984. That same year he received the most deserved award of all—the Horatio Alger Award given to the individual most personifying the entrepreneurial spirit. Monaghan is the personification of Horatio Alger and was given this award for his perseverance and rags-to-riches climb to the pinnacle of American business. He received the Napoleon Hill award in the same year. Tom Monaghan's simplistic approach to business proves that a highly focused dedication to a principle can work. His concentration on excellence in execution of goals gives testimony to his methodology.

Tom Monaghan is a great role model for anyone attempting to create a new business or master a detailed one on a national basis. He responded to a letter from the author by noting that "creativity is fostered through unobstructed brainstorming."

Everyone is creative. It's a matter of allowing it to express itself in thought and actions. I feel that lack of formal education was a contributing factor to the creation of Domino's Pizza and in the process, innovating many tools of the trade used throughout the pizza industry today.

Monaghan feels formal education is not necessary for achieving great success in business. This is a universal feeling among even the most educated entrepreneurs. Monaghan wrote, "Formal education is certainly not essential, and sometimes is even a hindrance to creativity."

Thomas Monaghan
born March 25, 1937
Ann Arbor, Michigan

Dominant Personality Characteristic: Competitive to a fault
Mottos: "I'm an optimist at heart." "The body is the temple of the soul." "I dislike moderation." "I try not to let power corrupt."
Nickname: "Pizza Tiger"
Firm Name: Domino's Pizza
Location: Ann Arbor, Michigan
First Innovation/Date: First "take-out only" national pizza chain, 1960
Products: Guaranteed home delivery—hot pizza in 30 minutes
Initial Investment: Borrowed $900 from credit union to open first store
Second Innovation/Date: Innovative pizza boxes, ovens, and vans with warmers

---

Sibling Status: First son. Brother two years younger
Personality Profile: Introverted Intuitive Thinking Perceiver (INTP)
Parents' Occupation: Truck driver father died when Tom was 4; mother a nurse
Childhood Data: Foster homes, orphanage, seminary. Poor and lonely. Voracious reader, dreamer, and terrible relationship with mother
Family Socio-Economic Status: Poor. Lower middle class
Formal Education: High school diploma, one semester college
Age, First Business Venture: Newstand/paper route as a teenager
Age, Big Hit: 23
Hobbies/Activities: Marathoner, pilot, racketball, fitness nut, Detroit Tigers, Indy racing car, 3 planes, 5 boats. Frank Lloyd Wright collection

---

Marital Status: Married
Children: Four daughters
Religion: Attends Catholic mass every day
Public Offering Date: Privately held—Monaghan owns 97 percent of stock
Revenues or Units of Big Hit: January 1993, 6,000 stores, 500,000 pizzas sold every day. Largest pizza takeout chain in the world
Revenues of Firm: $3 billion, 1993
Estimated Worth: Billionaire according to *Fortune,* 1990
Age Became Millionaire: 39 in 1976 when leisure lifestyles and football parties created the take-out bonanza for pizza
Heroes: Frank Lloyd Wright, P. T. Barnum, Ray Kroc, Knute Rockne, and Virgin Mary
Honors: Entrepreneur of the Year Award and Horatio Alger Award, 1984. Six honorary doctorates

9

Nolan Bushnell—Confident

A Wall Street Journal *article on entrepreneurship recently concluded, "Successful entrepreneurs have enormous contagious self-confidence." Dennis Waitley in* Psychology of Winning *said, "Winners have developed strong beliefs of self-worth and self-confidence." McKinsey & Company did a study on the entrepreneurial personality in 1983 which stated, "CEO's radiate enormous, contagious self-confidence." Maxwell Maltz in* Psycho-Cybernetics *wrote, "The most important psychological discovery of this century is the discovery of the self-image . . . behavior, personality, and achievement are consistent with your self-image." The personification of a strong self-image and confidence is Nolan Bushnell of Pong fame.*

Creative and innovative people "believe." They believe in themselves and their decisions, and are oblivious to those who do not have their same vision. They exhibit such confidence in their concepts that fear of failure never paralyzes them as it does other types of people. This behavior is exemplified by Nolan, who had an awesome self-esteem. Fortune *characterized his confidence as "egotistical charm." Bill Lear exuded this same confidence, as described by* Flying *magazine, "His confidence more than anything else defined him." Tom Monaghan's confidence was legend.* Playboy *described Akio Morita of Sony as having the "jaunty confidence of a man who knows where the world's buttons are and how to push them." Shakespeare said it well: "To thine own self be true—and it must follow as the night the day—thou can'st not then be false to any man." Creative geniuses understand this more than most.*

Alfred Adler wrote, "Man's opinion of self and the world influences all his psychological processes" (1918). Winners exemplify this psychologically driven mentality. When winners make mistakes they offer themselves a positive critique, "better next time," while losers tend to flagellate themselves and reinforce the negative. In fact, there is little difference between the top performers in any sport or business activity. The only difference is, "Winners concentrate

*on 'what must I do to win' while losers concentrate on 'how not to lose.' "
Warren Bennis, the educator-writer, has studied leadership at length. He con-
cludes, "Leaders are inner-directed, self-assured, and truly charismatic. . . .
These leaders have proved not only the necessity but the efficacy of self-
confidence."*

*Maslow established esteem needs as the second highest form of self-
fulfillment in his hierarchy of needs. Recent research has shown that self-esteem
is more and more responsible for the problems in dysfunctional children and
adults. Self-confidence is their only ammunition to fight adversity. It is what
the innovators use to stay on track and what Webster calls "Conviction,
Determination, Certainty, and Self-Assurance." It is what Maslow has labeled
prestige and power of the personality. Einstein flunked his college entrance
exams and was still able to rewrite the textbooks due to his unflappable belief
system. Howard Head couldn't ski or play tennis but was confident in his
ability, not the equipment, and changed it. Lear and Bushnell rode the roller
coaster of success and failure like no other and their self-confidence alone carried
them beyond the adversities. A positive self-esteem is necessary for innovative
and creative success. Dennis Waitley says, "Most successful people believe in
their own self-worth. . . . Perhaps more than any other quality, healthy self-
esteem is the door to high achievement and happiness."*

> The picture of the highly creative architect . . . emerged as *self-confident,*
> flexible, self-accepting, having little concern with social restraints or other's
> opinions, and strongly motivated to achieve.
> —Donald MacKinnon, Institute of Personality Assessment and Research

Father of the Video Game Industry

"King Pong" was the nickname given Nolan by the Silicon Valley media. The
name was appropriate as Nolan was the quintessential game player and acknowledged king of games. He had the impetuousness of a kid when it came
to games and the same dependability. Pong was created out of a passionate
desire to make a coin-operated computer game for the masses. Nolan conjured
up the name "Pong" to describe the sound made when the video paddle struck
the video ball. The name was also part of the contraction of Ping-Pong, which
was the essence of how the game was played. "King Pong" also denotes Nolan's
role as the acknowledged father of the video game industry in America.

Nolan is really a fun-loving free spirit who often lost his way back from
lunch if game buddies or a friendly lady accidentally crossed his path. His
temperament was that of a teenage, game-playing, frivolous spirit who appeared
to be masquerading as a middle-aged, bearded 6'4" man. Nolan's childlike love

of games and flamboyant spirit were instrumental in his creation of the video game industry. It was a labor of love played according to the script of Horatio Alger. Without this positive self-confidence, Nolan would never have attracted the faithful following of disciples who were intrumental in his innovations.

Pong was Nolan's second attempt at marketing a video bar game. His first attempt was a game called Computer Space that failed miserably because of its complexity and cost. The game required instructions that were far too sophisticated for the average arcade game player. Nolan simplified Pong by creating a game that everyone knew how to play. Introduced in 1972 it became a hit in 1973 and 1974. Pong changed the world of games in many ways. It changed the coin-operated games industry, the locations accepting of games, and the players of games. It became the pioneer of all mass-marketed, coin-operated video games. Pong changed the nature of *arcade* (pinball) games, *home TV* (cartridge) games, *computer* (PC) games, and more recently the *adult* ("Star Wars") games played by the Pentagon and NASA.

Pong was not the first computerized video game. The Magnavox Odyssey home TV game holds that distinction. However, it was the first computerized coin-operated video game that was mass produced. It created such a revolution that it in fact established a new industry. Pong also holds the distinction of being the first mass-marketed video game acceptable to a wide range of sophisticated players and route operators.

A Technology-based Innovation

The ubiquitous pinball machine dominated the coin-operated industry during the early 1970s. They were large electromechanical machines, technologically inflexible, service intensive, featuring a restrictive distribution system. The electro-mechanical firms who dominated this industry were not inclined to cannibalize their own manufacturing operations by attempting to change their technologies for a foreign technology. This myopic mentality of the industry leaders created an opportunity for new firms who understood the nuances of the newly emerging microchip technology.

Silicon Valley firms were conversant with and comfortable with the new integrated circuit microchip technology. This allowed them to be the first to recognize the vast opportunities in electronically designed video games. An identical scenario was being played out in other industries similarly affected by the power of integrated circuits and diving costs of memory. The calculator, digital watch, and phone industries were going through the same metamorphosis as the games industry during the mid-1970s. The microprocessor had just been invented by Intel in 1971. This development happened to occur coincident with Atari's beginnings—this technological breakthrough was the catalyst for the proliferation of the games industry.

The video game became the stepchild of the emerging integrated-chip technology of more and more power and memory in ever smaller packages at cheaper and cheaper prices. This evolution into the microcosm of micro-computer technology became the driving force of video games, hand-held calculators, digital watches, personal computers, and digital phones. These were all products created in the mid-1970s as a byproduct of the technology. Those firms that did not adapt to this electronic world did not survive. Bushnell was a child of the technology and thus became the father of the video game industry.

Bushnell and Atari actually created three market segments of the game industry. The first was the Pong arcade game, initially marketed in 1972. Second was the home TV version of Pong, which interfaced with the home TV. This game was sold by Sears exclusively during 1974 and 1975. The third segment was the cartridge-loaded game system, which allowed games to be changed and swapped in the likeness of the razor and blade concept. The Video Computer System became the industry standard and dominated the home TV game market from 1977 through 1983. It was the forerunner of today's Nintendo games, which made video game cartridges a must on every kid's Christmas list.

Expert Myopia

Nolan's initial intent was to sell the Pong game concept to Bally's Midway division in 1972. His initial strategy called for designing video games and licensing them to major manufacturers like Bally. That was Atari's original charter. When Nolan flew to Chicago and demonstrated Pong to Bally's executives, he was confident that they would see the potential of Pong and agree to a licensing agreement. Nolan received the same encouragement he was to give Steve Jobs and his Apple computer innovation just four years later. The executives declined his offer with the ignominious comment, "Who would stand in front of a TV screen and play a game with no physical action [like a pinball]?" Bushnell was not discouraged. He donned his supertech cape, flew home to Los Gatos, and placed Pong in Andy Capp's, a local singles bar in Sunnyvale. He was determined to show the world that his game was viable.

The Pong Revolution

Nolan expected the Andy Capp's test to prove the video game was as good at attracting young adult quarters as the ubiquitous pinball machines. The game would need to earn enough to pay back a distributor's investment in twelve to sixteen weeks. This meant Pong needed to earn forty to fifty dollars per week at a quarter per play. This would allow it to compete for location spots with the pinball machines. The owner of Andy Capp's called him two days later and said, "Take this fucking game out of here. It does not work and is upsetting my customers."

Nolan brought circuit boards and other sophisticated test equipment to fix the game. He couldn't find anything wrong with the game. As a last resort he checked the coin mechanism for a coin jam. When he opened the coin box (a breadpan in this prototype) quarters flew everywhere—1,200 of them. Pong had broken because of its success. The coin box held $300 in quarters, unheard-of earnings for any game in any era. Nolan's normal enthusiasm was always ten miles ahead of anyone else's. This Andy Capp's experience pushed him over the edge of rationality and he decided to forget about licensing and to proceed right into a full manufacturing operation immediately.

A Company of Hippies

The early days of Atari were a financial nightmare. The firm's lack of financial resources were only exceeded by its lack of manufacturing and managment experience. Nolan hired bikers, hippies, dropouts, and freaks as minimum-wage production-line workers. A walk through the production area was reminiscent of a stroll through the *Star Wars* bar scene. The attire was T-shirts and sandals. The employees were long-haired misfits who smelled of the cannabis plant. The mood was loose and crazy. Beer parties were rampant and meeting any production schedule was enough excuse to shut down for the day and party.

The spirit at Atari emulated Nolan's fun-loving demeanor. Once when customers with three-piece suits showed up for a plant tour Bushnell convinced his motley employees to jump into large shipping cartons and stay there until the plant tour was completed. Atari gained a reputation in the Silicon Valley as the land of the fruits and nuts. This reputation was tough to come by in those days of Gestalt psychedelia, which had been spawned just fifty miles to the north in San Francisco. However, the demand for Pong was such that it overcame all of Atari's incompetence, inexperience, and underfinancing. It was one of the few growth companies in Silicon Valley in those dark days of 1973 and 1974. It grew quickly, dodged bankruptcy through sheer desire and moxie, and Bushnell began twelve- to sixteen-hour workdays with little or no pay.

Atari delivered the first Pong arcade game in November 1972 and generated $3.2 million in games revenue for 1973. In 1974 eight thousand units were shipped at $1,200 each for $9.6 million in revenue. The top arcade game of this time earned approximately forty-five to sixty dollars per week in revenue on location. The average Pong game brought in two hundred dollars per week. This was a revolutionary change for the nongrowth coin-operated game industry.

The video game became an instant success and spawned numerous competitors, new distributors, and new players. Because the games were sophisticated they were found on college campuses, in airports, and other locations that had never accepted the pool-hall image of pinball machines. Competitors proliferated even faster than the games and helped expand the market faster than otherwise would have been possible. Ironically, Bally's Midway division licensed Pong and actually shipped more games than Atari in 1973-74.

Atari followed with a plethora of new games named Super Pong, Grandtrak, Quadra Pong, Space Race, and Touch Me. These were soon followed by Breakout, Sprint II, Night Driver, Lemans, and Grand Prix. The video game craze grew and was rampant by 1979. That was the year that Space Invaders hit the market. The timing was impeccable. The movie *Star Wars* was a smash hit and Space Invaders became the most-produced video game in history. It changed the game business more than any other game since Pong. Atari sold it as a cartridge, upright video, and as a cocktail game.

The video game became an acceptable entertainment vehicle to the majority of families in America. Fathers and sons played together in arcades and in hotels. Available locations were upgraded to include locations compatible with the me-too generation of game players—businessmen, families and college kids. The new high-technology, sophisticated games were both intellectually and physically challenging. Research proved that players' eye-hand coordination was enhanced by playing games. The pool-hall image of pinball and arcade games was nonexistent. Microprocessor technology had changed the image of coin-operated games and expanded the market to university student union centers and various traditional family-oriented environments like the local pizza parlor.

Atari broke the billion-dollar revenue mark in 1981. On its tenth anniversary in 1982, Atari grossed $2 billion in sales, making it the fastest growing company in history. Atari had an 80 percent market share of an industry that had penetrated 17 percent of American homes. In 1981, at the height of the video game frenzy, the video game industry generated $6 billion in revenues, more than double Hollywood's gross for movies. It was double the gambling revenues for all the casinos in Las Vegas combined, triple the combined TV and gate receipts of professional baseball, basketball, and football, and four times the revenue for all records and rock concerts. Seventy-five thousand man years were spent playing video games in that one year. Bushnell's video game dream had penetrated the psyches of a generation and made game-playing fun.

Personal History

Like Wozniak, Jobs, Morita, and Gates, Bushnell was a child of microprocessor technology. He was born in 1943 in Clearfield, Utah, and raised in a Mormon family that honored the classical European work ethic. His father was a hard-working self-employed mason who instilled the importance of hard work in Nolan. His motto was "Work hard and you can play hard." Nolan learned the lesson well. He was an inveterate tinkerer and built a ham radio at the age of ten. He repaired TVs, radios, and washing machines and worked at various jobs through school. He lost his college tuition money in a poker game and was forced to work the midway at the Lagoon Amusement Park. Nolan was a barker, guessed weights, and worked the milk-bottle pitch games. This experience gave him his "carny" craving for gaming. It also helped him understand the mentality of game players and their motivations and desires. This early experience was invaluable to the development of mass-appeal computer games.

Nolan worked his way through the University of Utah as manager of the games concessions for Lagoon Park. By his own admission he was a poor student. He became known as a game junkie, a label that followed him into adulthood. Games were to become his road to success. They were also the Achilles heal of his education, much like Akio Morita of Sony. When not managing the game department at the amusement park, Nolan spent most of his spare time playing games. Games were instrumental in Nolan graduating last in his class with a degree in electrical engineering at the University of Utah in 1968. When he was unable to get a job offer from Disney he accepted an offer to work in design engineering at Ampex in Mountain View, California, the heart of Silicon Valley.

Business and Personal Survival

Nolan's first game was Computer Space, which he created while working as a design engineer for Ampex. It was a commercial flop. He concluded the game was too complicated and that the world wanted a simple game without instructions. The computer games that he and his friends were playing on mainframe computers were for engineers, not the masses. His analysis of this problem was, "I had to come up with a game people already knew how to play; something so simple that any drunk in any bar could play." Pong met that criterion.

By this time Nolan had moved to Nutting Associates in Mountain View. After he had completed the concept for Pong he resigned and together with Ted Dabney, a former Ampex engineer, he formed Atari to design video games. It was at this time that he decided to take the prototype game to Bally Midway in Chicago. They were not interested and did not believe there was a market for such a game. They were pinball experts who made pinball machines with flippers, bumpers, solenoids, relays, and mechanical scoring. They were non-plussed by a game that had no moving parts and that did not fit their marketing distribution system.

That was when Bushnell and Dabney invested $250 each and began producing Pong games. They had no funding and were required to use their wits. The irrepressible Bushnell started a pinball route on credit and used it to generate cash for the production parts. He was able to conjure up a couple of consulting contracts and then talked Wells Fargo Bank into giving him a $50,000 line of credit. This represented the total capital investment in Atari until Don Valentine, a venture capitalist, put together a consortium of investors for $600,000 in 1975. During the interim Atari was forced to grow internally and by its wits.

The arcade industry was dominated by the pinball machine in the early 1970s. These coin-operated machines were blue-collar, electromechanical in design, and built to last for years. Bushnell's new high-tech video units were considered more white-collar, intellectually oriented devices that appealed to a whole different generation of players. The technology was new, the game play was new, the players were new, and the locations were new. These new electronic games were the byproduct of the microprocessor revolution, which became the driving force behind the video game and arcade industries.

Bushnell is an inveterate innovative visionary who is driven to create, invent, and innovate; as soon as a concept is a success he is off creating his next major creation. He is invariably working two years ahead in his head. The home TV version of Pong, Nolan's second market innovation, helped spread the game fever to the households of America. This game hooked to the home TV. Sears was given exclusive marketing rights and it sold 150,000 of these home units in 1975. During this time Nolan's fertile mind had already created a new cartridge-loadable game—the Video Computer System, introduced in 1977.

The VCS cartridge game provided a vehicle for testing new game types prior to releasing them to the arcades. This came to fruition with the popular arcade games like PacMan and Space Invaders, which were simultaneously marketed to the home market and the arcade market. In addition, tennis, car racing, star wars, and chess kinds of games could be offered as a commodity product to the masses. This concept created a new market opportunity to sell hundreds of millions of cartridges in the late 1970s and early 1980s. It was this marketing magic and a $200 million investment that launched Atari into a $2 billion enterprise.

Bushnell Sells His Dream

Atari was expanding faster than the company could manage or finance. It became immediately apparent that Atari needed massive infusions of capital to continue to market Bushnell's innovations. Atari, in 1976, was in the coin-operated arcade games industry, the consumer electronics industry, and was considering the personal computer industry. The fertile mind of Bushnell had strained the ability of the firm to finance the operation and Bushnell decided to sell instead of taking the company public.

Bushnell's first choice of a suitor was Disney, his favorite company. They were not interested. The next choice was MCI, who also passed on the opportunity. But Warner Communications was cash rich at the time and on an aggressive acquisition bent. They had not even been on Atari's list.

Nolan sold Atari to Warner Communications in September 1976 for $28 million in cash and long-term employment contracts for him and his key employees. Part of the deal included a further investment of $100 million to finance the growth envisioned by the ever-creative mind of Bushnell. Warner had already acquired *Mad* magazine and other high-profile and risk-oriented ventures that were of the same ilk as Atari. As a result, Warner was not deterred by Atari's free-spirit reputation. The sale rewarded Nolan with $15 million in cash. The first Pong game had been built less than four years earlier. Bally saw no opportunity for the video game innovation, motivating Nolan to take a $250 investment and multiply it sixty thousand times in less than four years. Such are the rewards of risk-taking innovators.

Nolan's Second Innovation—Family Entertainment

Nolan resigned under pressure from Warner in 1979 and assumed the full-time position as chairman of Pizza Time Theatre. He had acquired the Pizza Time operation from Warner for $500,000 in 1977, as Warner was not interested in pursuing another of Nolan's whimsical concepts. The first prototype of this fantasyland concept had been completed at Atari in 1977, but Warner didn't see any future in the concept.

Pizza Time grew faster than Atari, and ultimately Nolan made more money with this concept than he had at Atari. Pizza Time theaters were large restaurants featuring pizza, massive game arcades, stage shows of robotic animated characters, computer game rooms, kiddie playgrounds, and a furry rat MC and mascot named Chuck E. Cheese. The costumed character delivered pizza to birthday parties and danced with the children. The concept was an instant success, as it filled a market void for families with small children from three to fifteen years old. Revenues shot to $1.25 million per unit with 25 percent pre-tax margins.

During the 1970s there were no real opportunities for a mother, father and children to eat, play, and be entertained together. The traditional amusement parks, zoos, and national parks were seasonal and not always appealing to the adults in the family. They were also regional destinations not conducive to weekly family events. Pizza Time Theatre offered the family a small, localized eating/entertainment concept at a fraction of the cost of destination parks. The stores were located in or near shopping malls in every metropolitan market in the United States.

The Pizza Time concept grew in concert with the video game rage. It went from a single store in San Jose in 1977 to 250 stores in 1983. Revenues went from zero to $250 million with corresponding profits. Nolan's personal stock value at the public offering in April 1981 was $48 million. He had had two successive winners and became the darling of Wall Street. This was short-lived, however, as Nolan's creativite bent once again got in the way of his long-term success.

Nolan used the Pizza Time Theatre venue to satiate his desire to create and innovate. He was afflicted with the disease of most creative geniuses, who would rather create than operate. Nolan organized various divisions within the corporate structure of Pizza Time to build games (Sente to compete with Atari), create animated cartoons (Kadabrascope to compete with Disney), pioneer a new singles bar concept (Zapps to compete with TGI Friday's). Then he started working on a miniature amusement park concept. All of this was accomplished within the confines of Pizza Time and was financed with Pizza Time capital.

What is truly amazing, he created all of the above divisions within Pizza Time Theatre while simultaneously establishing a whole new series of businesses within the confines of an incubator company called Catalyst. This attempt at building a vertically integrated conglomerate was too much for the resources of Pizza Time. The firm was forced to file for Chapter 11 protection when these various divisions ate up all of the operating cash and capital from the Pizza Time Theatre operation. The firm was sold out of bankruptcy to its largest competitor, Show Biz Pizza of Dallas—one of Pizza Time's first franchisees.

Personal Behavior Characteristics

Nolan Bushnell is the only subject in this study who has an extroverted intuitive thinking perceiver (ENTP) personality type. According to Keirsey (1984),

> ENTPs wish to exercise their ingenuity in the world of people and things
> . . . thus they deal imaginatively with social relationships as well as physical
> and mechanical relations. They are very alert to what is apt to occur next,
> and always sensitive to possibilities.

Bushnell is the quintessential extrovert, drawing most of his energies from the external world. He innovates and makes strategic decisions with an obstinate intuitive belief in his vision. He makes tactical decisions with rational and impersonal thought processes. Bushnell operates in an open-ended, spontaneous way relative to all business and personal dealings. Structure is not his forte.

The one consistent personality trait of Nolan Bushnell is that he "never lets the 'given way' get in the way of a 'new and unknown way' when attempting new innovative opportunities" (quote to Landrum, 1976). Keirsey substantiates this behavior as a key characteristic of the ENTP personality:

> The ENTP is the most reluctant of all the types to do things in a particular
> manner just because that is the way things always have been done. They
> characteristically have an eye out for a better way, always on the lookout
> for new projects, new activities, new procedures.

Keirsey also paints these personality types as fascinating conversationalists. Nolan meets this description as well, as he was known as the ultimate "charmer" and "snake oil salesman" of Silicon Valley. Bushnell fits the mold of the "nonconformist who enjoys outwitting the system to win the game— whatever it may be." This iconoclastic attitude was never more prevalent than his admonition about parking meters. He was parking his Rolls-Royce in San Francisco in 1982 and said, "Don't bother feeding the parking meter Gene. These spots are the rich man's parking lots" (Landrum 1983). Another such Bushnellism was, "Let's not allow the truth to stand in the way of making that deal, Gene" (Landrum 1979).

Bushnell is the consummate optimist, to the detriment of his own well-being. He believes in his new ventures to such a degree he is willing to risk everything in the pursuit of his dreams. An example of his positive myopia was his venture into home robotics, to the tune of $8 million in 1982. This was his personal investment, not venture capital money. He was passionately convinced the era of the home robot was at hand. He told reporters these robots would replace the dog in bringing the paper to their owners—and believed it. When questioned about the viability of home robots, he responded, "Live entertainers are expensive. You don't have to pay robots." The operation closed with a loss of $15 million in the mid-1980s.

Bushnell was the inveterate "happy go lucky" game player. He would gamble on who would come through the door next. He would stand in the Chuck

E. Cheese game parlors and play games with friends for $100 per game for hours. His philosophy is that business is a game and all business should be conducted in the same manner as a game. He believes that the rewards at the end of all games or business are only an accounting of how well you have played the game.

The name "Atari" is a reflection of Nolan's game mentality and competitive spirit. The name was taken from an ancient Japanese game called Go. It means, "I'm going to attack you," in the same context of "checkmate" in the game of chess. It demonstrates Bushnell's aggressive and competitive nature and desire to keep games at the center of his world.

Risk-taking Proclivity

Nolan Bushnell is a game player and gambler in the vein of Turner and most other great entrepreneurs. He has a game room in his home and games of some variety in virtually every room including a movie theatre, ice cream parlor, tennis court, waterslide, boche ball court, crochet, volleyball, and swimming pool. This array of adult toys is used to placate his whimsical, childlike need for fun and frivolity and also to entertain his seven children.

The Catalyst—Bushnell's incubator for "mothering" new business concepts —was started in 1982. It demonstrates his vision and his risk-taking proclivity better than any of his other ventures. In some respects it surpassed Ted Turner's need for speculation and risk-taking. The first firm within this group was called Androbot. It designed and built robots for the home. This venture went through $15 million in a three-year period. Timbertech was a firm created to teach computers to young children. Bushnell's next venture was created while sailing the Transpak Race from Los Angeles to Hawaii. He and some crew members came up with a satellite navigational system for automobiles and commercial vehicles. On their return, Nolan started a company named Etak to design and market this space-age concept.

Nolan, the ageless kid, created a company called Axlon to enter the high-tech toy business with talking animals. He then started a retail vending machine company that he predicted would obsolete the department store, named Bi-Video. He tested his mind in the commercial microwave communications business with a firm named Magnum-Microwave. Nolan and his wife Nancy then opened a continental restaurant by the name of Lion & Compass and a singles club called Zapp's Bar & Grill. The seasonal color industry was in full force in the mid-1980s, which prompted Nolan's fertile mind to concoct a new color computer called IRO. This computer would scan the skin and hair of patrons and print-out a personalized color compatibility for customers. Sente became Bushnell's game company, established to compete with Atari and other coin-operated game companies.

Bushnell was chairman and invested heavily in most of these firms. He did not do well. He raised outside risk capital and also risked many millions of his personal fortune. Most of these ventures were never able to return their investment. His ability to conjure up new concepts and then go for it is reminiscent of Bill Lear and Bushnell unabashedly rolls the dice with the disdain of Ted Turner.

Bushnell had a net worth of $80 million before he was forty and lost much of it due to the above business gambles before he was forty-five. He continues to play the game in the same fashion as the entrepreneurial whiz kids like Lear, Delorean, and Trump. Nolan made a fortune and lost a fortune on games. Games are his identity, not unlike Trump's identity with the "deal." These high rollers have made their mark based on their strong conviction that business is a game and they play as if it were monopoly money.

Innovative geniuses often bet the farm on their intuitive beliefs and win big—and they often make monumental blunders with the same huge consequences. This was the case in the 1970s, when Nolan grossly miscalculated the potential of the PC market. Steve Jobs had worked on and off for Nolan in the frenetic days of 1973–75. Therefore, Bushnell was one of the first people Jobs contacted when he and Wozniak developed the prototype of the Apple I personal computer in 1975. Nolan, the consummate visionary, told Jobs that he did not see any market potential for the personal computer. This shows that even a visionary genius can be myopic when the idea is not his own.

Confident Success

Nolan Bushnell is a confident optimist with an awesome self-esteem. He takes all adversity in stride and does not allow the ups and downs to distort his vision or goals. The game of business is a game in his mind and games are fun. He plays them with vigor and a positive mental attitude. Defense is not part of his demeanor. He only plays offense.

Nolan is a fun-loving extrovert with a fertile mind and an extremely limited attention span. His philosophy on new business opportunities makes Norman Vincent Peale seem negative in comparison. His careless, fun-loving spirit includes a hyperactive libido as well. An example of this is an escapade that occurred at the Atari/Warner closing in New York City in the fall of 1976. Nolan was single at the time and was given a million-dollar check as an advance on his $15 million windfall from the Atari sale. In his inimitable fashion he partied much of the night at New York night spots with an eye on one of the female attorneys from Warner. Nolan lost the million-dollar check during his overzealous partying. His new employer must have been in shock when the chairman of the board of the new acquisition had to call and have a stop payment placed on a million-dollar check. To Nolan, the check was just another chip that he considered a reward for having played the "game" well. Life is a bowl of cherries for the ever-confident father of video games.

The early days of the video game found the establishment bad-mouthing the game as deliterious to the health and welfare of children. Local, state, and federal governments began banning them from various uses and environments. This witch-hunt mentality so pervasive in human history, from Galileo to Einstein, was rampant in the late 1970s and early 1980s in the video game industry. Dope use was attributed to game playing, as was poor vision, delinquency, and other behaviors not controllable by parents. The video game has since been vindicated, as reported by *U.S. News & World Report.* UCLA psychologist Patricia Greenfield did a study on the effect of games on the players. She says video games require a wide range of cognitive skills essential to learning, problem solving, creativity, and visual and spatial conceptualization. She found improvement in the "intellectual abilities among college students who frequently play video games." *Popular Science* has furthered the support, saying, "The old teaching machines reeked of routine. Computer toys give the user the experience of 'thinking well' " (February 1990).

King Pong, alias "The P. T. Barnum of Silicon Valley," has been accused of over-optimism. The accusation is true. He has also admitted to being less than interested or qualified to run a company's day-to-day operations. However, Nolan is the talented innovator who used an inviolable self-confidence and esteem to change the way the world plays games. The world is more fun because of Nolan Bushnell. His zero to $2 billion Atari run was not to last but it was a game that was fun and interesting.

Nolan K. Bushnell
born February 5, 1943
Clearfield, Utah

Dominant Personality Characteristic: Confident—an awesome self-esteem
Motto: "Innovation is 'pulling back the foreskin of creativity.' "
Nickname: King Pong
Firm Name: Atari, Pizza Time Theatre, Axlon
Location: Sunnyvale, California
First Innovation/Date: Atari, 1972
Products: Video games, arcade and home cartridge games
Initial Investment: $250 from savings and $250 from Ted Dabney, an early
    partner in Atari
Second Innovation/Date: Pizza Time Theatre, 1977

Sibling Status: Only son, second of four children
Personality Profile: Extroverted Intuitive Thinking Perceiver (ENTP)
Parents' Occupation: Father self-employed mason, mother housewife
Childhood Data: Working class. Built ham radio at 10. An entrepreneurial
    youth with jobs selling and repairing radios and TVs. Worked his way
    through college
Family Socio-Economic Status: Mormon home and work ethic. Middle class
Formal Education: University of Utah, BSEE, 1968 (last in class)
Age, First Business Venture: Worked through school. Atari at 29 (1972)
Hobbies/Activities: Competitive sailing (two Transpak races from L.A. to
    Hawaii—finished first in time, 1982), skiing, tennis

Marital Status: Married twice
Children: Seven children from two marriages
Religion: Agnostic, born Morman
Public Offering Date: Atari sold to Warner 1976. Pizza Time public April
    1981
Revenues or Units of Big Hit: Shipped 8,000 Pong games, 1973; shipped 100,000
    home TV cartridge games, 1975. Pizza Time Theatre reached 250 stores
    and $250 million, 1982
Revenues of Firm: Atari broke $1 billion in 1981, $2 billion in 1982
Estimated Net Worth: $80 million in mid-1980s
Age Became Millionaire: 32, 1975
Heroes: In business, Walt Disney; the intellectual philosophers
Honors: Father of the video game industry

10

William Gates III—Driven

Alfred Adler said all successful men are driven to strive for superiority. Bill Gates, the acknowledged father of the PC software industry, is the personification of Adler's personality profile of the successful man. USA Today characterized Gates as "competitive even when giving parties" and as a "determined, combative, and ruthless dealmaker." Inc. magazine portrayed Gates as a "fidgety bundle of energy." Even Gates says Paul Allen and he "were total addicts" when they got on their computer terminals. And on their early days at Microsoft he says, "Paul and I worked day and night writing a language called BASIC that could be used to program the Altair." Paul Allen said, "We used to take the bus over (to school) and program until 3:00 or 4:00 a.m."

David Silver, a high-technology venture capitalist and author, says, "Entrepreneurs make better use of time than any other group in society . . . place an inordinately high value on time . . . They drive quickly, take early flights, avoid time eaters, speak rapidly, and walk at a quick pace." A testimony to this behavior is Ted Turner's refusal to fly with anyone who checks bags. He believes it is a needless waste of time. Bill Gates is even more obsessive about time. He normally eats at his desk or in fast-food restaurants. He never eats at home because he doesn't want to waste the time to fix the food. He is single but only dates women who are involved in the software or computer industries. Time is of the essence at work and at play, a strange malady for a man of thirty-five with a net worth of $7.4 billion.

Creative personality researcher David McLelland says, "Achievement is the desire to do something 'better, faster, more efficient' and with less effort." Extensive research on the creative personality by Roe (1972) found that, "Willingness to work hard seemed to be the most general characteristic for creativity . . . emanating from the labor of a driven person." Venture magazine (1989) described "an all-consuming desire to succeed" as the most important personality trait for the entrepreneur. One example of this all-consuming desire to succeed or Adler's "striving for superiority" was when Gates decided to pursue IBM in the creation of DOS. He called his mother and told her he wouldn't see her for six months because he would be "working twenty-four hours a day to get the IBM deal." He made the deal and the rest is history.

The intensity and drive of Gates is legend and contagious according to Scott Oki, a senior vice president at Microsoft. He says the Gates influence is pervasive. "We have a maniacal work ethic here . . . Everyone has a sense of participating in a crusade." Inc. (1991) profiled Gates as a "ruthlessly competitive entrepreneur." Fortune magazine in 1990 said, "Gates is so intense that he rocks almost constantly during conversation." A girlfriend characterizes Gates as "going to the edge all of the time." Another says he is "consumed with winning" and uses his "force of will" to overwhelm his adversaries, not unlike the nineteenth-century industrialists like Rockefeller, Carnegie, and Mellon.

The ultimate compliment came from Bill's competitors, who told the media (1991), "We'd love to see Bill get married and have a few kids. We'd love to see him mellow out." The Los Angeles Times interviewed Microsoft's competitors, who said, "Bill Gates is a megalomaniac. He wants to win at everything he does." Forbes has said that Gates is massacring his competitors, to which they attribute the FTC investigation of Microsoft's virtual monopoly in the software industry.

The driven Type A behavior of Bill Gates is found in most great leaders and innovators, including those in this book. They have "rushing sickness," are notoriously impatient with lethargic employees, and are intolerant of stupidity or incompetence in the workplace. They are intellectually arrogant because of their drive for superiority and excellence. Their work ethic is beyond any rational norm for society but it is one of the major factors in their success. Their driven behaviors cause them to hurry through work, play, and life. Their idea of relaxing is reading The Economist while watching the news, having lunch while reading competitive reports, and visiting the Acropolis with a book on archeology. Bill Gates is their role model.

The genius's goal rivets his attention and puts order among his ideas. In fact, his concentration upon the activity . . . becomes an obsession. In this effort, not merely the mind and the will, but the whole organism—muscles, blood, nerves, and glands—are involved. This mad passion or passionate madness is the reason why psychopathic personalities are often creators and why their productions are perfectly sane.

—Jacques Barzun, *The Paradoxes of Creativity* (1989)

Software Innovation

Bill Gates will go down in history as the youngest self-made billionaire ever (early 1992 stock jumps have placed his net worth at an estimated $7.4 billion). And, according to David Bunnell, publisher of *PC World,* "When the history of the microcomputer industry is written, Bill Gates will be remembered as the guy who wrote the first successful program for the mass market." *U.S. News & World Report* (February 1993) characterized Gates as the present-day Rockefeller.

How did he do this? First, he became an expert on microprocessor programming in BASIC while still in high school. He and his high school buddy Paul Allen wrote the first operating software for the Altair 8080 computer kit as teenagers. By the time IBM decided to enter the PC race (July 1980), Gates had earned a national reputation as one of the top microprocessor software experts in the United States. This reputation gave him an entree to IBM, who gave Microsoft a development contract for the MS-DOS operating system in October 1980. This coup was consummated prior to Gates's twenty-fifth birthday and was a unique arrangement for Big Blue, which was not used to working with a group of counterculture hackers with few capital resources. This event preordained Gates's emergence four years later as the "Boy Billionaire."

Gates created MS-DOS—the industry-standard PC operating system (90 percent of the world's computers operating in 1993 were using MS-DOS)—for IBM, and in a stroke of genius reserved the rights to sell it to any competitor of IBM. This was not luck. It was based on the genius of Gates and the insecurity of IBM. IBM was not sure they could catch up to Apple at the time and was happy to allow the copying because they were fighting an uphill battle for industry supremacy. They were unaware of the monstrous "clone" and "knock off" market that was out there just waiting to be fed with the wherewithal to copy any IBM machine. History has shown that the clones are what has made Gates and Microsoft such a dominant force in the industry and removed IBM as the dominant force in the world of computers.

Gates started Microsoft in 1975 while in Albuquerque, New Mexico, writing BASIC software programs for the Altair. Altair sold out in 1977 and disappeared in 1979. Paul Allen joined Microsoft and they relocated to their home town in Bellevue, Washington. They continued licensing their BASIC software to the then-burgeoning personal computer makers. Gates admits Microsoft finally stabilized when they licensed software to Apple in 1977 for the Apple II. By 1980 they had written programs for Commodore, Radio Shack, and Apple, giving them a reputation as the gurus of personal computer operating software and enough credibility to open the tough doors at IBM. Their reputation, coupled with the disdain for IBM by Digital Research, the creators of the CPM operating system and Microsoft's chief competitor in the early days, is what led to Gates's fateful September 1990 meeting with Big Blue.

Microsoft dominates both operating and applications software for the personal computer industry throughout the world. Its MS-DOS operates on the IBM PC system, compatibles like Compaq, and the clones. Its Excel program operates on the Macintosh and the PC. Windows 3.0 and 3.1 are an emulation of the Macintosh system for the PC. The 1990 release of Windows 3.0 was a phenomenal success. Microsoft shipped three million units during the first year while IBM shipped only 300,000 units of its competing OS/2 system. In 1991 Microsoft shipped 40 percent of all the PC software in the world and MS-DOS was operating on over a hundred million PCs. By 1993 Microsoft was shipping a million copies of Windows every month.

Microsoft is now generating sales in excess of three billion dollars annually (1993). Bill Gates's dream of a PC on every desk and in every home is coming very close to reality. At the present growth rate America could have significant saturation by the millennium. When asked about the future of the personal computer, Gates made a personal prediction to *Inc.* magazine (December 1990), "Ultimately the PC will be a window to everything people are interested in— and everything we need to know." If Bill Gates is allowed to pursue this dream it could well happen based on his insight, energy, and drive.

Personal History

William Gates was born October 28, 1955, the first child and only son of a prominent Seattle lawyer and a socialite mother. He has two younger sisters. After attending private schools, he was expected to follow in his father's footsteps by attending Harvard Law School. Bill was a computer junkie by the time he reached the seventh grade, however, and dreamed of becoming a math professor. The Lakeside School Mother's Club bought time on a mainframe for the students when Bill and his school chum Paul Allen were in middle school. This changed Bill's life as he and Allen become so enamored with the ability to program they would skip gym class to play with the computer. According to Allen, they would program until 4:00 a.m. on school nights and all day on weekends.

As an eleven-year-old Gates was eager to win a trip to the Seattle Space Needle restaurant, which was being sponsored as a competition by his pastor. The challenge was to memorize the Sermon on the Mount, which included three chapters of the Gospel of Matthew. According to biographers Wallace and Erickson, Gates recited the sermon flawlessly. Later he was quoted as saying, "I can do anything I put my mind to." According to high school drama teacher Anne Stephens, Gates once glanced at a three-page monologue for a James Thurber play and memorized every line instantly.

Gates and Allen entered the world of entrepreneurship at the age of fifteen. They wrote a traffic program and formed a company to sell traffic programs that they named Traf-O-Data. Their destiny was in the making as they earned $20,000 on this project and had not yet entered high school. By the time Gates was seventeen his reputation had spread and TRW hired him to write software on power allocation for the Bonneville Dam. TRW paid him $30,000 for a year's work—his first and last salaried position. The enterprising young Gates accepted the job and negotiated a deal with the high school to substitute this work for most of his senior year course work.

Gates entered Harvard at seventeen as a pre-law major to follow in his father's footsteps in law or as a math professor. By his own admission he was there in body but not in spirit. He played pinball, bridge, and poker for much of his tenure at Harvard. He does recall "ace-ing" an economics test without ever having attended a class just by cramming.

Paul Allen eventually got a job with Honeywell in Boston and both he and Bill continued their all-night programming forays. At Harvard, Gates earned a reputation as a poker addict and techie freak. Steve Ballmer, a friend and now senior vice president at Microsoft, says Gates never even bothered to take time to put sheets on his bed during his two years there (Rebello, *USA Today,* January 16, 1991). Balmer also says Gates was "part poker addict (he would stay up all night playing cards) . . . We knew him as that crazy guy from Seattle with the messy room."

Harvard turned out to be a temporary stop for the impetuous Gates. A 1975 *Popular Electronics* cover story announcing the MITS Altair computer got his attention. He and Allen called MITS and arranged to write a BASIC program for the new hobbyist computer. They worked eighteen-hour days in a Harvard lab to produce the program, which Allen took to Albuquerque. At nineteen Gates took a leave of absence from Harvard as a sophmore and moved to Albuquerque, where he rented a motel room across the street from MITS. He wrote programs and found time to form Microsoft as the business entity with which to sell his output to MITS. He and Allen shared the same hotel room, with Allen working for MITS and Gates programming. According to Gates, he and Allen worked day and night writing those first BASIC programs.

The Albuquerque experience turned out to be very important for their later work with Apple, IBM, Commodore and other firms. The Microsoft operating systems were on the absolute leading edge of the personal computer technology during the late 1970s. *Byte* magazine has said that the Gates/Allen/ MITS experience will become a legend in the computer industry when the history books are written on the subject.

Business and Personal Survival

Microsoft's early days were fraught with danger and uncertainty. When Gates and Allen moved to Albuquerque to program for the MITS computer they were betting their careers on a start-up company that would in fact fail after a few years. Gates had dropped out of school and had bet his future on the software industry. After MITS filed bankruptcy they moved their fledgling firm to Seattle and began licensing BASIC software programs to other PC start-ups. These new firms began failing en masse in the late 1970s. Microsoft was not considered a viable entity in the market until it licensed software for the Apple II in 1977.

Gates and Allen were very enterprising entrepreneurs. They licensed many of the new home computer makers who were making inroads into the market during the late 1970s and early 1980s. Commodore, Radio Shack, and Apple were using Microsoft operating software when IBM finally decided it was time to enter the market in July 1980. Its target introduction of the now ubiquitous PC was August 1981.

Gates's genius was convincing IBM to allow him to write software for the PC using the new Intel 8088 chip—a sixteen-bit microprocessor—which allowed him to create a design structure for others. IBM changed its designs to fit the Gates-recommended MPU logic and gave Microsoft the development contract in October 1980. This contract was destined to change the history of the personal computer industry. Both IBM and Microsoft won. It is a matter of conjecture as to who won the most. Gates's major competitor— Digital Research—was preoccupied with other business and did not offer any competition. Gates walked off with the most lucrative design contract in the history of computers. IBM's crash program did not allow any extensive bidding and Microsoft was left alone with the MS-DOS development.

Gates had retained the rights to sell MS-DOS to other users, including competitors of IBM. Big Blue saw no risk in this and actually encouraged it, as it was convinced Apple was its only major threat. IBM was arrogant and not concerned with the small firms who might buy the operating system from Microsoft. But the strategy got IBM into the PC business, which they would dominate for the rest of the eighties. They made Gates and Allen billionaires. Gates's father must have been proud of this ingenious bit of negotiating, as it turned out to be a momentous coup. The contract was a first for IBM, because it had never allowed another firm to control the operating system of one of its key products. The move came as a total shock to most of the industry, especially since Apple had made such a point of keeping all operating software proprietary. The MS-DOS contract was a stroke of genius, luck, and hard work for Gates and has been worth billions of dollars to Microsoft.

A 1991 probe by the Federal Trade Commission, still ongoing, may end by breaking Microsoft up into two different operating entities—operating software and applications software. The monopolistic position that Microsoft gained during the 1980s scared the industry and the government. Microsoft competitors saw it as a way to compete more effectively and welcomed the help from the government, which is ironic for an entrepreneurially driven industry.

Microsoft dominates the industry with 44 percent of total software revenues. This dwarfs their nearest competitors. Microsoft is twice the size of Lotus and Borland together. Microsoft is even larger than the largest mainframe software firm. Mitch Kapor, founder of Lotus, conceded the software market to Microsoft. He told a reporter in 1991, "The revolution is over. Bill Gates has won. Today's software industry is the Kingdom of the Dead."

People magazine gave Gates the ultimate tribute for an entrepreneurial innovator. It said, "Gates is to software what Edison was to the light bulb, part innovator, part entrepreneur, part salesman, and full-time genius." *Playboy* added to Gates's accolades in a 1991 story that alluded to Microsoft as the savior for the United States software industry. "The role of DOS as a unifying component of most PCs has helped entrench the U.S. as the epicenter of worldwide software."

Forbes put Gates on the front page in April 1991 and asked the question, "Can Anyone Stop Him?" It concluded somewhat prophetically that a few top competitors will team up in an effort to derail the Microsoft express. Shortly after the article appeared IBM and Apple—two bitter rivals through the 1980s—have agreed to team up in a venture that appears to be more of a move to stop Bill Gates than anything else.

Personal Behavior Characteristics

Bill Gates is a compulsive workaholic. When asked if he really works until 4:00 a.m., Bill said he does occasionally but the media has exaggerated it. In a sincere attempt to show that his work ethic is just an ordinary day-at-the-office routine, Gates described a typical day. He told David Rensin of *Playboy,* "I generally work until midnight, with a break for dinner with someone from work. Then I go home and read a book or the *Economist* for an hour or so. Generally, I'm back in the office by nine the next morning." This is the work ethic of a thirty-something billionaire who could never spend his money if he tried. In 1993 he was still working six days a week, thirteen hours a day.

Gates's understated, casual description of his work habits is reminiscent of Tom Monaghan saying that three hours of strenuous exercise six days a week in all weather conditions is just a controlled regimen. Both Monaghan and Gates act as if they are functioning in a normal manner and honestly feel the media is exaggerating their actions with descriptions of "obsessive" and "compulsive" behavior. The mindset of driven innovators like these two is to believe their behaviors are normal when it is quite extreme or even bizarre to the average employee or manager who is less driven.

Bill Gates has been labeled a "nerd" by the *Wall Street Journal* and *Inc.* His youth, mode of dress, height, nonconforming attitude, intellectual precocity and introversion have led the media to characterize Gates as the consummate nerd who has made it in the land of high technology. However, Gates is very charismatic in his own way. He has little or no turnover at Microsoft and has a very loyal following of yuppie-type employees. Bernstein Research says Microsoft is "probably the most desired technology company to work for today" (1993). An arrogant intellectual impatience with employees has added to his mystique and his image. He is infamous for his "flame mail," which can berate and intimidate employees. Employees say, "Chairman Bill can be unnerving." This style and work ethic and a constant search for perfection have been responsible for his success and a not-always-fair assessment of his persona.

Gates is an intuitive/thinker based on Carl Jung's personality typology. He is an introvert and a strong judger or closer. His temperament type is Promethean, which is the one most frequently found in entrepreneurial visionaries. Bill "lives on the edge" using an intellectual precocity and competitive risk-taking drive that pervades everything he does. His mistress is work, and he has a penchant for math and rational thinking due to a high IQ. His intellect gives him an exceptional ability to analyze and resolve problems. Paul Maritz, one of Microsoft's programmers, says of him, "Bill is simply smarter than anyone else." Scott Oki, a Microsoft senior vice president, says Bill has the "cumulative intellect of an octogenarian and the hormones of a teenager." A testimony to his intellectual ability is the perfect 800 he scored on the math SAT in the seventh grade.

Gates is a passionate competitor who sacrifices personal pleasures and opportunities to meet his larger goals. He does not work for money and never has. The Wall Street analysts irritate him when they continually hound him about the potential for loss due to the FTC probe. Gates maintains that he will buy the same hamburger and pizza even if he loses a billion or two and cannot control the price and therefore isn't interested. He insists that he works because he likes to, which is lost on the bottom-line mentality of analysts. If the president of Lotus keeps worrying about the price of the company stock, why doesn't he? Gates's response is, "They are worried and their stock price is low, I don't care and the price is high." That is all too prophetic.

Gates, like Ted Turner, Arthur Jones, Soichiro Honda, Steve Jobs, and others, has no interest in a stylish wardrobe and often wears mismatched clothing. Clothes are functional only, which Gates also ascribes to the role of money.

Top: Steven Jobs (Reuters/Bettmann). *Bottom left:* Fred Smith. *Bottom right:* Tom Monaghan.

Note: Photographs of Marcel Bich, Solomon Price, Howard Head, and Arthur Jones not available.

Above: Nolan Bushnell. *Left:* William Gates III

Above: William Lear (UPI/Bett-mann). *Right:* Soichiro Honda

Akio Morita

Ted Turner

Bill does strive to be one of the guys and has altered his management style to that end. Gates has been criticized for his impatience with employees who are not his intellectual equal. This management trait is reminiscent of Honda, Price, and Jones, who had the same style. Gates is very sensitive to the criticism and feels he is improving with age.

Gates is similar to other visionary geniuses married to their jobs and innovations; their identities become their passion. This driven passion accounts for their success as well as the reason they are labeled Type A personalities and have something less than a typical lifestyle or family life. This causes Gates to eat most meals at his desk or in fast-food restaurants. He virtually never eats at home.

Gates refuses to fly first class (a la Ted Turner). Saturday nights are typically spent watching physics lectures on his VCR. Ann Winblad, a Silicon Valley venture capitalist, has been a frequent companion of his on vacations and at corporate events. She says, "He likes going to the edge all the time." An *Inc.* article titled "Triumph of the Nerd" appeared in 1990. It characterized Gates as a

> fidgety bundle of kinetic energy . . . Behind the boyish demeanor lies a ruthlessly competitive entrepreneur . . . Although he can be unyielding and intellectually arrogant—quickly losing patience with those who fail to absorb the nuances of sophisticated computer technology—his inner toughness has taken him to exceptional heights. (Stevens 1990)

Gates has a frenetic energy that causes him to be in perpetual motion when a deal is in the works. A Seattle friend, Vern Raburn, describes Gates's competitive nature, which appears to be the driving force behind his business dealings: "Bill is competitive-plus. Race-car drivers have a phrase for it: red mist. They get so pumped up, they get blood in their eyes. Bill gets red mist" (*USA Today,* January 16, 1991).

Catherine Duncan, a professional psychic, did a personality characterization of Bill Gates for *USA Today* in January 1991: "Gates has felt like a misfit since early childhood, always taking the unbeaten path . . . He has unlimited possibilities in the world. But like a torch, he burns hot and hard and could run out of gas."

Risk-taking Proclivity

Bill Gates is a competitive, self-made, and self-confident innovator of extraordinary talents. He has so dominated his industry that *Forbes* gave this editorial comment in April 1991: "Massacring its competitors, Microsoft may seem headed for a near monopoly in the software industry."

A further testimony to Gates's competitive nature is his fear of failure, which is apparently what drives him to overachieve even though he is one of the world's richest people. He told a reporter in a 1990 interview:

> I have a fear of failure. Absolutely. Every day that I come in this office, I ask myself: Are we still working hard? Is someone getting ahead of us? Is this or that product really good? Can we do more to make it good? (Stevens 1990)

Strange talk from the world's richest man. He also likes fast cars and fast boats. He owns two Porsches and two boats. He was a poker addict at Harvard and played for up to $2,000 a game. He still likes the challenge and is not deterred by risk. His risk-taking is very calculated but he still makes new product entries in much the same way he did when the firm was still a struggling start up venture.

"Type A" Success

By 1990 Microsoft had shipped over fifty million units of MS-DOS software. By 1993 it had over 90 percent of all computers using its software. What did Bill Gates know that IBM didn't? IBM was the dominant computer company. It had annihilated conglomerates like GE, Honeywell, RCA, Philco/ Ford, NCR, and numerous others. Why didn't Intel see this opportunity and exploit it? They had invented the microprocessor, which is the heart and soul of all microcomputers, and had the inside track and all the resources required. Bill Gates was at the right place at the right time with the right talent. He took on the giants and won and now IBM is faced with playing catch-up with the kid it helped launch into the world of PC software. In fact, in January 1993 the market value of Microsoft was $27.1 billion and IBM's was $27.7 billion. The kid is pushing his daddy for supremacy in the computer industry.

Bill Gates had no special gifts that allowed him to monopolize the software industry. He was smart, had a great work ethic, and superlative timing. Bill admits that serendipity played a part but always adds that it took a lot of intense hard work. He also had vision, an innovative spirit, and a risk-taking propensity that was foreign to the self-preservation mentalities that operate in large corporate enterprises like IBM and Intel. Gates was at the right place at the right time but with the right understanding of the needs of the industry. He exploited his opportunities as well as anyone ever. No one in the computer industry has ever made the money Gates has and ironically he could care less. The computer nerd beat the button-down Ivy Leaguers and the fight wasn't even close.

Fortune, in mid-1990, gave Gates credit for the Microsoft miracle. They said, "Microsoft's clarity of purpose, competitiveness, tenacity, and technological self-confidence emanate from Gates." The focus and drive of Bill Gates are the energy that drives Microsoft and the reason America controls the PC operating software industry. The success of Microsoft has made the industry also-rans nervous and ready to throw in the towel. They are anxiously awaiting the FTC investigation in hopes they may be able to extract some small advantage from Microsoft's misfortune.

If the spoils of competition are the barometer of success then Bill Gates is the consummate innovator success story in the computer industry. His "nerd" label has been overdone by the media. His refusal to capitulate to their image of the corporate executive has given them an unconscious desire to paint Bill as a maverick. He bewilders and beguiles Wall Street analysts because of his sincere disinterest in the stock price of Microsoft. If they only understood that if Gates were the type to follow the stock price, Microsoft would not be performing so effectively. Their role models of the corporate executive with the Brooks Brothers suits are not what success is made of in the world of innovation and creativity. A major contribution to that success is that two thousand Microsoft employees have a million dollars of stock. That's 18 percent of the company's work force.

The *Wall Street Journal* (1991) calls Gates, "the single most influential figure in the computer industry." Microsoft's $1.3 billion sales revenues in 1993 gives it such a dominant economic edge in the software business that the FTC is considering a breakup in the tradition of the Rockefellers and Standard Oil at the turn of the century. Success breeds fear in mediocre minds and in bureaucratic organizations. Bill Gates's omnipotence in the software industry has conjured up all the paranoia that the government needed to meddle in the industry.

Bill Gates has made more money than anyone his age in the history of business. According to 1992 *Forbes* and *USA Today* rankings, Gates is the richest person in America, with a net worth of over $7 billion. He is building a $10 million estate on Lake Washington which includes 45,800 square feet of living area, a 14,000-book library, a dining room to seat a hundred, a pool, theater, racquetball and volleyball courts, a twenty-car underground garage and 350 feet of waterfront for his speed boats. Not bad for a thirty-something bachelor who spends very little time at home. Mitch Kapor, the founder of Lotus, gave Gates the ultimate compliment: "When the history books are written, Microsoft will be the Standard Oil of the post-industrial empire. And Bill's got a place like Rockefeller had in the nineteenth century" (Silver 1985).

The miracle of Microsoft was without question the result of the passionate drive of Bill Gates and his ability to instill this drive in others. Roe (1972) concluded from extensive investigations of eminent men, "Creativity . . . does not come from any sudden inspiration invading an idle mind and idle hands, but from the labor of a driven person." And she never met Bill Gates.

William H. Gates
born October 28, 1955
Bellevue, Washington

Dominant Personality Characteristic: Driven, Type A behavior—workaholic
Motto: "A computer on every desk and in every home"
Nickname: Trey (home), "Boy Billionaire" (press), Megalomaniac (competitors)
Firm Name: Traf-O-Data and Microsoft
Location: Redmond, Washington
First Innovation/Date: Traf-O-Data in 1970 (age 15), $20,000 in revenues
Products: Software: Basic for Altair, 1975; Xenix, 1980; MS-DOS for IBM, 1981; Excel for Macintosh, 1985; Windows for PCs, 1986; Windows 3.0, 1990
Initial Investment: Gates savings, then venture capital
Second Innovation/Date: Microsoft, 1975, Albuquerque

Sibling Status: First son. Older and younger sister
Personality Profile: Introverted Intuitive Thinking Perceiver (INTJ)
Parents' Occupation: Father, Seattle lawyer; mother, socialite
Childhood Data: Private schools. Groomed to be lawyer or math professor. Photographic memory, perfect score on math SATs in 7th grade
Family Socio-Economic Status: Upper middle class
Formal Education: Private schools. Harvard pre-law at 18. Dropped out at 19
Age, First Business Venture: Traf-O-Data, 15; TRW, 17
Hobbies/Activities: Programming, reading, powerboating, fast cars

---

Marital Status: Single
Children: No children
Religion: Interested in Buddhism
Public Offering Date: Incorporated 1981. Public offering, March 1986
Revenues or Units of Big Hit: Market share, 74 percent, 50 million MS-DOS shipments
Revenues of Firm: 8,200 employees, $3.1 billion revenues and $1 billion profits, 1993
Estimated Net Worth: $7.4 billion, June 1992, *USA Today*
Age Became Millionaire: 25, 1980 IBM deal. He has since made more money than anyone his age in the history of business. Net worth $300 million by 1986
Heroes: Napoleon, Roosevelt, da Vinci, Alfred Sloan, An Wang, Edwin Land, David Packard, Richard Feyman
Honors: Time cover April 16, 1984. Acknowledged creator of first successful PC programs

11

Marcel Bich—Focused

"If you don't know where you're going, any road will take you." Innovative
visionaries know this better than most. Marcel Bich knew where he was going
to such an extent that he left the roadside strewn with the bodies of those
who crossed his path. One of those was Gillette, which was beaten twice by
Bich. Bich focused on the simple and obvious and let nothing get in his way.
His goal was to provide the masses with cheap, reliable products that could
be thrown away after reasonable use.

Bich's strategy was to find products used by everyone every day but so
expensive they had to be repaired instead of being thrown away. He estimated
the price at which the product was disposable yet extremely utilitarian. This
price for the first throwaway ballpoint pen was twenty-nine cents in 1950, when
competitive pens sold for between $9.00 and $12.95. Bich would ask, "What
kind of plant and equipment will it take to achieve the manufacturing costs
demanded by the low price?" He built enormous new manufacturing facilities
and automated processes to reach his price targets (this is just the opposite
of the large-firm mentalities). He would then saturate the market with a pervasive
distribution system and shout the price and reliablity to the world through
massive consumer ads (such as "Flick Your Bic"). This strategy repeatedly wiped
out all competition and made Bic pens, Bic lighters, and Bic shavers the standard
in the world for throwaway, mass commodity products. Marcel's pricing and
distribution strategy worked as well for him as it has for the Japanese. American
companies have been virtually inept at the process, except in a few areas like
semiconductors.

Marcel Bich's business philosophy was based on his focus on the macro
long-range demands of mass markets. He had a goal and concentrated on
it with the tenacity of a tiger. Dennis Waitley says most people fail to achieve
their goals in life because "they never really set them in the first place." This
is the difference between the successful innovators and the also-rans. Creative

people shape and control their environment while the average person is content to be shaped by it. Maslow confirms this with his research, which showed that, "Self-actualizing creative people are independent, autonomous, and self-directed." Only 10 percent of the population are "self-actualized."

George Bernard Shaw said, "Geniuses are masters of reality." He was referring to their ability to simplify complex events and make them elegantly simple. Innovators have this ability and Marcel Bich more so than most. They seem to have an intolerance for complexity and a powerful drive to make things simple. Chaotic environments such as our present future shock world require more people with this talent. Dr. Illya Prigogine, a Nobel Prize winner, said, "The more complex a system the greater its instability." He said that all organizations are perpetually teetering between "self-destruction and reorganization." All thirteen subjects in this work were able to focus on the reorganization of a market or product and simplify it to fit the needs of the marketplace. They were able to extract simple and elegant solutions out of the clutter and complex. This ability is critical for all aspiring innovators and entrepreneurs and is best personified in this work by Marcel Bich.

It's not as important to know where the puck is now as to know where it will be.

—Wayne Gretzky

Innovator of the Throwaway Culture

Baron Bich created the first throwaway or disposable ballpoint pen. He spent two years developing a cheap but very reliable pen in 1950 and tried to sell the concept of a throwaway ballpoint pen to the major pen manufacturers of the day. They turned him down—an oft-repeated scenario—saying he did not understand the nuances of the sophisticated world distribution system. He was left with three choices: to forget his idea, to develop the product on his own and sell it to small distributors, or to build his own pen company and distribution system. In the tradition of the classic entrepreneur, Baron Marcel Bich decided to create his own brand and market distribution and the world of writing has never been the same.

Bich was an inveterate entrepreneur who was convinced his assumptions about the world markets for commodity products were correct. History has vindicated Bich's market assessments. He now sells over three billion ballpoint pens a year (a million a day in the United States) and his company, Societe BIC, dominates the pen and lighter markets in most countries of the world. He has maintained a 60 percent market share in the United States since his revolutionary pens first appeared in 1957. Bich replicated his pen success with lighters and shavers, and is now attempting the same with a disposable perfume product.

Baron Bich did not invent the ballpoint pen. A Hungarian, Lazlo Biro, invented the first ballpoint pen and called it a "birome." Bich was not the first mass producer of the ballpoint pen either. The European and United States markets were initially penetrated in 1946 by an American named Milton Reynolds. However, Bich's creation—the BIC Stic pen, introduced at 29 cents in 1953—was the first throwaway or disposable pen in the world. Prior to the BIC Stic, the ball-points were high priced specialty products. By the mid-1960s, Marcel was producing over a billion pens a year and had successfully reduced the price to under ten cents. Societe BIC has since dominated all world markets for mass-produced throwaway pens.

This "throwaway culture" was the brainchild of a rebellious and iconclastic workaholic who refused to listen to anything but his own intuitive beliefs. He ignored the dissenters who predicted his demise in virtually every market he entered. For example, the industry experts in the shaver market, including Gillette, said the potential market for disposables represented less than 10 percent of the total razor potential. Bich maintained the potential for disposable razors was 50 percent or more of the total razor market. Bich was proved right as both he and the industry were shocked when disposable razors grew to over 60 percent of the total market within a few years of the Bic introduction.

Marcel Bich is the acknowledged innovative genius behind the "throwaway culture." His prescription for successful innovation is to attack new and unknown markets with a philosophy of: "Concentrate on one product, used by everyone, every day!" and "Build 'em strong, and sell 'em cheap." His prophetic advice to the innovators of the world is to ignore the experts and listen to your own counsel: "My success is due to my refusal to listen to almost no one's advice but my own."

Baron Bich's vision included a remarkable feel for the sales distribution required to market disposable products to the masses. In the United States he penetrated 300,000 retail outlets for the Bic products, which represented an amazing 93 percent of all U.S. retailers (most of his competitors like Gillette were satisfied with just 30 percent of the retail outlets). This is a remarkable success story in sales distribution for any firm, but unheard-of for a foreign firm. Bich then implemented a strong pull-through sales program with the use of a massive $4 million advertising campaign that created the consumer demand that moved the products off the shelves of those 300,000 retailers.

Personal History

Marcel Bich was born in Turin, Italy, the French-speaking, northern part of Italy. He was born with Italian nationality and did not become a French citizen until a teenager. His father, Emmanuel, was a civil engineer who traveled extensively. Marcel spent his youth traveling and learning the idiosyncrasies of the southern European nations—Italy, Spain, and France. This travel experience offered him an opportunity to see the world at an early age. Research has shown that early travel experiences are highly correlated with creativity and an innovative personality.

Marcel was educated in Italy as a child, followed by two years at the Lycee Francais in Madrid. He completed his secondary schooling at a Dominican school in Bordeaux, France. The enterprising Marcel began selling flashlights door to door in Paris at the age of eighteen while he attended the well-known Lycee Carnot in Paris. He believes the door-to-door sales experience was critical to his entrepreneurial success:

> I began work right away. I believe that to be what I am, a "money-maker," one must start at it young, as with sport, in order to acquire the necessary reflexes as soon as possible. (Dewhurst, 1981)

Marcel studied mathematics and philosophy at the university and after graduation began work as a production manager for an office machine company. He was sure this was not to be his long-term vocation and continued his education at night. He received a law degree in 1939, just prior to the outbreak of war in Europe. By this time Bich was a production executive at Stephens, the largest French pen company. Stephens was Waterman's major competitor in France at the time and a major force in the national pen business. The war interrupted Bich's career and when it was over in 1945 he was determined to strike out on his own.

Business and Personal Survival

Following the war Bich and a friend, Edouard Buffard, raised $1,000 and bought a leaky shed in Clichy, a Paris suburb. They started manufacturing ink refills for the new ballpoint pens that were just hitting the market. These were high-priced and unreliable novelty products. This experience gave Marcel the ammunition needed to create the throwaway pen. He spent four years refining the functions and operations of the first Bic pen.

Most industry leaders tend to be too conservative to enter the dangerous waters normally traveled by innovators like Marcel Bich. They fear the unknown and continue to operate in a left-brain–dominated world that uses quantitative analysis to examine market opportunities. This strategy predictably leads to a refusal to enter new, unknown markets since there is no data to validate market size or to eliminate risk. Establishment executives refuse to believe in the potential for new market opportunities unless they are quantifiable. Therefore they tend to stay with the known, safe, and existing markets, where the comfort level is consistent with their thinking processes. Visionaries like Marcel Bich were not of this ilk.

Bich experienced the same resistance to the new and untried as had Turner, Jones, Bushnell, Jobs, and Lear, as well as Galileo, Edison, and Bell in past eras. Bich began the disposable ballpoint research and development effort in 1949. His target design criteria were focused on designing a "maximum service— minimum price" ballpoint pen. It was expected to write well for a specified time and then be thrown away because of its inexpensive purchase price.

Marcel finished the first prototype in 1950 and offered it to the top six pen firms for which he built pen refills. One of these firms was the old-line American giant Watermans, a firm Bich eventually purchased. He offered these six firms the opportunity to market his idea first, with only a royalty for Bich's firm. They refused in the risk-averse tradition of industry experts and Bich decided to go it alone and, in his words, "to stake everything on the ballpoint."

When Marcel introduced the first Bic disposable pen in France in November 1953 it was an immediate hit. Within three years he was selling a quarter million pens a day for a fraction of the price of his competition. This startled the status-conscious, high-priced, traditional pen companies, who were left at the gate in the race for the mass writing market. Bich was actually startled himself by the magnitude of the demand for his new pen:

> In my most optimistic estimations, I had been reckoning on selling 10,000 ballpoint pens a day. In less than three years, we had reached a level of 200,000 to 250,000 pens a day. It was so successful that it seemed to me we must not delay by a single day before we tackled foreign markets. (Dewhurst, 1981)

And attack he did. Marcel immediately embarked on an aggressive plan to dominate the world of writing. Without delay he licensed the patent rights from Biro to avoid any patent infringement suits. He then acquired a British firm, Biro-Swan, that was dominant in the English-speaking markets of Europe and Australia. The Biro-Swan acquisition brought Marcel both management expertise and distribution know-how for the huge British markets. He utilized the licensing rights for the British markets to gain knowledge for his planned launch into the States. The purchase cost him 1.5 million francs ($300,000) but it gained him immediate access to the Australian, New Zealand, and Canadian markets.

Within a year Bich had acquired a Swedish firm, Ballograf, and began a strategy to enter the huge American market. He bought Watermans Pen Company of Connecticut in 1958. Within a decade Bich was selling 330 million ballpoints a year in the United States—more than one and half pens for every American.

When Bich entered the huge American market for pens in 1957 he had to face enormous competition from Gillette's PaperMate. His biggest challenge was overcoming the terrible reputation ballpoints had earned in America. Early entrepreneurs and opportunists sold shoddy merchandise and disregarded irate customers. These pioneers had exploited early opportunities and took a short-term attitude towards consumers, who became quite skeptical of ballpoints. Bich turned this negative into a positive in the classical style of an innovative visionary. His $4 million "torture test" ad campaign was designed to offset the poor quality image of ballpoints. This national TV campaign depicted the Bic Stic ballpoint drilled through wallboards, scraped along ice, pounded by flamenco dancers, baked in a fire, and shot from a gun. The commercial then demonstrated how the quality Bic pen would still write perfectly, and for an unbelievably low cost of twenty-nine cents!

Once the pen market was safely in Bich's hands he launched an attack on the cigarette lighter industry. He proved that his amazing pen innovation and promotion was not luck but genius. He penetrated the disposable lighter market with a Bic throwaway priced 30 percent below the competition. Bich then replicated the pen advertising ingenuity with another, even more successful ad campaign. The "Flick Your Bic" TV commercial became a source of jokes and was frequently used in comedy routines. The cute slogan was used to kick off the competitive wars against Gillette's Cricket lighter.

Bich was extremely aggressive with this marketing campaign because he was faced with the task of selling a product competing with a "free" resource—matches. Matches caused many industry leaders in the cigarette lighter business to think that the disposable lighter idea was not sound. Bich, in his inimitable fashion, ignored the experts and introduced his throwaway lighter product to immediate success. The lighter success proved even more dramatic than his pen innovation, as he eventually forced the powerful Gillette to capitulate and leave the business. Gillette finally admitted that the intense price competition from Bic was formidable by leaving the market in the mid-1980s.

Bic entered and won the same battle for market dominance with Gillette in both pens and lighters. These successes gave the indomitable Bich the self-confidence to enter the domain of Gillette's major business—shavers. Marcel Bich, the inveterate competitor, could not resist the challenge of creating a disposable razor market, which Gillette had purposely avoided. A disposable razor would have jeopordized Gillette's bread and butter blade products, so it had carefully avoided the market. When Bich started test marketing his new disposable razor in France, Gillette and the other industry experts said he was crazy. Bich countered with predictions of a sizeable market (40 to 50 percent) for disposable razors. The industry experts were convinced he was "nuts" and insisted the market was less than 10 percent of the total razor market.

Marcel Bich ignored the experts and ultimately proved them wrong by introducing Bic throwaway shavers in 1976. The market exceeded even Bich's optimistic predictions and now represents approximately 62 percent of the total razor market in the United States. It is even greater in some Third World nations. Marcel Bich did not immediately dominate this market as he had the pen and razor business. Gillette was afraid of Bic's entry and countered with a strong product (Good News) in 1976. The Bic razor has held its own even in Gillette's home market and had a 45 percent market share in 1990. Gillette was successful in keeping Bic market share in check and has since maintained dominance in this market.

Without Marcel Bich Gillette probably would not have entered the disposable razor market. It was playing the self-preservation game of protecting a market it owned. Gillette's key executives perceived the disposable market as cannibalizing the company's blade business. This mentality is what loses markets and is why Marcel Bich is the real father of the disposable razor business. Creative destruction was Marcel's forte and razors his third stroke of innovative genius in the throwaway culture.

Personal Behavior Characteristics

Marcel Bich has been described as a dynamic workaholic. He is competitive to a fault. Four attempts at the America's Cup race are a testimony to his perseverance. He is an introvert, which means he derives his energy from his internal world of ideas, emotions, or impressions. He has the sixth sense of the intuitive personality, which gives him a macro or large picture view of the world. According to the Jungian typology, Bich is an INTJ, which makes him "a relentless innovator in thought as well as action." Bich's personality has also been described as representative of the "culture's foremost visionaries and pioneers." Research has also shown this personality type as "tending to be logical and ingenious." A psychologist's description of Bich's personality type sounds like a biographical sketch of Marcel Bich:

> NT leaders see new ventures to get involved in, new programs to develop, new organizational structures to design, or new buildings to erect. NT leaders can galvanize staff, mobilize energies, and create dramatic and long-lasting change. NT leaders have their own brand of charisma—idea charisma. The

powerful and articulate expression of a new vision is the source of their greatest strength. (Berens, 1988)

The above profile is quite descriptive of Marcel Bich, the businessman. His personal life is a different story. He emulates Howard Hughes, Fred Smith, Sol Price, and Steve Jobs in protecting his private life. He shuns interviews and refuses to be photographed. He once did an interview with a French magazine called *Face to Face,* yet refused to have his picture taken and the "Face" page had to go to print blank. Bich is a reclusive, innovative genius who qualifies for the classical definition of maverick, rebel, iconoclast, and, according to *Time* (December 1972), "a stubborn, opinionated entrepreneur."

It is this stubborn and aggressive attitude that has driven Marcel Bich to dominate his businesses throughout the world. This indomitable *self-assurance,* resolute *self-esteem,* and an uncanny *intuition* have been guided by a *focus* on his goals that is nonpareil. His personality is based on an unflappable self-confidence that led him to charge into new markets with new ideas and concepts never before considered. A Promethean temperament gave him the vision not often seen by the normally conservative French.

Risk-taking Proclivity

Bich was competitive, and like most competitors, not afraid to take enormous risks for huge potential gains. His sailing exploits have demonstrated this predisposition for risk-taking. A look at his infrequent quotes to the media show a pattern that is athletic and competitive. He used metaphors about athletic competition as analogies for his business successes. His focus was always on winning, which did not necessarily endear him to the establishment.

French bankers continually turned Bich down for loans, characterizing him as "too imprudent." He has since had his measure of revenge as he only uses them when absolutely necessary. *Time* magazine, in a 1972 article, said he "abhors technocrats, computers, and borrowing money." Bich combined a mastery of vision and insight in creating the throwaway culture for a society that was in a hurry. The "future shock" generation was being formed and Bich contributed immensely to its growth. His market philosophy of building cheap, reliable, and disposable products was timed perfectly for a society not inclined to spend the time to repair commodity products.

When people or firms move quickly towards a goal or market they are more prone to make mistakes. In other words, the classic risk-reward curve of life dictates that speed incurs risk and slow is safe. This is as true in business as it is on the road. Marcel Bich was always accused of going too fast. The *New York Times* called him a "fast-moving entrepreneur," his competitiors continually were overwhelmed by his speed of market entry and penetration, and his bankers were disenchanted by his speed. This speed was his strength and just as it scared others it became Bich's road to success.

The "Throwaway" Success

Marcel Bich is more responsible for the creation of the throwaway culture than any other single person in the world. His highly focused ingenuity changed the buying habits of society and impacted the way the world writes, lights up, and shaves. His creative destruction of old and static markets were innovative and ingenious.

Bich's compulsion for detail extended to his competitive pleasure in sailing. He competed in the America's Cup race four times. His desire for victory led him to spend $3 million on the 1970 race in his sloop *France*. He and his crew spent relentless fourteen-hour days preparing for the event only to be ignominiously lost in the fog off Newport. Bich has ten children from two marriages and a past mistress. His innovative vision can be summed up with this quote from him on the entrepreneurial process:

> You know about wind-surfing? Well, that's my method. Success at wind-surfing demands absolute mastery of the surfboard, and also that you exploit its capabilities to the maximum. Above all, you must have total freedom of movement; no shareholders or bankers coming along to put a heavy foot on your surfboard. (Dewhurst, 1981)

Marcel Bich was a master of anticipating societal needs. He was an innovative visionary who ignored the establishment in a persistent march to create a new and better way. His vision was based on a focused passion to reach his goals at whatever cost. Destroying the existing way was part of his equation for success. This was coupled with an enormous ability to convert complex products and markets to simple ones.

Baron Marcel Bich
born July 29, 1914
Turin, Italy

Dominant Personality Characteristic: Focused—goal-oriented to a fault
Mottos: "My success is due to my refusal to listen to almost no one's advice
but my own." "Build 'em strong and sell 'em cheap." "Concentrate on
one product used by everyone, every day."
Nickname: Baron
Firm Name: Societe BIC
Location: Paris, France
First Innovation/Date: The first throwaway pen, 1953
Products: Bic pens, lighters, and razors, Bic parfume, sailboards
Initial Investment: Edouard Bufford and Bich borrowed $1,000 in 1945
Second Innovation/Date: Lighter, 1972—"Flick Your BIC"

Sibling Status: Two younger brothers
Personality Profile: Introverted Intuitive Thinking Judger (INTJ)
Parents' Occupation: Father, civil engineer
Childhood Data: Italian childhood and nationality; Spain for 2 years, Bordeaux
school, 2 years; Paris, where he became a French citizen
Family Socio-economic Status: Middle class
Formal Education: Philosophy and math, Lycee Carnot; law degree
Age, First Business Venture: Sold flashlights at 18
Age, Big Hit: 39, 1953
Hobbies/Activities: America's Cup 1970, 1974, 1977, 1980. Famous for having
been lost in the fog in the 1970 race off Newport

Marital Status: Married twice, plus a mistress
Children: Ten children: three by his first wife, one by his mistress
Religion: Roman Catholic
Public Offering Date: November 1972, offering at $208 per share.
Revenues or Units of Big Hit: 3 billion ballpoints a year in 1979. Dominated
market with 93 percent saturation of the 300,000 retail stores in the United
States
Revenues of Firm: 1989 United States revenues, $330 million. Market share:
pens–60 percent, lighters–60 percent, wet shavers–45 percent
Estimated Net Worth: $200 million in the early 1970s
Age Became Millionaire: 41, 1955
Heroes: Unknown
Honors: Chevalier Legion d' Honneur. Virtually created throwaway culture

12

Solomon Price—Impatient

Patience may be a virtue for some pursuits in life, but for the innovative vision-
ary it is a liability. Entrepreneurs "have the patience quota of zero," accord-
ing to one study of successful leaders. Soichiro Honda was so impatient he
earned the nickname of "Mr. Thunder" due to tyrannical outbursts toward
less aggressive or incompetent workers. Ted Turner was so impatient he refused
to fly with anyone who checked bags and his biographer said, "He had the
attention span of a gnat." Bill Lear's turbulent nature was legendary as he
was intolerant of people less driven than he. Nolan Bushnell would get up
and leave meetings that became tedious. Research has shown that entrepre-
neurs tend to receive an inordinate number of speeding tickets, take red-eye
flights, grow beards in order to save shaving time, and walk, talk, eat, and
think fast. They are impatient with life and see time as their enemy.

Sol Price personifies the impatient leader. He is intolerant of inefficiency
and waste. He is frugal to a fault and loses patience with those not holding
his same values for efficiency and frugality. These traits have made his firm
eminently successful. A New York consultant researching the Price Club inno-
vation concluded, "It's the most efficient retail machine ever invented." One
reason was Price's dedication to excellence and his intolerance for anyone not
so inclined. Sol's son confirms, "He is not the most tolerant person in the
world. If you do something wrong, whether to him or someone else, he will
never forgive you." Friends have said, "He is widely known as a man who
takes no prisoners, in business or in his personal life."

Impatience and intolerance are traits commonly found in creators, entre-
preneurs, and visionaries. Studies of the gifted show they have an intolerance
for useless conformity. This is what made Edison a poor student and led Honda,
Lear, and Jones to drop out of school in the ninth grade. Psychologist David
Keirsey says the individual with an intuitive/thinking temperament "has little
patience for redundant or needless paperwork or for nonproductive meetings."

144

He also found that the visionary leader "expects a great deal from himself and only a little less from others." This demanding nature causes entrepreneurs and innovators to be insensitive to employees and others who must interact with them on a regular basis.

Maslow points out that self-actualizing creative people are independent, autonomous, *and* self-directed. *These traits drive the innovator personalities to expect excellence from their associates and themselves. Because of this obsession with excellence, they have a low amount of tolerance or patience. Ray Kroc exemplified this in running the McDonald's chain. Sol Price used the same driven obsessions in creating the Price Club. At seventy he continued to visit a different store every day to checks the toilets, signs, and floors for cleanliness. Sol is highly sensitive, gracious, socially conscious, and philanthropic. He lives by the Golden Rule and demands the same from all employees. He preaches self-sacrifice and judicious evaluation of every detail. In business he demands perfection and total obedience to the mission of the firm. He tolerates no waste or inefficiency in himself or in his people. Sam Walton said he learned more from Sol Price about retailing than any other person—quite the compliment from the creator of the world's largest retail operation.*

> The intuitive/thinking visionary can be quite oblivious to the emotional responses of others and may not always be sensitive to the complexities of interpersonal relations.
> —David Keirsey and Marilyn Bates, *Please Understand Me*

Father of the Wholesale Club Industry

Sol Price says, "Merchandising is not a science, it is an art." Price has lived up to this prophecy and his name by using an artful pricing strategy to outperform the giants of the retailing industry. He created an industry that reached $30 billion in 1991 and is projected to surpass $50 billion by the mid-1990s. Howard Davidowitz, a New York–based retail consultant, said of Price's creation, "This is probably the fastest growing, most exciting concept in retailing in the past twenty years, and it's continuing to grow." How did Sol Price, an ex-lawyer, create the most awesome new retailing concept of the era and not Sears, Penneys, K-Mart or even the innovative upstart Wal-Mart?

Sol Price inherited a warehouse in 1950 and while looking for a tenant accidentally ended up in the retailing business. Sol had been a practicing lawyer for seventeen years and had no prior experience in the retailing trade. He created a discount retailing concept—Fed-Mart—that challenged the price protection laws of the time. Fed-Mart was a mass merchandising and supermarket chain that pioneered selling national brands at a discount. He built Fed-Mart into a $300 million chain over a twenty-five-year period and then sold it in 1975 to West German retailer Hugo Mann. He was fired less than a year later.

Sol founded the Price Club in 1976 at a time when he was unemployed, sixty years of age, and walking the streets of San Diego looking for some new opportunity to salve his crushed ego. Both he and his sons were unemployed and his creative search for atonement was as much for them as it was for himself. He began by interviewing small retailers, who told him about the inefficiencies of purchasing commodities like candy, cigars, and liquor through wholesalers. The high cost of distribution had obsoleted traditional two-step wholesaling methods of a bygone era. The small retailer ended up getting squeezed out by the inadequate distribution systems. Wholesalers could no longer support the small retail accounts because it entailed too much labor for the potential return. Sol describes this antiquated distribution system in explaining the creation of the Price Club:

> It cost a lot of money when somebody called up to order twenty cartons of cigarettes and ten boxes of candy. They take the order, pick the order, stage it, get it on a truck, deliver it, and collect the money for it. It's not an effective way to get merchandise from the manufacturer to the consumer. (Bragaw, 1990)

Sol decided to find a solution for this inefficient system. He had discovered a problem and in the inimitable fashion of the innovative visionary began searching for an elegant solution. Sol evaluated the elements in the distribution equation and concluded that there were too many layers between the manufacturer and the consumer. He decided to create an operation where the retailer could buy brand-name products at wholesale (8 to 10 percent over cost) but would have to come to the warehouse to eliminate the cost of delivery. The wholesaler had a 20 to 25 percent markup in the old system, but was required to perform many extraneous functions for the small retailer.

Sol reasoned that the small retailer could buy brand-name merchandise for cash (no accounts receivables or credit), buy larger quantities (better price breaks from manufacturers), perform the pick-up and delivery function (eliminating the trucking and delivery costs), and totally eliminate the sales and advertising functions by having stores regionally located in giant warehouses. If viable, this concept would work in every major metropolitan market in America where the inefficient wholesale distribution systems were still operating.

Sol's Prototype

Sol decided to test his warehouse club concept in a vacant airplane hanger with a prototype unit named the Price Club. The products were brand-name products marked up just 8 to 10 percent over cost. He offered a limited number of items—3,000 in contrast to the 80,000 to 100,000 carried by a typical K-Mart. Sol's major contribution was a dramatic deviation from traditional retailing principles. He eliminated advertising, credit cards, customer service personnel, distribution warehouses (the store is the warehouse), and all shopping frills and decor. Sol's concept violated most of the traditional rules of retailing. His creative destruction proved a case study on the innovative process. The old ways must be destroyed in order to create a new and better way. This was a basic economic principle first devised by Schumpeter fifty years ago to describe the innovative process and Sol at age sixty became its master implementer.

The Price Club became an industry sensation two years after its beginning. Why did this innovative concept meet with such unbelievable success? One of the reasons was the fundamental precept of offering high-quality *brand* merchandise at wholesale prices. This allowed the small retailer to become an end-use customer without affecting required markups. An unexpected coup was the attraction of the upscale consumer who desired low prices on brand-name merchandise. These "yuppies" were conspicuous spenders who desired brand-name merchandise but were content to purchase the items in a no-frills environment. They were willing to dispense with the other services and amenities of traditional retailing. The name "wholesale club" was coined to describe the concept of middleman to the local businessman or retailer. Ironically, the consumer attraction (the word wholesale) became the merchandising vehicle that drove masses of people to seek out brand-name merchandise at unheard-of low prices.

The reason for the Price Club's success is often lost on an unsuspecting buying public. A specialty store or department store like Macy's operates on a margin of 50 percent on most items to cover the cost of expensive real estate and an even more costly customer service operation. A mass-merchandiser like Sears, Penneys, or Wards operates on a 35 to 40 percent margin for many of the same reasons. They limit the services and thus require a lesser margin. A discounter like Wal-Mart or K-Mart cuts operations ever further and needs only 25 to 30 percent margins. Sol Price decided to charge only 10 percent on the identical products offered by these traditional retail outlets. Advertising was unnecessary since the manufacturers created the demand through their national advertising campaigns. The stores were not shopping intensive, demanding foot traffic to achieve high sales volumes. They were destination locations that could utilize distress or tertiary warehouse space, which saved many thousands of dollars in monthly rent.

The Price Club's pricing philosophy met two different distribution criteria. It coincided with the spartan needs of small retailers. It also met the demands of self-employed and other individuals who desired high-quality but low-cost products. Sol Price's concept eliminates the needs of wholesaling to the small retailer while offering a variety of national brand products at extremely low prices for the individual willing to sacrifice the services.

The Price Club grew to seventy stores by the early 1990s, with revenues approaching $10 billion. The industry was producing $25 billion in revenues; one New York analyst predicted $55 billion by 1995. By any barometer the warehouse club is a revolutionary concept with offshoots now affecting other industries, like office equipment, computers, drugs, eyeglasses, hardware, and the auto industry.

Personal History

Sol Price was born in New York City in 1916 and moved to San Diego with his parents at the age of thirteen. He was the middle child, having an older brother and younger sister. Sol's father was a union negotiator in New York (instrumental in Sol's extreme social consciousness) during Sol's youth. His father became a distributor of women's garments in southern California and was successful enough to send Sol to law school at the University of Southern California.

Sol received a law degree from USC in 1938 and practiced law in San Diego until 1955. Former student friends of Sol say that he always had a strong work ethic in addition to very liberal political views (Mullich, 1988). They described Sol as very strong willed and opinionated. Others found him extremely frugal. David Block, a former school friend of Sol's, says, "He either loves you or hates you. He is not the most tolerant person in the world."

Business and Personal Survival

Sol Price and his two sons were the key executives at Fed-Mart when he sold the firm in 1974 to German Hyper-Mart retailer Hugo Mann. He received an employment agreement as part of the sale but his innovator temperament and autocratic style were not compatible with the German entrepreneur. The marriage did not work. Hugo Mann fired him in 1975 after a year of squabbling. Sol and his sons walked the streets of San Diego, depressed, mad, and concerned over their future. It was this crisis that turned out to be the catalyst and the inspiration for the creation of the first Price Club.

Sol and his sons opened the first Price Club store in an old airplane hangar in San Diego in 1976. Sol invested $800,000 of his proceeds from the Fed-Mart sale. He raised another $1 million from local businessmen and sold $500,000 worth of stock to ex Fed-Mart employees who joined him in his new venture. They sold annual memberships to local retailers for $25. The concept was fluid and kept evolving. The owners were learning as well as the customers during the first year. Consumers were not welcome during that first year and the store had few customers and even slimmer sales. Sol refused to advertise the operation and the firm almost folded during the first year.

Sales were $16 million for that first year, with losses of $750,000. Certain sectors of the general public were then invited to join the club (government employees and all self-employed individuals) and there was a stampede to join. Brand-name offerings at just over cost appealed to the cost-conscious. Real estate sales people and other individuals with a sideline business became the Price Club's biggest boosters. These people were price conscious and willing to drive greater distances to make a good buy on brand-name products. A nuance lost on the highly ethical Sol Price was a subtle but effective method of circumventing taxes. The Price Club concept makes it convenient for small business people to purchase products for use by their business entity, but which are actually for personal consumption. Appliances, food, and sundries make up 77 percent of the sales at a Price Club and a consumer can acquire electronics devices or food products and pay for these consumer items through their business.

The Price Club success story swept through San Diego County. Bargain hunters spread the word and the Price Club was on its way to remarkable growth. By 1981 sales reached $230 million and topped the billion-dollar mark by 1984. The firm went public in 1982 and a stock purchase of $1,000 would have been worth $12,247 by 1990. There were just four stores operating at the public offering. That grew rapidly to seventy-five stores in the United States and Canada at the end of 1991.

Price Is King

The innovative ingenuity of Sol Price was oriented around a business philosophy of giving the consumer the best possible goods at the lowest possible price. This magic formula made Henry Ford a hero and has made the Price Club eminently successful. This same mentality has been instrumental in the success of the Japanese, who have used the same pricing philosophy to make inroads into new industries. In order to offer the lowest prices, Sol had to eliminate many cost elements. In Sol's mind many costs were unnecessary frills of retailing because they did not add anything to the value given or received.

Other retailers had lived with these frills for so long it was difficult for them to eliminate them. Sears has since attempted such a change and become more discount-oriented, but it has met with little acceptance by a consumer grown accustomed to being waited on, scanning product ads, using credit cards, and leisurely meandering through upscale shopping areas. Sol Price changed all this, which has not endeared him to the old-line retailers, who have lost enormous business to the wholesale club industry.

Sol's pricing philosophy has probably been the single most critical factor in the Price Club's success. Sol's pricing philosophy is summed up in this analysis given to a reporter in 1990:

> Pricing decisions should be based on correct buying . . . Price products as though you were buying it right and then you'll find out whether you can do the buying right! . . . Other retailers ask, How much can we get for this item? I ask, How can we sell this item for less?

Sol's pricing strategy was aimed at negotiating better and better prices and passing on any and all cost reductions to the customer. This strategy is foreign to most American executives and nonexistent in bureaucratic chain operations. The traditional executive will typically allow all cost reductions to drop to the bottom line, making themselves look better in the process. This traditional executive strategy is adhered to in most organizations because it looks good to the shareholders. This is a very short-term mentality and ultimately dooms the perpetrators to long-run failure. Sol often philosophized about these classical executive types who tended to optimize the short run instead of the long run. He told an interviewer that this self-preservation mentality is one of the biggest problems with the operations of most retailers:

> Wall Street wants your profit numbers to be a little better, so why not just cheat a little bit? Cut quality and charge the same price. The customer won't know the difference. (Bragaw, 1990)

Personal Behavior Characteristics

Sol Price has a personality dominated by a strong introversion and judging bias. He is energized by his own internal drives and tends to be more territorial than sociable. Structure is his forte as he likes closure and firm commitment on most things. His temperament is Promethean as classified by David Keirsey, which makes him an intuitive/thinker type. This is consistent with the findings for most innovative visionaries.

In a letter response to the author, Price said he considered high self-esteem a critical factor in any innovative success. Price also credited intelligence and perseverance along with a keen sense of intuition as the factors contributing to innovative success. He said he did not believe formal education was a very critical factor to his success. This is also consistent with most findings on other innovators. When asked about the most critical factor for innovation, Price responded, "maybe necessity" and "maybe rebelliousness" (letter of March 15, 1991). Price lists his father as the most instrumental person in his success. And he said he didn't know what motivated him to take such risks in his accomplishments.

Sol has an ethical system similar to that of Tom Monaghan. He operates with the Golden Rule as the governing determinant for all business decision-making. He believes that businesses or individuals must "give" before they can "receive." He admires Ghandi and often quotes his philosophy of humility and passivity.

Sol was adored by most of his employees, who speak of him in godlike and reverent terms but would not consider crossing him. His executives describe him as "paternal" and with messiah-type undertones: "When people speak about him, it is almost like mortals speaking about Zeus" (Mullich, 1988). His social consciousness has been legendary. He once set up a Fed-Mart store on an Arizona Navaho Indian reservation and another in a Houston ghetto. Sol has an intuitive sense about new concepts like most innovative visionaries and said it was his "gut" decisions that led him to the Price Club success. Sol was notorious for paying the highest wages in San Diego and he unionized his firms without any outside coercion or formal organizing efforts. He would not allow credit cards in his business because "it is against my religion for people to go into debt to shop." A company newsletter quoted him on an idealistic set of values that he holds dear: "Sturdiness, frugality, leadership, and self-service."

Sol always maintained tight-fisted control of his operations and allowed this principle to overlap his personal life. A terrible divorce and family squabble led to a notorious legal battle with his youngest son Larry. Larry says of Sol, "My father is obsessed with controlling the lives of his family" (Mullich, 1988). Larry retained Marvin Mitchelson to file a $100 million lawsuit against his father and the Price Club. He maintains that his father interfered with his business career (his operation of the Price Club's tire division) because of his decision to leave his wife.

Risk-taking Proclivity

Sol Price was known as a "crusading liberal" in southern California for his history of circumventing and fighting the antiquated price protection laws of the 1950s and 1960s. The government had enacted these laws to protect the public during World War II and was slow to repeal them. Sol Price tried to help the process along during his days at Fed-Mart. He was constantly in legal battles with manufacturers or other government agencies for having circumvented the price protection laws. This attempt at overturning antiquated price protection laws was a very risky part of Sol's life and caused him much anguish and many lawsuits.

Sol's philosophy of giving the consumer the lowest possible prices on high value goods was in line with his social philosophy. This low-price ideology was also instrumental in his creation of the wholesale club industry. Sol often quoted Gandhi, "You must give before you get." In Sol's case he "gave" by assuming the consumer's fight with the federal government for years to foster better consumer pricing. He finally "got" when he used these hard-earned pricing principles to create the eminently successful Price Club operation. Sol's pricing ideology is unheard of in traditional retailing operations and would never be practiced by a career-oriented executive in one of the establishment organizations. Negotiating a better price and passing on all excess margins to the customer is not the nature of the retailing mentality. For Sol Price it has worked eminently well.

One of the amazing factors in the success of the Price Club, according to one Wall Street analyst, Michael Extein, was its charging an annual fee for the opportunity to spend money. He was in awe of Sol's concept and said so to the *Wall Street Journal:* "It was unimaginable, this idea that you could charge people to shop" (Mullich, 1988). Another of Sol's iconoclastic principles has often been attacked by the establishment. He has insisted from the beginning on allowing only a very limited line of products in his stores. This is one of the major differences between a wholesale club store and a discount store like K-Mart. Sol's succinct and incisive response to these charges was, "The essence of merchandising is the intelligent loss of sales. You can't be everything to everybody."

Impatient Success

If imitation is truly the sincerest form of flattery, as Shakespeare said, then Sol Price has been eulogized by the retailing giants of America. Wal-Mart has been the recipient of the greatest amount of Sol's talent. Sam Walton, just before his death in 1992, told *Fortune,* "I guess I've stolen—I prefer the word borrowed—as many ideas from Sol Price as from anybody else in the business." Wal-Mart operates Sams and Wholesale Club stores and at this writing is by far the largest wholesale club operator in America, with over three hundred stores. K-Mart emulated the Price Club with its Pace and Macro stores. Costco of Seattle was started by Price Club ex-employees. The Home Club emulates Price's formula in the hardware field, Sports Club does so in the athletic goods business, the Office Club and Office Depot do so in the stationary/office equipment industry, Vision Works follows the formula in the eyeglass field, and the Software House uses the concept in the burgeoning computer software industry.

Price says the secret of his success has been in deciding what products he can do without. He never looks back or discusses his competition. Sol is always single-focused and admits that his major failing has been an insensitivity to dedicated employees. He admits to finding fault without giving compliments. However, the Golden Rule has always been his Bible in all dealings, both business and personal. Sol's ethical system was integrated into his business philosophy, as summed up by this quote to a reporter in the spring of 1990:

> We learned that you can do very well in the retail business without cheating, lying, being cute, or spending a lot of money on advertising. (Bragaw, 1990)

Sol Price has been well rewarded for his frugality and altruistic business ethics. In 1991 the *Forbes* issue on America's 400 richest individuals listed Sol with a $335 million net worth. Sol is the acknowledged father of the wholesale club industry and is revered by most of his employees. He certainly qualifies as one of the great innovators of the last half of the twentieth century. His tempestuous impatience and intolerance for waste has made the Price Club a major factor in the retailing business in America. This ex-lawyer and unemployed discounter has changed the world of retailing more than anyone else in the last hundred years.

Solomon Price
born January 23, 1916
New York City, New York

Dominant Personality Characteristic: Impatient and intolerant of mediocrity
Mottos: "The essence of merchandising is the intelligent loss of sales." "Merchandising is not a science, it is an art."
Nickname: None, but known as a "crusading liberal philanthropist"
Firm Name: The Price Club
Location: San Diego, California
First Innovation/Date: Fed-Mart Corporation, 1953
Products: Wholesale club retail chain—premium merchandise at 10 percent over cost
Second Innovation/Date: The Price Club, 1976
Initial Investment: Price, $800,000; employees, $500,000; private investors, $1 million

---

Sibling Status: Second son, with a younger sister
Personality Profile: Introverted Intuitive Thinking Judger (INTJ)
Parents' Occupation: Father, union negotiator and women's coat manufacturer
Childhood Data: Born in New York City, relocated to San Diego at 13
Family Socio-Economic Status: Upper middle class
Formal Education: University of Southern California, law degree, 1938
Age, First Business Venture: 37, Fed-Mart, 1953; 60, Price Club, 1976
Hobbies/Activities: Philanthropy and social consciousness

Marital Status: Married once
Children: Two sons, Laurence and Robert
Religion: Judaism
Public Offering Date: 1980, with four stores and $148 million in revenue
Revenues or Units of Big Hit: Average customer purchase $100 to $300. Average store revenues of $100 million annually, with $200 million for top units
Revenues of Firm: $7 billion, 1991—22nd largest retail chain in America
Estimated Net Worth: Approximately $300 million
Age Became Millionaire: 40, with Fed-Mart
Heroes: Gandhi and his philosophy "You must give before you can receive"
Honors: Father of the $22 billion wholesale club industry, projected to hit $55 billion by 1995

13

Howard Head—Intuitive

"Without intuition we would still be in a cave," says futurist writer Marilyn Ferguson. Einstein said, "The really valuable factor is intuition." Webster defines intuition as "direct knowing" and "learning without reasoning." Weston Agor, a management researcher, has concluded, "Managers who have developed their intuition will have an advantage over those who have not." Fred Smith of Federal Express says, "If you want to innovate, you have to be capable of making intuitive judgments."

Intuition is one of four key dimensions of personality, according to Carl Jung. Keirsey and Bates (Jung's disciples) have described intuitive thinkers as culture's foremost visionaries and pioneers. They have a need for competence, work efficiently, and even tend to work at playing. Additionally, they say, these individuals have superior skills for designing and planning, and a typical motto for them is "be excellent in all things." They are pragmatists focused on autonomy, use their power for the sake of expediency, and pursue knowledge and truth with vigor and ingenuity.

Intuitors like Howard Head prefer to solve new, complex problems via their inner vision of reality. They accomplish this by using their right brains to picture their goals, wins, and successes before attempting them. Dr. Garfield, a NASA research scientist who did pioneering research on astronauts, demonstrated that peak-performing athletes and overachievers are visualizers who, in his words, "see it, feel it, and experience it, before they do it!"

Intuitive people prefer the abstract to the rational, insight to hindsight, quality to quantity, holistic to linear, macro to micro, sixth sense to common sense, long term to short term, hunches to hard data, analog to digital and the future to the past. These "patterns" and "visions" of reality are right-brain characteristics that allow us to explore the abstract and unknown. It is a prerequisite for creative thought and large-scale innovation.

Mihalsky's 1970 research revealed that exceptional leaders (his subjects

155

had doubled their firms' profits over a five-year period and 80 percent of them demonstrated intuitive skills) have above-average precognitive powers (intuition). Agor, in a different study, also found that intuiting top managers perform the best. Most contemporary research has shown that entrepreneurs have a better chance of success if they are intuitive. These studies have also shown that intuition is not genetic; it is a learned ability. This would indicate a crying need for more management students interested in learning how to refine the skill of using intuition to manage effectively. Intuitive ability is acquired by programming and imprinting and the lack of this skill is based on early conditioning that can be changed.

One indication of how imprinting has influenced intuitive skills is women. For centuries women have been considered superior at the intuitive process. This has not been a function of their gender but because they have been conditioned to believe that showing emotion is an acceptable form of behavior. Men have been conditioned in just the opposite way. They have been taught to repress their emotions. Women have had cultural permission to be feeling, sensitive, and therefore intuitive. Most men have repressed their potential intuitive abilities and have been taught that to be manly is to behave according to their role as "strong, in-control quantitative managers" of the status quo. Free expression has therefore become the province of the feminine mystique, artists, and rebels, leaving the male gender to live in the world of (culturally acceptable) composed self-control.

Innovative visionaries have classically overcome cultural roadblocks to utilizing their intuitive skills. They have become right-brain and holistically driven in their creative endeavors. Howard Head personifies this talent. More intuitive leaders like Head are needed to protect our organizations from the self-serving number-crunching incompetents who use the NIH factor to destroy the innovative process.

> The extroverted-intuitive is uncommonly important both economically and culturally . . . he can render exceptional service as the initiator or promoter of new enterprises. He brings vision to life, presents it convincingly, and with dramatic fire, he embodies it."
>
> —Carl Jung

Two World-class Innovations

Howard Head revolutionized two sports. He accomplished this with an intuitive approach that is seldom found in business. Howard Head was the quintessential left-brain-educated (Harvard engineer) and -trained (Martin Aircraft) innovator who invented and operated with a right-brain intuitive vision. Head used his gift for vision to revolutionize two industries, not because he wanted to change the industries but because he wanted to improve his own ability. He was inept at both—skiing and tennis—and admittedly only created these two extraordinary innovations to solve a personal performance problem. He was grossly incompetent in both sports and blamed his incompetence on the equipment. He believed if he had a problem, then others like him had the same problem and he set out to solve the problem. Therefore, he changed the equipment, which had been considered inviolable for a century in each sport. First, he replaced the antiquated hickory skis with his precision, state-of-the-art Head metal skis. Second, he revolutionized the tennis industry with his Prince oversized tennis rackets.

Head's dramatic innovations changed both sports for amateurs and professionals. *Sports Illustrated* dubbed both his inventions "cheaters" since those individuals using his equipment were said to have a competitive edge. It called his tennis innovation "the most successful racket in tennis history." This was not a difficult assessment since Head's innovation had been the first major change in racket technology in over a hundred years. A final tribute to Head's contribution to the tennis industry was the comeback attempt of Bjorn Borg in 1990. Borg decided to play with his old wooden racket, which made him number one in the world in the 1970s and early 1980s. Borg was derided by the media and tour players who predicted his rapid demise because of his obsolete racket. Borg's comeback lasted less than a month.

Tennis industry leaders who led the charge into the use of space-age materials—metal, aluminum, and graphite—during the early 1970s changed the traditional wood frames into metal frames. This was a dramatic change that unbelievably left everything else about the racket intact. These industry leaders fell into the classic trap of attempting to create a new product without tampering with the status quo of their existing technology. Their defensive approach to the innovative process created a product using new materials with old concepts. They were not willing to destroy their old products in order to create a totally new product. Only a new innovator outside the industry was able to do so because he had no investment financially or psychologically in the old.

The industry experts were afraid of violating the traditional ways of things. These experts did not have the perspicacity to question the size of the tennis racket. It took a non–tennis player who was not protecting the old to create the new. Head "creatively destroyed" the wooden racket. He was experienced in such revolutionary development by "creatively destroying" the hickory ski industry with his metal ski innovation. This conditioned him to the rejection and naysaying that he was to encounter from the traditionalists who would decry his attempts at destroying their sacred icons.

Every one of the industry leaders—Wilson, Dunlop, Spalding, MacGregor—

applied the new space-age metal and alloy materials to the old manufacturing principles, assuming the old way was inviolable. Not one of these industry leaders had the vision to question racket size, hitting area, or any other facet of tennis lore in the creation of their new designs. Howard Head did. He gave credence to his intuitive mentality with this quote to *Sports Illustrated* on what made him succeed when others failed:

> The invitation to innovate went unanswered because the traditional geometry is so fixed in people's minds that it just never occurred to anyone that bigger might be better . . . there is more wisdom in the gut than in the head. (Kennedy, 1980)

Head, in the traditional fashion of the innovative visionaries of the world, did not reinvent either the ski or the racket to make money. He wanted to improve his personal performance and solve a problem that he found interesting. He became very wealthy as a result of each innovation but his passion was directed toward problem resolution, not monetary reward. This appears to be a consistent pattern in virtually every innovation of any magnitude.

Head encountered a strong resistance to change in each of his endeavors. This obstruction to the innovative process permeates our society, which Head confirmed to *Ski* magazine in 1964: "The more innovative the concept, the greater the resistance." The industry leaders had repeatedly told him, "I told you so" with every failure he faced. And he experienced failure after failure on both the ski and tennis developments. His skis took four years of heart-wrenching development in which he was emotionally crushed every time a new ski design was broken by a ski pro. The pros broke forty pairs of skis that Head had handmade; each time he was convinced they were perfect, only to hear them crack and shatter in the hands of the nonbelievers. After years of heartbreak and disillusionment he finally succeeded when a pro in Vermont came flying over a hill, made a fast turn, jumped over a mogul, and told Howard the product was better than his hickory skis.

At Prince Howard was further ridiculed when his oversized racket was called a joke, a flyswatter, and a tool for incompetents. Howard had bought the company and was chairman. The vice president of engineering told him, "If another inventor had come in with a crazy-looking racket like that, we would've turned him away" (Kennedy, 1980). Even after he knew he had a successful racket design that improved the game of tennis, the U.S. Patent Office told him the racket wasn't really different and didn't qualify for a patent. They said he needed concrete evidence that it wasn't just larger in size, but performed differently and more effectively. They continually refused to believe he had created anything worthwhile for the industry and denied him a patent three times. When they told Head that a racket is a racket is a racket, and that his designs did not warrant a patent, Head became driven. Howard describes this period: "When I first applied for the patent, the inspectors—who act as both judge and jury—refused the application, claiming that my idea was no more than an obvious state of the art in tennis-racket design" (Kennedy, 1980).

Head persevered in the inimitable fashion of the entrepreneurial visionary. He took the lemons from the Patent Office and made innovative lemonade. Head built a laboratory testing machine with high-speed cameras and documented on film that his revolutionary design provided a 20 percent increase in power with a "sweet spot" hitting area four times that of traditional rackets. He provided these nonbelievers statistical and engineering proof of the dramatic difference between the performance of his racket and traditional rackets. Head even found that the Patent Office rejection forced him into creating some worthwhile benefits that he may not have discovered on his own. He said, "We were startled to discover that the best place to hit the ball was in that three-inch area of added length, an area that doesn't even exist on conventional rackets." His perseverance paid off. After two years of intense work and statistical analysis the U.S. Patent Office issued Howard Head patent #3,999,756 (1976), good for seventeen years.

Head's intuitive approach to problem resolution resulted in two breakthrough innovations that ultimately changed the worlds of skiing and tennis. Head said, "With both my skis and my racket I was inventing not to just make money, but to help *me*. I invent when it's something I really want. The need has to grow in your gut" (*Sports Illustrated,* September 1980). Skiing and tennis have been dramatically altered by the vision and "gut" of this consummate innovator.

Personal History

Howard Head was born in Philadelphia on July 31, 1914, to an upper-middle-class family. His father was self-employed as a private-practice dentist. (Research has shown that most great innovative personalities have had fathers who were self-employed.) His older sister was an accomplished writer and he had strong desires to follow her into the literary writing field as a screenwriter. This motivation was so strong Howard spent years studying writing and working at it (three jobs) as a career path before discovering that it was not to be his calling.

Howard attended Harvard with the intent to pursue these writing aspirations, but became disenchanted after a few semesters. In his second year he changed to engineering sciences and in 1936 graduated with honors with an engineering degree. He still wanted to write and went to work in the publishing field with various positions as a scriptwriter, reporter, and copywriter. He was fired from jobs as a scriptwriter for two news publishing firms and from a reporting position at a newspaper. Howard pursued a writing career until he was so crushed he had to face reality. After three years he had never earned more than twenty dollars a week. In 1939 he decided to take an aptitude test and "to my great anger and disbelief, I found that I had the lowest potential for creative writing they had ever tested." Yet he had the highest score ever tested in structural visualization. His ability to think in three dimensions was enormous. He had found his niche as an intuitive thinker and went to work through the war years at Glenn Martin Aircraft Company in Baltimore. He worked in the engineering department with structural engineering materials and designs that ultimately helped him with his ski and tennis developments.

Business and Personal Survival

Howard Head will be remembered as one of the great innovative visionaries of the twentieth century. Howard constantly faced failure in those fields in which he most wanted to succeed. He failed at everything he cherished most. Howard wanted desperately to write and failed miserably. He passionately wanted to master the art of skiing and failed. Tennis was to become his retirement pleasure and he failed at it as well. These failures drove him and became the catalyst to achieve great things, where a lesser temperament may have given in to the failures. He pursued tennis and skiing with the tenacity of a hungry animal right up to his death in 1991. He ended up eminently successful, not at the sports, but as the one who changed these sports more than anyone in history. His desire to personally conquer these leisure activities resulted in two great innovative breakthroughs. He became a reasonable skier and tennis player, but his real success was using his intuitive talents to redirect his personal incompetence into creative success. He dramatically changed the way two sports were played by both amateurs and professionals.

Howard spent much of his time partying and playing poker during the years of World War II. His social behavior led him to a life-changing ski vacation to Stowe, Vermont, in 1946. He was terrible and blamed his inept skiing on the hickory skis. This trip was to prove a fortuitous prelude to his future:

> I was humiliated and disgusted at how badly I skied, and characteristically,
> I was inclined to blame it on the equipment, those long, clumsy hickory skis.
> On the way home I heard myself boasting to an Army officer beside me
> that I could make a better ski out of aircraft materials than could be made
> from wood (Kennedy, 1961).

Howard later admitted that if he had known it would take him four years and forty versions of ski design he would probably have given it up. Howard resigned from Martin on January 2, 1948, rented a room in a Baltimore store, and entered the world of entrepreneurship. He took $6,000 in poker winnings from under his bed and financed the equipment and supplies required to build the first prototypes. He worked day and night for the first year perfecting six pairs of skis that were his pride and joy. Howard was convinced he was destined to ski on metal Head skis in 1949. He took the skis to Vermont and the ski instructor broke every one of them within an hour. Head said, "Each time one of them broke, something inside me snapped with it."

Head persevered for two more winters through forty different designs and by 1951 had created an aluminum ski with a plywood core for strength, steel edges for turning, and a plastic running surface for smoother runs. The ski instructors could not break it. He called it the "Standard" and sold it for $85, which was an exorbitant price at the time. The ski took a while to catch on but within a few years it had become the status symbol of skiing. The patents he received on the metal Standard ski placed Head Ski years ahead of the other firms, who were convinced Head was nuts and attempting the impossible. Howard built Head Ski into the dominant firm in the ski industry. He never enjoyed the corporate management game and finally sold Head Ski to AMF in 1969 for $16 million. Howard Head had used his intuition and perseverance to the tune of a $4.5 million personal windfall from AMF.

Howard Head retired, built a tennis court in his backyard and took up the game of tennis at the tender age of fifty-five. An inveterate perfectionist, he spent $5,000 on tennis lessons. He was so inept his pro refused to give him more lessons unless he bought a ball machine and practiced every day. Head bought a Prince ball machine and, in his inimitable fashion, found it technically unacceptable. Since it was not functioning to his standards, he tore it apart and proceeded to redesign it. He then called Prince and suggested the company modify the machine to his new standards. After frustrating encounters with the noninnovative types at Prince, he became exasperated and bought controlling interest in the company in 1971. Within a short time the redesigned Prince ball machine captured 50 percent of that market. But Howard Head was still a lousy tennis player.

Still determined to improve his game Howard built lighter and heavier rackets with no tangible results. He awoke from a dream in the mid-1970s with a "Eureka" flash of intuitive genius that told him to "make it bigger." He assumed like everyone else that there were racket size regulations that were inviolable. A compulsive perfectionist, Howard decided to research the U.S. Tennis Association rules on the subject and found that the USTA had rules on everything from the width of the lines on the court to the length of the hair on the balls. There were rules on racket stringing to restrict spinning of the ball and on the thickness of the strings. However, there were no rules on the size of the racket. He was shocked to discover that rule number four said specifically, "a racket is the implement to strike the ball," with no other restrictions. Howard could use anything from an ironing board to a fly swatter to hit the ball and improve his game.

Howard's Ingenuity

Howard immediately set out with the use of his right-brain intuition and his left-brain engineering training to improve his tennis game and to solve the problems encountered in racket designs. One of the engineering principles he utilized in his racket innovation was the fact that "the polar movement of inertia increases with the square of the width," which simply says that a wider racket will resist twisting more easily than a narrower racket. Head designed a racket that was two inches wider and three inches longer. This increased the "sweet spot" by four times, the hitting area by three times, and the power by 20 percent. The racket size was 60 percent larger but, with the use of the new space-age metallic materials, it was not any heavier.

Howard made some rackets, called his friends, and set out to see if this larger racket could in fact change his game. He was amazed at his improvement. Head said, "I could play much better immediately." Friends who were never eager to play with him (they called him "old scatterball") were inviting him to play. If this new racket could help a sixty-year-old who had little experience at the game it should be a boon to others. His business acumen went into motion and in Head's words, "As soon as I found out that the racket helped me, I thought I might as well try it on the market."

Head's patent covered all rackets between 85 and 130 square inches of hitting area (conventional wooden rackets were 70 square inches). Howard said of his design, "I was hoping for improvement, but I never dreamed of such a profound improvement." His persistence as an engineering fanatic had allowed him to succeed beyond his wildest dreams. His technical elegance and perfection utilized some esoteric concepts that solved some very simple problems. He described the ball velocity improvement as "coefficient of restitution," which translates simply as the velocity of the ball rebounding off a racket relative to its incoming speed. Normally, a tennis ball will come off a racket at about 57 percent of the incoming speed. The initial testing of the new Prince racket produced a 52 percent coefficient of restitution, which frightened Howard into believing that the experts might be right about his racket. Had he created a "monster racket" that was grossly inefficient?

Howard persisted with more testing and found that the "sweet spot" created a dramatic improvement in return velocity. The return speed of a ball struck by the racket was 67 percent in the "super sweet spot" of the Prince racket, or 20 percent greater than on a standard racket. This intuitive genius had created what *World Tennis* magazine was to call "one of the most innovative concepts in tennis."

Personal Behavior Characteristics

Carl Jung said, "The extroverted intuitive personality fits many of today's leading innovators." Howard Head could have been Carl Jung's prototypical role model. He was a party animal in the classic style of the extrovert. His intuitive skills were documented by the Stevens Institute years earlier, when Head resorted to aptitude testing to find out why he was a failure as a writer. Howard used his rational—engineering—thought processes to resolve macro problems uncovered by his intuitive mind. His elegant solutions were the result of using a holistic approach to the problem. His perseverance was described by his daughter: "If he gets annoyed with something he changes it." His wife confirmed this with, "Howard never gives up."

Howard Head was an avid gambler, drinker, and partier as a youth. He was always a perfectionist. Head had a desire to "fix" things that weren't broken. He wanted to make them perfect, orderly, and excellent. Quality consciousness was high on Howard's list of requirements for any new design or innovation. He would never err on the low side of quality and efficiency. He sought perfection even if it violated the given order of things. Employees at Head Ski thought of Howard Head as extremely bright and charismatic.

Head's macro vision allowed him to create new concepts that left-brained "adaptor" types might not even consider. This quality also kept him from pursuing long-term management opportunities, as he never considered himself a talented executive. In the classic style of the innovator he preferred to create and invent, then move on to other opportunities. This led him to sell his firms to other operating entities once the products were perfected. He had no desire to operate the companies once the creation was complete.

Risk-taking Proclivity

Head, like all great entrepreneurs, was a high risk taker. He had a passion for poker—recall the $6,000 in poker winnings he had stashed under his bed that provided the seed money used to start Head Ski in 1948. He took the money—his total savings—quit his engineering job and proceeded into the world of entrepreneurship. *Ski* magazine reasoned that Head's success against the large, old-line companies was based on his personal determination and resolve:

He was obsessed, to be sure, and being relatively unencumbered by stockholders, high overhead, and strong yearnings for luxurious living, he was well braced for the long haul. (*Ski,* January 1964)

Head's personal life was also surrounded by risk. He not only loved to gamble, his idea of leisurely fun was Alpine skiing, competitive tennis, and scuba diving. Most of these pursuits were acquired after the age when most men of his education and training were relaxing in more sedate activities. Ocean cruises were not his forte. He enjoyed competing against nature and had an adventuresome and gambling spirit that seems to possess the great innovators of the world.

When Head was interviewed about his success at the innovative process he said, "People who go around trying to invent something fall on their tails. The best inventions come from people who are deeply involved in trying to solve a problem" (Kennedy, 1980). Head sold Prince Tennis to Chesebrough-Ponds for $62 million in 1982. His second big risk had resulted in a windfall of $32 million, far greater than that of his first innovation. He finally had the time and money to pursue his loves of skiing, tennis, and snorkeling, as well as his more intellectual pastimes of bridge, chess, and Plato's *Dialogues.*

Intuitive Success

Pam Shriver did for the Prince oversized tennis racket what Jimmy Connors had done for the first Wilson metal rackets. Pam was an unknown seventeen-year-old when she made it to the semifinals of the U.S. Open in 1978. Her vivacious personality and endorsement of the Prince racket helped the oversized racket achieve some much-needed credibility and launched it into an internationally known product. The rest is history. One indication of the impact of the Prince racket is Howard's technical description: "The potential for improvement with a Prince is inversely proportional to the ability of the player, ranging from 150 percent for the beginner down to 3 percent for the world-class player." Both the professional and the amateur has been improved by Head's invention.

Head believed that function preceded form as a design strategy: "I deeply believe in sticking to function and letting style take care of itself" (Harvard case study, 1967). Needless to say, his dedication to function over form is a technical description of problem resolution over aesthetic considerations. This was never so evident as in the Prince oversized racket product. Howard Head used a passionate desire for perfection and an irresolute intuition to change the sports of skiing and tennis. He followed his own personal desire to excel and when he couldn't, blamed his equipment. Then he proceeded to change the equipment rather than admit personal failings or inadequacies.

Vic Braden labeled his creation, "The Butterfly Chaser." *Sports Illustrated* gave it somewhat higher marks—"The most successful racket in tennis history." *Tennis* magazine said, "The genius of Howard was his ability to imagine with his mind and tinker with his hands." Howard Head was extremely introspective and at times his own worst critic. He said, "If you open yourself up, wisdom is going to flow in. . . . I consider myself primarily a creator, an innovator, and possibly a possessor of unusual vision. I do not think of myself as a businessman. . . . You have to believe in the impossible (Kennedy, 1980).

Burton Klein of Harvard gives testimony to the intuitive powers of entre-preneurs and innovators like Howard Head. In *Dynamic Economics* (1977) he said:

> If the entrepreneur wants to give himself the best chance of putting the law of large numbers on his side, he will use his *intuition* to leap to new hypotheses. The entrepreneur's riches are his hints. But if his hints are not to be squandered the entrepreneur must trust his intuition.

Howard Head
born July 31, 1914, Philadelphia, Pennsylvania
died March 4, 1991, Baltimore, Maryland

Dominant Personality Characteristic: Intuitive—a right-brain vision
Motto: "You have to believe in the impossible."
Nickname: "The Cheater"
Firm Name: Head Ski
Location: Baltimore, Maryland
First Innovation/Date: First metal ski, 1950
Products: Metal skis and oversized tennis rackets
Initial Investment: $6,000 in poker winnings
Second Innovation/Date: Prince oversized tennis racket, 1976

Sibling Status: Only son, older sister
Personality Profile: Extroverted Intuitive Thinking Judger (ENTJ)
Parents' Occupation: Father, dentist
Childhood Data: No detail
Family Socio-economic Status: Upper middle class
Formal Education: Harvard, engineering with honors, 1936. He wanted desperately to be a writer but failed miserably
Age, First Business Venture: 34, Head Ski, 1948
Age, Big Hit: 38, 1952
Hobbies/Activities: Skiing, tennis, scuba diving, poker, Plato's *Dialogues*

Marital Status: Married three times
Children: One daughter
Religion: Agnostic. Believed in a universal intelligence, Esalen, and philosophical metaphysics
Public Offering Date: Sold Head Ski to AMF in 1969 for $16 million
Revenues or Units of Big Hit: Dominated ski business for 10 years and the tennis business for 15 years
Revenues of Firm: Head skis, 300,000, $25 million revenues, 1967. Prince rackets, 200,000 annually, 1981, dominating world markets
Estimated Net Worth: $4.5 million on sale of Head Ski to AMF in 1969, $37 million on sale of Prince to Chesebrough-Ponds in 1982
Age Became Millionaire: 38, 1952
Heroes: Plato, Carlos Castenada, philosophers
Honors: Ski patents and tennis patents. A Head ski hangs in New York's Museum of Modern Art.

14

William Lear—Passionate

In 1916 Freud published a psychosexual study on the personality of Leonardo da Vinci. He said, "Leonardo transformed his passion into inquisitiveness." Freud's thesis is, "What is repressed in sexual life will reappear—in distorted form—in daily life." The creative individual will sublimate repressed psychosexual energy into enormous bursts of creativity. Bill Lear was a contemporary role model for this Freudian theory of psychosexual energy. He had enormous vitality and talent that emanated from a deep-seated sensual desire to seduce markets and women. He had an insatiable appetite for new creations and new female conquests. Lear was a classic satyriasis personality. His obsessive behavior and compulsions have been found in many overachieving entrepreneurs (Turner, Bushnell, Jones, Honda) as well as some of the world's great leaders like Napoleon, Roosevelt, Mussolini, and Kennedy.

Great artists like Balzac also had enormous passionate energy that drove them to great creativity and peak achievement. Balzac's biographer said of him, "Everything he did seemed to have a tenfold intensity. When he laughed the walls trembled." Jacques Barzun researched the creative personality, resulting in this conclusion: "The genius's goal rivets his attention and becomes an obsession. . . . This mad passion or passionate madness is the reason why psychopathic personalities are often creators and why their productions are perfectly sane."

Virtually every great artist, creator, and innovator has a hyper, almost volatile, passionate, driven nature. They exhibit a "will to power" or "vital force" evocative of Nietzsche's "Superman" or Maslow's self-actualizing or transcendental man. Creative superstars and dynamic leaders are intensely driven overachievers. Some internal search for truth drives them to a potent frenzy. Turner's biographer described him as "having the most unbelievable energy"; Gates has been labeled "a bundle of kinetic energy"; Head was said to have been "obsessed"; Jones was "hyper energy incarnate"; Steve Jobs was portrayed

167

as "possessed"; and Lear was characterized as "a genius driven by the need to give birth to his ideas at all cost."

Frederick Herzberg, the famous behavioral psychologist said, "Innovative people are passionate." Einstein said, "The emotional state which leads to such achievements [creative breakthroughs] resembles that of a worshipper or 'lover.' " Irving Taylor, a researcher on the creative personality, describes the metamorphosis of the personality: "The creative individual turns from reality to fantasy, where he gives full play to his erotic wishes."

Napoleon Hill spent thirty years of his life researching the lives of Carnegie, Ford, Edison, Rockefeller, Gillette, and others. He concluded, "Sex energy is the creative energy of all geniuses. There never has been and never will be a great leader, builder, or artist lacking in the driving force of sex." Freud's pioneering research on creativity was a "life force" or "libidinal psychic energy" in pursuit of the "pleasure principle." Freud's theory proposed that all ingenuity flows from recharged sexual energy, creative energy is sublimated libidinal drive, and creativity is a function of the individual's desire to resolve sexual conflicts.

Research on the gifted substantiates many of Freud's theories. The gifted have been found to have enormous sexual energy, vitality, and drive, which is directed to the seduction of markets and women. The founder of Success magazine, Dr. Marden (1897), said, "Sexual energy is the foundation of mental as well as physical fertility. It awakens, enriches, and vitalizes all the faculties and develops creative energy." The doctoral research for the subjects of this book substantiates the passionate nature of these entrepreneurial visionaries. Bill Lear epitomizes this behavior. Flying magazine (1989) described Lear as "entrepreneurial energy incarnate." Lear had an insatiable need for creative fulfillment as the result of an unhappy and insecure childhood. His ideas were his tranquilizers, his conquests his catharsis, perfection was his solace, and passion his obsession.

> Sex and power are inextricably intertwined.
> —Michael Hutchison, *The Anatomy of Sex & Power*

> Big T's [thrill-seekers high in testosterone], as a group, tend to be more creative and more extroverted, take more risks, have more experimental artistic preferences and prefer more variety in their sex lives.
> —Frank Farley, psychological researcher

The media dubbed this "Stormy Genius" King Lear, since he personified one in total control of his destiny while dissension ran rampant all around him. He was the consummate Renaissance man and maverick inventor. Lear was best known for the Lear jet, which he created at the age of sixty. He had already developed the first car radio (1924), airplane transceiver (1935), airborne direction finder (1946), autopilot (1949), and, coincident with the Lear Jet innovation in 1963, the first eight-track stereo tape system (1967). Lear was volatile, impatient, inventive, and extremely passionate in everything he did.

Lear generated over 150 patents, most of which were for high technology electronic or aeronautical products. He accomplished this with an eighth-grade education, an innate ingenuity, and a colossal risk-taking mentality. One of his favorite expressions aimed at motivating less passionate employees was, "Don't tell me it can't be done" (Rashke, 1985). A Lear jet coloring book was published in the 1960s that included some tongue-in-cheek but incisive descriptions that give insight into how Lear employees saw their passionate and flamboyant boss:

> Color Bill: Angry, genius, unpredictable, kind, dynamic, genius, generous, raging, intelligent, genius, happy, ridiculous, friendly, genius, mad, inquisitive, absurd, bothersome, and genius. (Rashke, 1985)

When Lear was asked what made him create the Lear jet his response was a classic one for the innovator personality: "I built the Learjet because I wanted one." He bought his first biplane in 1931 with monies from Motorola radio royalties. The ensuing cross-country flights fueled Lear's already fertile mind. This tempestuous creator/entrepreneur kept getting lost and became frustrated because he had no way of locating his position or direction. He solved the problem with the creation of the Learoscope. This product, like most he was to create, became the industry standard, with more than half of all U.S. planes using Lear's invention by 1939.

The Learjet Project

Bill formed Lear, Inc., in Grand Rapids, Michigan, in 1939 to produce his miniature autopilot. The unit dominated the market through the 1940s and during the war he shipped over $100 million worth of aeronautical instruments. America's jet fighters used his products exclusively. He amassed a personal fortune and spent a great deal of time in Switzerland at his 27,000-square-foot Le Ranch retreat. It was on one of these sojourns to Switzerland that Lear ran across an abandoned Swiss fighter that was to become the basis for the Learjet design.

When Bill decided to build the Learjet he was chairman of a very successful enterprise. The board of directors was used to Bill's tempestuous personality and desire to jump into various projects without notice or approval. But Lear's proposal to enter the business jet market was too much for the board, as the plane would compete with their largest customers. In addition, aeronautical engineers had told them the plane was a huge risk and that it probably never would fly. The capital cost of the jet aircraft business was enormous and beyond the financial scope of Lear, Inc.

Lear was not easily dissuaded from pursuing his dreams. He gave the board an ultimatum to accept the project or he would sell out and finance the project himself. They accepted his offer and Lear sold out in 1962 for $14.3 million and a long-term consulting contract. He then invested most of the money from Lear, Inc., into his new company, LearJet of Wichita, Kansas. Lear was convinced the plane would fly and was a viable business risk. He was so passionate in his belief that he was willing to bet his total new worth on the project. Bill Lear was sixty years old but still willing to bet it all on his "gut" feelings because of an inviolable belief system.

Lear modified the designs of the P-16 Swiss jet fighter to produce the Learjet. His designs were for a plane that could outperform any commercial plane ever built by a wide margin. It would fly at 50,000 feet and cruise at 500 m.p.h., with the ability to accelerate from the ground to 41,000 feet in eighteen minutes. His target price was $649,000 fully equipped, making it the lightest and fastest plane of its type in history. After he flight tested it in November 1964 and obtained Federal Aviation Administration approval he received orders for fifty-two planes within six months. This success catapulted LearJet from no market share to a dominant 80 percent market share worldwide. He had gone from a nonplayer in the executive plane market to the dominant supplier in just twenty-four months. Such a Herculean task could never be performed by anyone without the passionate drive and ingenuity of a Bill Lear.

Aeronautical engineers said the Learjet would never fly. Aerospace industry experts said it was a ludicrous concept. Bankers would not finance the project and predicted his demise. Lear became jaundiced by the naysaying experts who knew so much. He said, "Bankers all went around to my competitors asking, 'Can he make a jet?' And they'd say, 'Well, he doesn't know anything about aviation. He's not really an accredited aeronautical engineer. He doesn't have over ten million dollars. . . . He probably won't be able to do it' " (Rashke, 1985).

When Lear was asked why industry leaders were not as perceptive as he was on the Learjet he would espouse the truth without thought of discretion. He was a gregarious, extroverted rebel who had an opinion on most subjects and pulled no punches in discussing his successes and his failings. He often characterized the establishment as narrow-sighted self-preservationist numbers crunchers. One such diatribe is remindful of Turner and Jones, who were cynical of all experts and market researchers:

> They don't ask the right questions. The trick is to discern a market before there is any proof that one exists. If you had said in 1925 that we would

build nine million automobiles a year by 1965, some statisticians would have pointed out that they would fill up every road in the U.S. and, lined up end to end, would go across the country eleven times. Surveys are no good. I make my surveys in my mind. (Rashke, 1985)

Personal History

William Lear was born in Hannibal, Missouri, on May 14, 1902. His mother, Gertrude, was a dominating German woman who was to play a major part in his driven insecurities and passions. She had a violent temper and divorced his father when Bill was just a child. After living with various men during his formative years, she remarried in 1913, when Bill was eleven years old. She became a reborn Christian, which created an environment guaranteed to cause psychological repressions of a normal teenager's sexual desires. Gertrude's newfound religion caused her to deal with Bill's adolescent hormonal flowering in a counterproductive manner.

Gertrude would treat Willy like a prince one minute and a wastrel the next. She told him he was fantastic and was capable of any undertaking. The next minute she could be a raving tyrant who treated young Willy like a villain by telling him he was the devil. To retreat from her, Willy buried himself in both reading and tinkering. He built a radio set at twelve and mastered the Morse code. He was a voracious reader of books on electricity and technical innovations. Fictional characters and fantasy-type larger-than-life characters were his favorites. Horatio Alger and Tom Swift became his heroes and flying his fantasy. He withdrew from an unhappy childhood by vicariously identifying with these fictional characters. They became his escape route to a happy exciting world.

Lear's dying words in 1978 were, "Mommie! Mommie! Finish it, Mommie, finish it." An Oedipal unconscious relationship was still indelibly imprinted on Willy's psyche at the age of seventy-five. One of the reasons for Lear's Oedipal associations was Gertrude's unusual behavior during his formative years. She watched him bathe and have bowel movements until he was eighteen (Rashke, 1985). In the sixth grade she beat him severely with a broom handle because she saw him with a girl on his bike, and then she took his bike away from him as punishment for playing with girls. She continually abused him both verbally and physically.

Because of her personal marital problems she warned him that marriage was just a prison and that girls were wanton and promiscuous. She constantly reversed her roles with him, telling him he was wonderful minutes after having flagellated him. Little did she know that she was creating one of the most incorrigible womanizers in America, a man who would lead a life of debauchery that would have been the envy of Errol Flynn. Lear was imprinted and conditioned in early life with such a hyperactive libidinal drive that it could only be satiated with an uncontrollable desire to create. His passion for creating and inventing was obviously influenced by his early repression of psychosexual energy.

Bill loved to tinker but was not enthralled with formal schooling. He had an inveterate desire to learn everything about electronics but was disenchanted with school and quit in the ninth grade. Bill loved flying and spent his time loitering around Chicago's airfields. He was badgered by his mother and finally could not tolerate the volatile home life and ran away at seventeen to find his niche in Hollywood. He never made it. Lear found himself broke and alone in Denver in 1920, where he lied about his age and joined the navy. The navy taught him wireless and radio technology. While in the navy he coupled his tinkering skills with the world of communications. This became his introduction to the world of electronic transmission, which was to be his forte for the next two decades.

Business and Personal Survival

Lear developed the Learjet in the same fashion that he lived his life. He violated all custom, tradition, and past methodologies. The Learjet transcended all certification parameters of the FAA because Lear had exceeded anything the FAA had ever encountered in state-of-the-art aviation designs. According to Stanley Green, an FAA engineer and lawyer, "It just boggled everyone's mind. Everyone at the FAA was adding regulations" in order to assure its safety and performance.

Lear classically operated in the netherland of development, which left him alone and vulnerable. His charismatic salesmanship and charm usually saved him. An example was his design criteria for the Learjet, which violated all of the traditional dogma of the time. He was ostracized by the traditionalists but always had a solid argument justifying his actions. His critics assumed he had missed the market because the plane did not meet the demands of the executive airplane market as the experts perceived them.

These experts said the speed of the Learjet was exorbitant and overkill for the small corporate customer. Lear's response was incisive and emphatic: "An executive used to 500 m.p.h. planes like the DC-8s should have a plane of equivalent speed." The experts said a walk-around cabin was required. Lear responded with, "You can't stand up in a Cadillac." The experts felt the heating and cooling systems were excess baggage. Lear said, "It is ridiculous for an executive to arrive at the airport in his air-conditioned $5,000 automobile and get into a $500,000 airplane that, until it becomes airborne, has all the comfort of a sauna bath." The experts said a bathroom was necessary. Lear's response, "A restroom is an admission you're spending too much time getting where you want to go" (Rashke, 1985). Lear usually had a poignant answer to his critics and was not shy about expressing his feelings.

Creativity and Financial Security

Lear ran into a severe cash flow bind in late 1966 because of his fertile mind (reminiscent of Bushnell). This caused him to sell LearJet to Gates Rubber in April 1967. Lear lost $12 million in 1966 primarily because he could not control his desire to continue creating and innovating and just focus on building the Learjets that were in such demand. He had concocted three more planes to design and build when he still had not completed the manufacturing cycle for the eminently successful Learjet.

Lear was appeasing his compulsion to create, create, create as a way of proving his worth psychologically. His genius became his demise. He had created the world's most successful corporate jet aircraft but was incapable of completing its production cycle prior to embarking on a whole new creative enterprise. He was not willing or capable of dealing with the more mundane aspects of implementation and commercialization of the product. He was compulsively driven to satiate his need for creation. His psyche drove him to fullfill some unrequited love and leave the spoils of business to others more inclined to that particular expertise.

Gates Rubber paid $11.89 a share for LearJet, which amounted to $21 million to Bill Lear plus another $3.5 million in debentures. He had once again emerged as a Phoenix rising from the ashes of his impetuous adventure. He was enormously wealthy and at sixty-five was expected to retire to enjoy the spoils of his ingenuity. As a testimony to the gambling mentality of the innovative visionary, Lear invested much of the LearJet windfall into a new steam engine car company he established in Reno, Nevada. After spending five years and $17 million in the steam car debacle, Lear created a new Lear Fan Jet in 1976. He put another $10 million into this venture at the age of seventy-four. Once again Lear went through all of the monies, as he had done on three other occasions. His estate was worth less than a million when he died in 1978.

Personal Behavior Characteristics

Bill Lear was an extroverted intuitive, the type that Jung had characterized as the quintessential inventor tycoon. Lear met all of Jung's criteria and then some. He was extremely sociable, hobnobbed with the Hollywood elite, and ate with presidents. His good friend Bob Cummings had agreed to play his part in the movie, *The Honor and the Glory*. The movie was never released because Columbia studios insisted on a crash scene involving one of his auto-pilots that Lear would not approve. He once again allowed his psychological need for perfection to interfere with something he wanted to do.

Lear was energized by the external world. He loved the "big picture" and macro vision of things. He never would allow himself to be constrained by the "little things" in life. This is an indication of his intuitive abilities, which he used in a holistic way. His decisions were based on analytical analysis of the problem regardless of any popular opinion on the subject. One example of this iconoclastic nonconformity was naming a daughter Shanda so she could be known as "Shanda-Lear."

Lear lived his life pursuing creativity and action whether right or wrong. He desired closure and completion in all things. An example was signing his last will and testament without reading it.

Flying magazine in September 1989 characterized Bill Lear as "Mister Bill" and portrayed him as a wacky, unpretentious individualist who exuded confidence:

> It was his confidence more than anything else that defined him; it was an absolute confidence, the confidence of the sun before clouds, an irresistible confidence that created a dauntless, positive feeling in people around him.

Lear's libidinal drive was virtually without equal. He had seven children from four marriages and another child from a long-time mistress with the pseudonymn Scarlet A. He kept mistresses in Chicago, Dayton, New York, Santa Monica, and wherever he found himself stranded for any period of time. Charlene, a mistress for years, would move in with him when his wife left to visit the children or to stay in one of their many vacation homes. He kept one mistress for over twenty years in both Santa Monica and Switzerland. Her code name was "The General." His wife, Moya, in an attempt at sanity, embroidered the various names of these mistresses in needlepoint (only those she knew about) and her list included Casidy, Margaret, Ethel, Madeline, Nina, Kathy, Deede, Scarlet, Jill, Eilleen, Jackie, Beth, and her nemesis Charlene (Rashke, 1985). Lear even invited his sons, John and David, along for many of his soirees with these various women.

Lear was a maverick in business and a renegade in his personal life. He once saw an Air Force jet coming to examine his plane. Lear sat his three-year-old son in the pilot's seat and hid in the back. The FAA wrote him up and the unflappable Lear promptly wrote to President Nixon, recommending the FAA be abolished. His daughter Patti talks of having lived in twenty homes in sixteen years and attending twelve schools in twelve years.

His impatience and intolerance with employees was legendary. Vern Benfer, his autopilot engineer, describes him as "mercurial, depressive, enticing, alluring, and masochistic." His wife of thirty-six years, Moya, became Lear's surrogate mother figure, according to his biographer, Rashke. "She understood Bill's darkest fears—not being loved, being thought of as worthless, being abandoned. She became everything that his mother hadn't been."

Bill Lear's talent was a mixture of innovative creativity coupled with the flair and flamboyance of the consummate salesman. He had the charisma of a snake charmer and the gambling propensity of Evel Knievel. Indefatigable passion and drive were his strengths. His biography, *Stormy Genius* (1985), and the media paint Lear as a frenetic innovator who worked twenty-four to thirty hours nonstop to create a concept. When less-driven employees were unable to keep up with his frenetic pace, he would become perturbed and frustrated and would often lash out at them. Rashke gives a characterization of him by the Swiss just prior to his LearJet project:

> an eccentric who could fire people with enthusiasm; a genius driven by the need to give birth to his ideas at all cost—family, friends, business; a visionary, conscious and confident of his place in history; an entrepreneur, blessed with a gift to generate both ideas and money and burdened with *la folie de grandeur*.

Lear considered every person in every company his direct employee in the autocratic tradition of other innovative geniuses like Steve Jobs. He demanded and received control over all facets of his operations. When questioned about the logic of this operating style, he replied, "Could five hundred men have painted the Sistine Chapel?" One description of Bill Lear's volatile personality was made by a friend who had heard his ashes had been thrown out of a plane into the Pacific off the Los Angeles coast: "I ain't going near that ocean for a month. It's going to be so mean and turbulent, it won't be safe" (Rashke 1985).

Risk-taking Proclivity

Lear made and lost millions but it was the game of creating and problem resolution and not the money that drove him to excel beyond the ordinary. He was notorious for taking risks for the sheer pleasure of solving a problem that others had determined was insoluble. When Ampex founder Alexander Pontitoff told him the eight-track tape for an automobile was an impossible task, Lear became passionately determined to make it happen. When he was frazzled about a dilemma or could not resolve a problem he would take to the skies and do a few rolls in his plane (an illegal maneuver according to the FAA) to salve his psyche. Bill Lear was Horatio Alger in disguise, a salesman without parallel who was equipped with a belief system that would boggle the mind of Norman Vincent Peale. Rashke gives validity to his positive attitude with this quote from *Stormy Genius:* "They said I would never build my plane. Well, I did. They said my plane would never fly. Well, it did. They say we won't succeed. Well, we will."

Lear's risk-taking nature was equivalent to Ted Turner's of a later vintage. He risked everything he had on every new idea until the end. The board of directors of Lear, Inc., voted down his idea for building the Learjet in 1961. They were convinced it could never be built and if it were, it could never be sold. Lear was dismayed but undaunted. He immediately arranged for a sale of the firm he had started (grossing $100 million annually at the time). He sold the firm to Siegler Inc. on February 8, 1962. His share of the proceeds was $14.3 million. He invested all of these monies in development of the Learjet project. Within two years he had gone through all of the money. He was deeply in debt, virtually bankrupt. He hocked his Le Ranch estate in Switzerland, his home in Wichita, new homes in Greece and Palm Springs, and his wife's Rubens paintings to keep himself afloat as the Learjet was being completed. (This is reminiscent of Honda hocking his wife's jewelry to finance his Honda operation.) Lear did this while awaiting FAA certification, which was not a sure bet since it was shocked by the Learjet's revolutionary design.

Lear was so strapped during the mid-1960s that he sold a Learjet test plane—which he was not authorized to sell because it was not certified by the FAA—to a personal friend to raise cash. When things looked dire he got lucky. Supreme optimists like Bill Lear seem to have Lady Luck on their side. When the situation looked the bleakest for his new firm, fate intervened, and one of his test planes crashed and burned. Insurance monies from the accident were enough to keep the company alive until the FAA certification. By this time Lear had no money left to build the plane and was forced to pursue a public offering or see everything evaporate. A tribute to his sales ability, Bill raised $5.5 million in November 1964 by selling stock at $10 per share for 40 percent of the company. Within twelve months the plane became the largest-selling commercial jet ever.

Bill Lear crashed on his first flight as a teenager and crashed at least two other planes. He was forever violating most FAA regulations on landing and flying. He was infamous for meeting a new lady friend and flying over Lake Michigan and making her an offer she couldn't refuse—to join his "mile high club." His methods normally included setting the plane on autopilot and retiring to the back to consummate his new relationship. These romantic interludes occurred during the 1940s and 1950s when such behavior took a great deal of verve and panache. Another Lear maneuver was ignoring air controllers and landing with zero visibility. He flew as he lived, with a wild abandon.

Bill Lear easily cavorted with Hollywood stars, royalty, and politicians. He phoned Alexander Pontitoff, the father of magnetic recording and founder of Ampex, in 1963, when he was deeply immersed in the design of the eight-track stereo recorder. Lear had decided to build a stereo to fit in the radio slot of his personal car and plane. The space and fidelity problems were major obstacles to the design. When he reached an impasse he called on Pontitoff for help. The inventor of magnetic recording was of no help as he told Bill, "Don't try to put eight tracks on a quarter-inch tape. You can't do it. Just can't squeeze that much information on it." That was all Bill Lear needed to hear. Pontitoff's advice turned out to be motivational, even though it was not intended as such.

Bill decided to embark on the eight-track tape design concurrent with his Learjet development. This was not necessarily the most rational strategy but it was Lear's style. He would become passionately involved in an idea and could not wait to complete the design or solve the problem. Once he had solved it he was off on another tangent. He worked day and night on the eight-track problem in 1963–64. He finally succeeded in overcoming all of the design problems and had a working model of the new "Lear Stereo Eight" by the fall of 1964.

This creation was years ahead of the industry leaders in the field. He sold the Lear Stereo Eight to Ford for its 1966 model cars and then convinced Motorola to manufacture and distribute the product. He also convinced RCA to manufacture the software recording tapes for the unit. This revolutionary development created a new market that reached $4.5 billion in revenues by 1975. Lear's fertile mind had created another breakthrough product of global proportions. He once again had no interest in merchandising the product or staying around to participate in its long-term commercialization.

Passionate Success

The Learjet hangs in the Smithsonian Air and Space Museum in Washington, D.C. According to the *Smithsonian Book on Flight* the "executive jet revolutionized the world. . . . It remained for William Lear to set off the revolution. Against all advice and prediction."

Bill Lear received many accolades over the years. This ninth grade dropout was given the highest honor in aviation, the Collier Trophy, by President Harry Truman during a lunch at the White House in 1950. This tribute to Lear's genius was given for his autopilot invention, a key system on the Air Force's F-5 jets. He was awarded an honorary doctorate in engineering in 1951 by the University of Michigan, and received a much-deserved Horatio Alger award in 1954. Ultimately, five other universities gave Lear honorary doctorates, the most prestigious being Notre Dame and Carnegie-Mellon. Lear is in the Aviation Hall of Fame and was recipient of the Thailen Medal in 1960.

Bill Lear is an innovative genius of the first order. His passionate pursuit of perfection is without equal. His vision and intuition overcame all attempts at control by the establishment or his four wives. He lived life to the end betting everything on his vision of the future. Lear never ran out of ideas and even when dying in Reno he made out a will establishing a trust that would carry out the plans for his new Lear Fan Jet. He died with less than a million dollars but with dreams of new and better ways of flying and living. A quote from him on the reasons for his success is appropriate for all innovators to observe: "If I'd done a market survey like they do for known products . . . the airplane would never have been constructed. . . . Listen to your own counsel."

William (Powell) Lear
born June 26, 1902, Hannibal, Missouri
died May 14, 1978, Las Vegas, Nevada

Dominant Personality Characteristic: Passionate pursuit of perfection
Motto: "If I'd done a market survey, the airplane would never have been
    constructed. . . . Listen to your own counsel."
Nickname: "King Lear," "Aviation's Stormy Genius," "Wonderful Wizard"
Firm Name: LearJet Corporation
Location: Wichita, Kansas
First Innovation/Date: Built first car radio, 1924, sold to Motorola
Products: Car radio, air compass, autopilot, Lear Jet, eight-track stereo
Initial Investment: Sold Lear, Inc., to Siegler for $14 million to fund the Lear jet
Second Innovation/Date: Lear jet, 1963, within 12 months the largest-selling
    jet

Sibling Status: Only child
Personality Profile: Extroverted Intuitive Thinking Judger (ENTJ)
Parents' Occupation: Father, carpenter
Childhood Data: Parents divorced when he was six. Mother lived with various
    men and remarried when he was eleven. Lear unhappy at home, fled at
    seventeen
Family Socio-economic Status: Lower middle class
Formal Education: Ninth grade dropout. Pilot. Inveterate reader
Age, First Business Venture: 20, an electronic repair shop
Age, Big Hit: 61
Hobbies/Activities: Flying, golf, and chasing women. Built his own plane in
    1925.

Marital Status: Married four times plus mistresses
Children: Seven children from three different marriages
Religion: None
Public Offering Date: November 30, 1964
Revenues or Units of Big Hit: Lear jet became largest-selling business jet within
    12 months. Revenues $52 million in first year
Revenues of Firm: Eight-track stereo he designed had $4.5 billion in revenues
    in 1975. Gates Rubber bought LearJet.
Estimated Net Worth: Made and lost millions
Age Became Millionaire: 29, based on first car radio designs, 1931
Heroes: Horatio Alger and Tom Swift
Honors: 150 patents. Collier Trophy, Aviation Hall of Fame, University of
    Michigan honorary degree, Swedish Thailen Medal, 1960

15

Soichiro Honda—Persistent

"PERSISTENCE PROPELS POTENTIAL TO PERFECTION"—the motto of great innovators from Edison to Honda. Edison insisted that creativity was based on 99 percent perspiration and 1 percent inspiration. Honda agreed and credited his successes on his "failures." He believed a lot of "failures"—trial-and-error heuristic experimentation—were required for successful innovation. This persevering attitude proved to be the difference for Honda and Edison as it has for most great innovative visionaries.

The ability to experience failure after failure without quitting is a fundamental behavior characteristic of the innovator personality. It is necessary for creating large-scale breakthrough innovations. Cy Young symbolizes this almost better than any scientist or inventor (the Cy Young Award is the annual award given to the highest-achieving baseball pitcher). Young personifies the essence of winning because he won more baseball games than anyone in history. In fact, his 512 wins exceed his nearest rival by 150 games—a record that will probably never be broken. Most baseball fans are familiar with this record just as assuredly as they are not familiar with the record dealing with the most losses by any pitcher. Guess who holds this unenviable record? Right! Cy Young. He lost 313 games, far more than his nearest rival for this ignominious distinction. Persistence paid off for Cy Young as it has for Soichiro Honda. It is a critical behavior trait for anyone who desires to change the world through innovation.

There aren't any "quick fixes" or "free lunches" in the world of large-scale innovation. Only a highly focused and persistent personality can overcome the continual crises and detours encountered on the road to any goal. Bill Lear made and lost four fortunes but he never quit. Tom Monaghan flirted with bankruptcy four times and was ousted from Domino's but refused to quit. Howard Head spent eighteen months building six pairs of metal skis that were all broken by a nonbelieving ski pro in just thirty minutes. He persevered

180

and built forty more pairs of skis until he had a pair that could not be broken. Henry Ford went bankrupt twice prior to his big win, the Model T. Lincoln lost virtually every race he entered. He persevered until he finally won the big one, which didn't happen until he was sixty. Ted Turner says, "Never get discouraged and never quit. Because if you never quit, you're never beaten." Honda gave this succinct and philosophical advice to all would-be innovators. "Entrepreneurs must be free to set improbable goals and to fail." Honda, like Edison, considered every failure one step closer to ultimate success, no matter what the challenge.

> Many people dream of success. To me success can be achieved only through repeated failure and introspection. In fact, success represents the 1 percent of your work that results from the 99 percent that is called failure.
> —Soichiro Honda, from a 1974 speech in Michigan
> on receiving an honorary doctorate

Honda had a dream as a child. His dream was to one day own a machine like an automobile. Little did he realize that he would not only own such a machine, he would be one of the titans of the industry that built them. Honda was destined to change both the motorcycle and automobile industries more than any other person in the world. His influence was not only in making radical changes in the products but in changing the very market for the products. He was single-handedly responsible for making the motorcycle socially acceptable to a whole new market segment. Honda's products were unisexual and appealed to the middle class, which had never before considered such a product.

Honda's forte was engineering elegance, packaging grace, and marketing insight. Yet he had no engineering background or education (he had only an eighth grade education). He knew nothing of marketing, finance, or distribution, as he was a child of rural Japan with none of the trappings of big business or international trade. And his accomplishments were made over the opposition of the *zaibatsu* (Japanese conglomerates), who considered him an outsider and rebel. Not only were the Japanese flabbergasted at his success, so were the perfectionist Germans, who owned the luxury market and the snobbish Americans, who owned all other markets.

Honda's elegant solutions to difficult problems were accomplished in the most simple ways. This appears to be consistent in many of the world's great innovators. He was not educated in the nuances or disciplines of engineering, which allowed him to use heuristic trial-and-error techniques in the tradition of Edison. By the eighties Honda had become the third largest car maker in Japan and by the end of the eighties he had become the third largest in the world. In motorcycles Honda dominated the market with over 70 percent market share during the sixties and by the nineties he was shipping over three million cycles per month and still maintaining a 60 percent worldwide market share. Not bad for an eighth-grade dropout who had a dream and then had the persistence and wherewithal to execute it. George Gilder describes Honda as "the world's single most brilliant and successful entrepreneur of mechanical engineering since Henry Ford." The British *Sunday Times* auto critic in the eighties wrote, "The precision of Honda's engineering, almost like a jeweled watch, has astonished every engineer I have spoken to."

Honda pulled another impossible breakthrough when he proved the experts wrong about American workers not being capable of building a high-quality car in the same genre as the Japanese. He built a plant in Marysville, Ohio, in the mid-seventies and destroyed this myth by producing a car with the identical quality standards as the Japanese. In fact this car—the Honda Accord— was to become the best-selling car in America during the late eighties and nineties, and was instrumental in Honda becoming the first Japanese executive ever inducted into the American Automobile Hall of Fame.

Personal History

Soichiro Honda was the first-born child of a very poor family in Japan's remote Hamamatsu province. He was born on November 17, 1906, not many miles from Akio Morita, the founder of Sony. Morita was born into a wealthy family with tennis courts and every advantage, but Honda was the son of a poor blacksmith who repaired bicycles on the side. This early environment was to prove beneficial to Honda in his early motorcycle days. His father's tutelage along with his mechanical aptitude for problem resolution were instrumental factors in his early training. The family was so poor that five of the nine children died of malnutrition before reaching maturity.

Soichiro was a poor student and habitual truant from school as he hated the formal learning process taught in the schoolroom. He preferred the techniques of experimentation and always learned best through trial and error. He always loved machines and mechanical devices and was mesmerized when he first saw an automobile as a child, as illustrated by this quote from his biography:

> Forgetting about everything else, I went running after the car. . . . I was deeply stirred. . . . I think it was at that moment, though I was a mere child, that the idea originated I would one day build a car myself. (Sanders, 1975)

Honda launched his company into the crowded motorcycle industry in the early fifties and within five years had successfully elminated 250 competitors in that industry (50 were Japanese). His "Dream" machine, introduced in 1950, was a realization of his childhood fantasy of building a better machine. This was followed by the "Super Cub" product launched in Japan in 1955 and America in 1957 with the now famous advertising slogan, "You Meet the Nicest People on a Honda." These unique products, coupled with an inspirational advertising promotion, made Honda an instant success and changed this one-time stagnant industry. By 1963 Honda had become the dominant force in the motorcycle business in virtually every country of the world, leaving Harley-Davidson and the Italian bike companies in the dust.

Honda became a juggernaut that propelled the motorcycle business into a $3 billion motorcycle annual market. His original approach to design and marketing was a catalyst that changed the industry from a "black leather jacket, Harley Hog crowd" to the "middle-class fun family crowd." Honda pioneered in products, thereby changing the industry, and dominated it like no other firm has ever done then or since.

After securing the motorcycle industry, the energetic and ambitious Honda decided to invade the automobile market and did so with a strategy of building and racing cars. His racing car debuted in 1962. The Japanese Ministry of International Trade and Industry told him that Japan did not need another automobile producer. Honda, in his inimitable style, ignored them as he did all industry experts who predicted his early demise. In 1970 he entered the competitive car business, which had not seen a successful new entry since 1925, when Walter Chrysler entered the capital-intensive and difficult automobile market. During the intervening years between Chrysler's entry and Honda's, no less than ten companies had failed, including the likes of Packard, Hudson, Studebaker, Kaiser, Willys, Tucker, Crosley, and, more recently, Delorean. Honda not only made it, he buried those in his way.

One of the first areas that Honda attacked was the weakest link in the industry—the clean air emissions engine standards imposed by the American government. Not one of the giants in the industry had been able to cope with this gigantic problem, not the American manufacturers—General Motors, Ford, and Chrysler; the Japanese giants—Toyota and Nissan; or the German high-performance manufacturers—Mercedez-Benz, BMW, and Porsche. Their solution to the problem had been the use of a catalytic converter. Honda approached the problem head on and actually embarrassed these titans of the auto world by creating the very first pollution efficient engine—the CVCC. He launched this elegant solution to pollution in the Civic, introduced in 1975, and the car became an immediate hit in the low-end marketplace.

Honda graduated from elementary school in 1922, and left immediately for Tokyo as an apprentice in an auto repair shop. He spent six years as an apprentice before borrowing the money to open his first repair shop in his home town in 1928. He received the first of his hundreds of patents that year—for a metal spokes design replacing the wooden one used for automobile wheels. This was Honda's first excursion into the world of creativity, which was to lead to some incredible technological accomplishments. Virtually every one was a simple solution to a complex problem. Honda was a simple man but his genius was in utlizing simple solutions to every product problem.

Business and Personal Survival

Honda became enamored of piston rings in 1938 and started a new company to design and build them for Toyota in Tokyo. He did this during the war until a bomb crippled his factory and then in 1945 an earthquake destroyed it completely. Honda was dismayed, sold out, and went into semi-retirement. His entry into the motorcycle market occurred quite by accident.

Honda was faced with no gas for his car in 1946, so this visionary took one of the many surplus motors left by the GIs and attached it to his bike for transportation. The engine was fueled by kerosene. This simple but elegant solution to a fundamental problem was Honda's way. His friends asked him to make them one of his motorbikes. After a dozen such requests, it occurred to the ever-innovative Honda that there must be a larger market for such a machine. He incorporated Honda Motor Company in 1948 with a charter to design and build motorbikes.

Honda introduced the "D" (for "Dream") motor for connection to a bike as his first product. The Dream-type "E" machine was introduced in 1951 and by the time the Super Cub was introduced in the United States in 1958, Honda had become the largest motorbike manufacturer in Japan, having passed by fifty other competitors. The Super Cub model had a unique step-through entry that appealed to the teenage and female market. This bike then revolutionized the motorcycle industry in America via the "You Meet the Nicest People on a Honda" campaign. This $5 million advertising promotion hit in 1962 and became an overnight success, wiping out the biker image for the motorcycle. Until this time the Hell's Angels image with the black leather jackets dominated the industry and hurt its expansion. This marketing move proved to be as ingenius as his step-through unisex bike had been a technological breakthrough. The market expanded by the millions due to an acceptable image and a low price with superb performance.

By 1961 Honda was shipping 100,000 cycles per month and by 1968 it had shipped its millionth cycle to the United States. By the mid-eighties Honda had 60 percent worldwide market share and in 1990 was shipping over three million motorcycles annually. The kid with the dream saw it come to realization and was then ready to attack the auto market.

Honda entered the auto market in 1970 with the Civic to the chagrin of MITI. He made the same innovative moves in this competitive arena as he had in the motorcycle field and was not the favorite son of the Japanese car industry. He was a true rebel and especially so when in 1974 the oil crisis caused the Japanese auto makers to agree to cut back production and raise prices. Only Honda refused and did just the opposite in the tradition of Henry Ford. He did the unthinkable in denying the Galbraithian economic model that said the industry should retrench. Honda doubled production and cut prices to an even greater degree than the legendary Ford had done fifty years earlier. Honda, who could not even spell price elasticity, had been right. Nissan and Toyota had seen their sales drop by 40 percent; Honda's sales rose by 76 percent and continued its upward spiral. By 1983 Honda was the fastest-growing auto company in the world.

Personal Behavior Characteristics

Soichiro Honda was a frivolous spirit and ladies' man as a youth. He was known as the "Playboy of Hamamatsu," a man who would party at the slightest provocation. His fun-loving, gregarious behavior led him to drive off a bridge with two geishas. He saved them by throwing them out a window.

This extroverted personality was known as "Mr. Thunder" to his employees for his emotional explosions when an employee did something stupid. They loved him but were wary of his emotional outbursts. This behavior was similar to that found in Bill Lear and Arthur Jones.

The freedom of spirit in Honda's many designs epitomized the truth that Honda constantly sought in all his products. He was a free spirit and fought convention his whole career. He refused to allow college graduates to work at Honda for many years, as he felt their dogmatic training would deter them from exploring the unknown. His dream of truth and vision is reminiscent of the best-selling novel by Pirsig, *Zen and the Art of Motorcycle Maintenance* (1974), which used the motorcycle as a metaphor for freedom. "The real cycle you're working on is a cycle called yourself." This statement epitomizes the innovative-visionary Soichiro Honda, who knew this truth better than most and was persistent in pursuing perfection in himself and his products.

Honda was an extrovert with an intuitive perception for business who used an analytical thinking approach to problem resolution. He was a Promethean temperament with a strong judging or closure attitude to life. He was impatient, rebellious, and persistent to a fault and just never gave up on a problem. Honda was intolerant of the establishment and traditional methods. In fact, he outlawed the use of the word *tradition* in Honda Motors as being counter to the principles of the firm. He blamed formal education for the traditional risk-averse behavior of technicians and management. He felt it biased and prejudiced individuals from taking initiative and exploring new and creative means of solving problems. He accepted mistakes, as illustrated in his doctoral acceptance speech at Michigan Technical University:

> Looking back in my work, I feel that I have made nothing but mistakes, a series of failures, a series of regrets. But I also am proud of an accomplishment. Although I made one mistake after another, my mistakes or failures were never due to the same reason.

Honda encouraged experimentation and resisted any attempt to control him or his firm through the traditional caste system. He told the *New York Times*, "Government officials should always act to protect the public interest. But they tend to become an obstacle when you try to do something new." This right-brain driven innovator drove the establishment crazy by allowing free reign to experimentation. He was against the hierarchical form of management, as indicated by this quote: "Generally speaking, people work harder and are more innovative if working voluntarily, compared to a case when people are being told to do something." What insight. Psychologists have since proven him right and the new management styles are moving toward the Honda methodology.

Risk-taking Proclivity

Honda was a consummate risk-taker. He was almost killed racing a car in the mid-thirties. He won the race, crashed at the finish line, and was in the hospitial for three months and was told never to race again. He learned to fly his own helicopter at the age of sixty and so frightened his passengers that he was persuaded to leave piloting to the professionals.

His competitive spirt was legendary. He would not admit defeat and would be willing to risk everything on his belief in an idea. His mid-seventies refusal to cut back production during the OPEC oil crisis was as gutsy as you can get. Honda Motors would have been history had he been proven wrong. He was not and Honda became a giant force within the industry.

A story from Akio Morita's biography, *Made in Japan* (1986), is poignant proof of the competitive nature of this man. Morita tells the story of Honda's indomitable risk-taking competitive spirit. When he was about to enter the auto market, Yamaha, his mortal enemy in motorcyces, saw an opportunity to take the market away from Honda due to Honda's extreme financial vulnerability. Yamaha tooled up many new models and cut prices dramatically, knowing that Honda was too preoccupied with the automobiles to retaliate. Wrong. Honda responded with all its resources as if it were engaging in a war to the death. In Morita's words:

The Honda management responded instantly, despite its heavy financial burden. It struck back with a new model introduction every single week for over a year! Yamaha could not keep up, and in the end there were top-level resignations at Yamaha.

Persistence Personified

Honda did for motorcycles what Henry Ford did for automobiles. He took a stagnant and dormant market and made it dynamic and exciting. His persistent pursuit of his dream of motorized perfection has been actualized through his elegant automobiles. Honda consistently led the world in motorcycle design from the mid-fifties through the early nineties. Honda's Acura had the distinction of becoming the best-selling automobile in the world for the years 1989, 1990, 1991, and 1992, according to *Car and Track* magazine. In 1991 they also built the most popular sports car—the NSX. In 1993 they once again won accolades from J. D. Power when the Acura was once again named the top luxury model in the United States. The company has the distinction of being the largest firm in Japan started after World War II.

In March 1988 *Motor Trend* magazine ranked the top cars in the world and the top three finishers were Honda cars—the CRX, Civic, and Prelude. The ultimate tribute came from *Car and Driver* magazine, which named the Accord as one of the top ten cars in the United States. When told that Honda planned to overhaul it, the editor wrote, "Short of remodeling the Sistine Chapel or overhauling the Acropolis, we can't conceive of a tougher undertaking."

These accolades and successes were all due to a small-town, impoverished maverick who behaved with an American flair for innovative risk-taking. He has been a controversial nonconformist in Japan, where conformity reigns supreme. His nickname, "Mr. Thunder," belies his small stature and the inscrutable behavior attributed to the typical Japanese executive. He personifies persistence, a trait magnified by a humble and gracious manner and his ability to see his mistakes as his greatest asset.

Soichiro Honda
born November 17, 1906, Hamamatsu, Japan
died August 5, 1991, Tokyo, Japan

Dominant Personality Characteristic: Persistent through failure
Motto: "Success represents the 1 percent of your work that results from the 99 percent that is called failure." "Love shortens distances."
Nickname: "Mr. Thunder"
Firm Name: Honda Motor Company
Location: Tokyo, Japan
First Innovation/Date: Dream "D" motor, 1949, clipped to a bicycle
Products: Dream "D," Cub, 1952; Super Cub, 1958; Civic, 1975; Accord, 1976; Prelude, 1978
Initial Investment: $3,200
Second Innovation/Date: Civic compact car with low-pollution engine

---

Sibling Status: First son—5 of 9 siblings died due to poverty and lack of medical care
Personality Profile: Extroverted Intuitive Thinking Judger (ENTJ)
Parents' Occupation: Father, blacksmith and bicycle repair shop owner
Childhood Data: Very poor agrarian life where survival was a win. He left home at 15 to become an apprentice mechanic
Family Socio-Economic Status: Peasant class from rural Japan
Formal Education: Poor student. Tenth grade only. Fearful of degreed types
Age, First Business Venture: 22, machine shop in hometown
Age, Big Hit: 47
Hobbies/Activities: Race car driver, avid golfer, helicopter pilot

---

Marital Status: Married once
Children: Two sons and two daughters
Religion: Buddhist
Public Offering Date: 1954
Revenues/Units of Major Innovation: Largest motorcycle producer in world. Largest selling auto in world, Accord, 1989, 1990, 1991, third largest car manufacturer
Revenues of Firm: $30.5 billion, 1991. Largest firm in Japan started since WWII
Personal Windfall/Estimated Net Worth: Honda Foundation established
Age Became Millionaire: 48
Heroes: Competitive risk-takers and nontraditionalists
Honors: Responsible for 470 inventions, over 150 patents, received honorary doctorates from Michigan Technical University and Ohio State University. Japanese Blue Ribbon, 1952.

16

Akio Morita—Persuasive

To be persuasive is to present compelling arguments in communicating a belief system to another person. That talent is tough enough when one speaks a similar language and is from the same culture as one's listeners. Akio Morita, a charismatic Japanese who cofounded Sony, has the reputation as one of the Western world's greatest salespeople. This is an unlikely role for an inscrutable Easterner and mindboggling for a Japanese engineer. The Japanese are not known to excel in the art of salesmanship. In fact, the Japanese invented the famous, or infamous, Japanese Trading Company to handle the demeaning tasks of selling. Japanese culture honors and respects the engineering and manufacturing functions and finds the sales function a necessary evil. Sales of any product is fraught with rejection, a totally negative and unacceptable proposition in Japanese culture. Therefore, the Japanese created the trading company to handle sales and the accompanying rejection.

Sony and Akio Morita are considered rebels in Japan. Morita discovered that the label "Made in Japan" had a negative effect on sales in the Western world during the early 1950s. He decided to change that image by ignoring tradition, discarding his engineering hat, and becoming one of the world's great salespeople.

David Silver studied the entrepreneurial personality for his book Entrepreneurial Megabucks *(1985). He included Morita as one of the world's great entrepreneurs, of whom he said, "Morita stepped into a proverbial phone booth, changed clothes, and blasted out as one of the greatest salespeople the electronics industry has ever seen." Other writers have concluded that all great entrepreneurial visionaries from Edison to Ray Kroc were persuasive sales talents. This author has found that the thirteen whiz kids in this work were all gifted salespeople. McKinsey & Company did a study on successful entrepreneurs during the 1980s: "The study found that our CEOs are almost inevitably consummate salesman." George Gilder called Morita "one of the world's para-*

mount salesmen." Ted Turner was known around his Atlanta television station, TBS, as its greatest salesman. The same was said of Bill Lear, Nolan Bushnell, Steve Jobs, Arthur Jones, and Fred Smith.

Morita says the reason for Sony's success is that "we do what others don't; we lead, others follow." His favorite story is a sales story about positive thinking. It describes two salesmen dispatched to sell shoes to an underdeveloped African nation. One salesman cabled his office, NO PROSPECT OF SALES BECAUSE NOBODY WEARS SHOES HERE. The other salesman cabled, SEND STOCK IMMEDIATELY INHABITANTS BAREFOOTED DESPERATELY NEED SHOES.

Innovators cannot be successful without being persuasive. They must convince the financial community that their concept is viable. Key personnel must be sold on joining the firm and then become convinced to sacrifice the present for the future. Suppliers and distributors must buy into the dream, and ultimately the products must be sold to the consumer. None of these will ever occur without a persuasive leader who can empower and motivate others to buy into an unknown and obscure future.

Jay Conger has done enormous research on charismatic leaders. He says, "Leaders can create this perception of extraordinariness through their prior successes, personal talents, and persuasive skills." *Passion and enthusiasm are fundamental to effective communication and sales of a concept. The creative, entrepreneurial and innovative personality appears to have mastered this ability more than most. Such people believe, and their belief fires up their enthusiasm to such a pitch that they cannot be denied. Akio Morita epitomizes those characteristics of persuasiveness and is a model to emulate for those wishing to become successful at the innovative process.*

> All major breakthroughs in transistor radios, from pocket-size to FM, and on to the first transistor TV—and most of the commercial successes—would henceforth come from [Sony]. . . . Sony, more than MITI or Nippon Steel, epitomizes the spirit of enterprise that infused and informed the miracle of Japanese growth.
>
> —George Gilder, *The Spirit of Enterprise*

Consumer Electronics Innovator

"Sony is the most well-known Japanese brand name in America, and Sony's cofounder, Akio Morita, is the most well-known Japanese businessman in America" (Moskowitz, 1990). Akio Morita's affinity for music led Sony and Morita to incomparable achievments deserving of the above accolades. Morita led Sony to the status of a world leader in consumer electronics through his burning desire to reverse the image of "Made in Japan" as a cheap copy. More than any other individual or company in Japan, Morita has been responsible for achieving that objective. Ironically, it is America who is now attempting to copy the "Japanese Way" in order to regain lost markets.

Morita was the first male child of a fifteenth-generation sake empire. In other words, he represented the embodiment of the tradition-steeped Japanese gentry. Morita was expected to head the family sake business, but he rejected that role to become world renowned as a flamboyant businessman. As a consumer electronics executive, he led the Japanese resurgence in world markets from the early 1950s through the 1980s. The innovative and imaginative products from Sony made Morita wealthy and one of the most visible Japanese personalities in the Western world.

Morita's salesman role at Sony was one reason he was considered a maverick in Japan. The Japanese originated the "trading company" to avoid any hands-on association with sales and marketing. They venerate the scientific/engineering image in their society. Sales and marketing are avoided because of the huckster-image of Hong Kong and the Near East and the ability to "lose face" in a sales environment. The irony is that Akio Morita has probably done more for the Japanese product image and economy—by becoming the world's most prolific salesman—than all of the nation's technologists put together. He helped establish Japan as a worldwide technological leader through the production and distribution of high-technology products that always led the industry in design and function. He accomplished this with business skills more normally ascribed to the Iaccocas, Perots, and Turners of the Western world.

Sony has been credited with starting the postwar Japanese juggernaut into motion. Its catalyst role started with development of the first transistor radio in the middle 1950s. Sony was not the firm best postured in 1955 to have created this innovation. Many other firms in Japan (Toshiba, Canon, and Matsushita) and America (Texas Instruments, General Electric, RCA, and Westinghouse) were securely entrenched in consumer electronics products and distribution. MITI—the Japanese government trade body—didn't think Sony could compete with these giants of industry who dominated the domestic and world markets. MITI refused to approve Sony's $25,000 license agreement with Bell Labs to import the new transistor technology into Japan. Morita and Ibuka spent a year attempting to convince MITI they were capable of competing in the highly competitive world markets. MITI was not convinced and told the company to work on less ambitious projects.

MITI was probably correct in its assessment of Sony's inability to compete with the consumer eletronic giants. However, Morita and Ibuka didn't know it and neither did the industry leaders. The American giants had a 98 percent market share worldwide in consumer electronics during the mid-1950s. They lost 90 percent of it over the next two decades, with a major share going to upstart Sony. Sony was a neophyte firm that should not have defeated Westinghouse, Texas Instruments, and General Electric at their own business in their own country.

Morita and partner Ibuka persevered in their struggle with MITI. In 1954 MITI finally approved their transistor license agreement. Bell Labs told these presumptuous newcomers that the transistor would only function for hearing aids because it was not powerful enough to drive a radio. Once again Sony didn't listen to the experts who had created the technology and proceeded to create their own transistor that would drive a radio.

During the mid-1950s the firm was known as Tokyo Telecommunications Engineering Corporation. This name did not convey Sony's mission, communicate a global image, or sound Western enough for Morita and Ibuka. Their vision was much grander than a Tokyo company, as they believed they would become a world leader in electronic sound products. Sound was and still is Morita's passion. This passion led him to name his company Sony, based on the Latin word for "sound." The Western etymology was not an accident. It was critical to the co-founders' long-range plans for their "sound" products. Most people still think Sony is a Western company because the name sounds Western.

Sony proceeded to develop the portable "radio that works," introduced in 1955. From the beginning it was high quality, priced above the Texas Instruments "Regency," and diminutive in comparison to all other radios. Sony's early experience building a tape recorder, which didn't sell, had a positive influence on their radio designs. Morita was to say, "You cannot sell what people do not want to buy." He was certainly correct on this first mass consumer product, which was so critical to Sony's long-range success. The product was revolutionary. It dominated the portable radio market from the beginning, even though it was a foreign entry and priced at $29.95, 50 percent more expensive than the popular Regency model.

Sony's initial product was followed by the world's first shirt-pocket-sized transistor radio in 1957. The shirt-pocket unit established the tradition of Sony products as small and high quality. This unit was a tribute to Morita's salesmanship. He felt it very important that the size was demonstrated by putting the unit in a shirt pocket. The first unit designed would not fit in the pocket so Morita had shirts made with extra large pockets to effectively demonstrate the small size of the product.

Small size and high quality were traditions destined to last for the next three decades. These first products are considered by most historians and economists to have marked the start of Japan's unparalleled post-war expansion. Economist-writer George Gilder is one of those who believe Sony's innovations were the catalyst for Japan's dominance in the world consumer markets:

All major breakthroughs in transistor radios, from pocket-size to FM, and on to the first transistor TV—and most of the commercial successes—would come from [Sony]. Sony's success would leave Hitachi and Matsushita some three years behind. (Gilder, 1984)

In *Spirit of Enterprise* (1984) Gilder goes on to describe Sony's tremendous success in the mass-consumer electronic markets:

Since 1950 Japan has outperformed any other country in the history of the human race. . . . Sony, more than MITI or Nippon Steel, epitomizes the spirit of enterprise that infused and informed the miracle of Japanese growth.

Sony has had a plethora of successes since the transistor radio. *Forbes* ranked it the forty-seventh largest firm in the world and twenty-fifth in Japan for 1990. Sony's sales had reached $29 billion in 1992. The company achieved this success by developing the first transistorized TV (1959), the first lap TV (1962), video recorder (1964), Trinitron single-beam TV tube (1968), VCR (Betamax, 1976), 8mm recorder (1983), Watchman (1984), and Discman (1986). In addition Sony created and produced the first high-capacity floppy discs for personal computers. Morita's passion for sound made Sony the consummate producer of state-of-the-art "sound" products. The culmination of Sony's success came in 1987, when Morita engineered the purchase of CBS records for $2 billion, and then two years later acquired Columbia Pictures for $4.9 billion. These acquisitions have made Sony a dominant force in the entertainment industry, with a large library of audio, film, and TV recordings.

Sony has always been known as the "guinea pig" company in the electronics industry because of its repeated leadership in technological breakthroughs. Sony created the first tranistorized radio and TV, always led with the smallest products, and followed with the first Walkman. And it was the first to commercialize the home video recorder, with its Betamax system released in 1976. When American companies like RCA, Zenith, and Admiral were moving production offshore during the early 1970s in order to get lower labor costs, Sony elected to come to America. What irony.

When asked about his move to open a San Diego manufacturing facility to make Trinitron TVs, Morita admitted the move made no sense in the short run, especially if one looked at the immediate profits. He emphasized that the move was based on manufacturing where the market was located. He believed that Sony could overcome the productivity problems associated with American workers and meet the cost demands of such a price-sensitive product. His strategy was correct and in his words, "proved to be a wise one in the long run." No American executive would ever be so bold as to make such a decision. We should learn from this philosophy of short-term sacrifice for long-term opportunities. Sony now owns the Rockefeller Center, Columbia Pictures, and CBS—a testimony on how to sacrifice the present for the future.

Personal History

Akio Morita was born in Nagoya, Japan, on January 26, 1921, as the first child of a fifth-generation family of sake producers. He had a keen interest in electric phonographs from a very young age. Morita says, "I was obsessed with this new discovery." It caused him to spend all of his spare time on electronics, at the expense of his schooling. By his own admission, "I was spending so much time on electronics that it was hurting my schoolwork." His father was grooming him to take over the sake business while the young Morita was feverishly learning all he could about electronics. The elder Morita taught Akio management skills from early on and by the age of ten he would attend company board meetings. He had a relatively comprehensive understanding of the family business and knew such things as how a leader was expected to motivate employees to achieve higher productivity. Morita admits this training was invaluable to him later on, even though he hated it as a child.

As with most innovative visionaries, Akio Morita was a voracious reader as a youth. *Popular Mechanics* was to change his life, as it did that of Bill Gates. Morita read an article on new tape recorders that could reproduce music through sound recording and reproduction. The dream of the future Walkman was borne at this early age. Morita's reading was limited to technical magazines and books on electronics and technology, in contrast to other innovators who fantasized about great world leaders.

The electronics diversion almost caused Morita to miss out on the higher school. This school is the equivalent of the Western prep school. "I became the lowest-ranking graduate of my school ever to be admitted to the science department of the Eighth Higher School and it took me a year of extra study to make it," he said. Morita was then accepted by the Osaka Imperial College, where he received a degree in physics in 1945. After the war he began teaching physics and working part time with Ibuka, an electronics genius who wanted to start a new firm to build electronic parts. Ibuka, Maeda, and Morita became partners in the formation of Tokyo Telecommunications Engineering Company in 1947. The firm became Sony in 1958.

Business and Personal Survival

Akio Morita and his partners incorporated on May 7, 1946, with a capitalization of $500. Their first product was rice cookers. They produced a hundred and sold none. Their second product was Japan's first tape recorder, which used paper tape since there was no plastic in Japan at the time. Once again they had a decent product but no sales. The company flirted with bankruptcy through this period and through the first eight years of operation. Morita's father saved the company numerous times. It became apparent that Morita was not to pursue his dream by engineering electronic products. The company knew how to design and build products but had no ability to sell what had been designed and built. This function was to become the express responsibility of Akio Morita.

Morita became the head of worldwide sales and marketing for Sony. He had no training in these areas. He was a technologist but had decided that sales and marketing differentiated successful firms from the also-rans. During this same introspective period in the 1950s the firm decided to establish Sony's identity as the "product innovation company." The name Sony has since became synomomous with innovative breakthrough products. For the next forty years Sony pioneered new concepts in virtually every market segment of the consumer electronics industry. This romance with the new and innovative made Sony the greatest product innovation company for three decades, from the 1950s through the 1970s, and took Sony from $2.5 million in revenues in 1955 to over $29 billion in 1992.

The Sony Walkman became one of Sony's most famous products. It was introduced in 1979 and became the world's ubiquitous sound machine with seventy-five models and over twenty million in use. Morita tells the story of how he had to threaten to quit his job to have it built. His engineers had done their own research and did not believe anyone would buy a unit that could not record sound in addition to playing it. Morita's intuitive feel for what would or would not sell prevailed. He said, "If we don't sell 100,000 pieces by the end of this year, I will resign my chairmanship of this company." This is not the classical Japanese way but it worked and the world is better for it. When asked about the market research function he said:

> I do not believe that any amount of market research could have told us that the Sony Walkman would be successful, not to say a sensational hit that would spawn so many imitators. (Morita, 1986)

Personal Behavior Characteristics

Akio Morita has an action-oriented innovator temperament. His intuitive-thinking personality is classical for the innovator. He is energized by external events in the world, which in Carl Jung's system of personality typing makes him an extrovert. He perceives the world of business with a view to the big picture. He sees the forest rather than the trees when evaluating opportunities. Morita makes decisions in a thinking or impersonal manner typical of his educational training. Morita's intuitive-thinking temperament classifies him as a "visionary-architect or systems-builder." This is consistent with reports on his behavior at Sony and from excerpts from his biography.

Morita lived his life in a structured manner, in contrast to the more spontaneous manner of a Nolan Bushnell or Tom Monaghan. Morita always sacrificed the present for the future in every business decision. "If management focuses only on quick profits, it is working only for its own short-term interest," he said (Range, 1982). He believed management should always make decisions on the basis of a long-term perspective, which was apparent with his decision to set up a manufacturing plant in San Diego years ahead of the need to do so. He was always competitive. He said, "We Japanese are competitive, not only in business, but in life." He says you should defeat your competitor but not destroy him: "You must leave him his honor." Akio was especially competitive when playing tennis and invited friend Virginia Wade to play with him at sales conventions (Jung interview, March 1991).

Morita took up tennis at the age of fifty-five, downhill skiing at sixty, and water skiing at sixty-four. He received a helicopter pilot's license while in his mid-fifties. He enjoys traveling fast, rides a motorcycle, likes roller coasters, and has done aerobatics in a plane over Germany. Morita and his wife are avid golfers and tennis players. He commutes between Tokyo and New York like others commute from Washington to Boston. Morita is viewed as an aggressive risk-taker in the mold of the innovative visionary. His work habits and time values are similar to that of Ted Turner and other Type A visionaries. One of his four secretaries would record a videotape of the news each day so he could watch it while driving between home and work and not waste valuable time.

Morita attributes much of his personal success, Sony's success, and Japanese business success to competitive drive. He believes this drive is a direct function of the insecurity of the Japanese people. Their insecurity, he says, is based on a daily fight for survival. The Japanese people are faced with daily extinction since they are all born on top of a turbulent volcano, face annual typhoons and tidal waves, and their land is constantly shaking with life-threatening earthquakes. Their land has no raw materials except for water and less than a quarter of it is arable or inhabitable. He believes that these life-threatening forces have been indelibly imprinted on the Japanese psyche, thus causing them to be fierce, overachieving competitors and frugal preservers of their assets.

Risk-taking and Cultural Nuances

Morita wrote a controversial bestseller in Japan in the 1960s called *Don't Mind School Records,* in which he called for a more pragmatic approach to recruiting and hiring (one of Honda's principles). This created a furor in Japan, where education is revered. Morita, however, does not capitulate to authority or tradition, which is one of the traits that has made him eminently successful at innovation.

Morita always listened to his own counsel on new product development and was constantly saying, "Sony creates markets." He believed that supply created its own demand; and he decried the market research used by large American firms to justify their every business decision. When asked why Sony had been more successful than American companies Morita replied, "America has been a society of justification. No one takes responsibility. American management no longer likes to make decisions" (Range, 1982).

Morita understood the nuances of the technology that made Sony so successful (he was a trained scientist) but he did not personally invent any of the products. His contributions were innovative marketing strategies and vision for potential market opportunities. His strengths were a resolute belief in action that took risks, especially long-range risks with high rewards.

> Management must be willing to take risks. And top management should all be experts in the business. . . . I think the Americans listen too much to the securities analysts and the consultants. (Range, 1982)

Morita attributes much of Sony's success, as well as that of other Japanese companies, to the Eastern egalitarian approach to business. He said, "Japan management does not treat labor as a tool but as a partner. We share a common fate." One of his axioms for successful market penetration was, "Share of market is more important to Japanese companies than immediate profitability." . . . Despite some of its darker aspects, "competition, in my opinion, is the key to the development of industry and its technology."

The essence of the egalitarian attitude has been reflected in the lifelong employment mentality of the Japanese. Morita feels very strongly that this factor has been instrumental in the changing fortunes in Japan and America, which he attributes to a lack of loyalty by American workers. His philosophy on layoffs is:

I cannot understand why there is anything good in laying off people. If management takes the risk and responsibility of hiring personnel then it is management's ongoing responsibility to keep them employed. (Morita, 1986)

Morita was always candid in his remarks to the media. He flirted with annoying Wall Street in a 1986 quote to the *Wall Street Journal.* He said that if he were made dictator of America, his first act would be the elimination of the quarterly report. This is probably one of the more astute observations he would ever make on America's problem of lost markets. Another quote from the loquacious Morita was on America's layoff policies:

In Japan, we think of a company as a family. You can't lay off people because of a recession. The recession is not the workers' fault. Management must sacrifice profit and share the pain. (Range, 1982)

Morita reiterates this point in his biography by describing a young executive in Japan championing a product idea that would not come to fruition for five to ten years. Japanese firms are very accepting of early year losses for potential long-term gains and Japanese executives are willing to wait years to see the fruits of their creativity. In America an executive would not consider a five- or ten-year project because of his limited employment life, which would preclude his seeing the benefits of the innovation. In Japan, executives are always around for ten or twenty years to see the fruits of their efforts. In America it is quite likely that a manager predicting a five-year loss would be terminated immediately for jeopardizing the organization. Morita feels this cultural difference has given Japan the edge in all long-term innovative endeavors and caused America to lose many major mass markets to the East.

Morita makes the observation in his biography that America has in excess of 500,000 lawyers. Japan has 17,000. He says, "While the U.S. has been busy creating lawyers, we have been busy creating engineers." He says Japan graduates four times as many engineers per capita as the United States—24,000 each year compared to the U.S.'s 17,000. The same disparity exists in the ratio of U.S. accountants and engineers. The United States has many more accountants than it needs, according to Morita.

Persuasive Success

George Gilder in *Spirit of Enterprise* gives Morita and Sony their due respect:

In the end it was salesmanship, sensitivity to consumer needs and responses, rather than technology, that allowed Sony to outdo such technically superior companies as Texas Instruments in selling transistor radios and other consumer goods.

Of the Japanese, he adds with elegance, "We [U.S.] landed on the moon. They landed in the United States's living rooms and dens."

Akio Morita is considered a rebel in Japan, as was Soichiro Honda. They both violated sacrosanct Japanese traditions. They established their own sales organizations when their distributors were insufficient for the task. They ignored the traditional trading companies and created their own vehicles to success with the flamboyance of the Western entrepreneur. In America, Morita would have been considered a true visionary on a par with Ted Turner, Fred Smith, Steve Jobs, and Bill Gates. He has the same philosophical approach, work habits, and business acumen.

The flamboyant Morita flies the world like most people go to a movie. He and his wife Yoshika own a twenty-four-room home in Tokyo and belong to golf and tennis clubs in both Japan and the United States. They lived in the United States in the early 1960s and two of their three children are graduates of American universities.

Akio Morita was totally focused on winning the game of business instead of worrying about his competitors or the vagaries of world problems. He has dined with presidents, prime ministers, and kings. He counts Henry Kissinger as a personal friend. He has been a constant advocate of bringing the West and East closer together. To this end he has spoken regularly of the idealistic problems faced by the two nations. A syndicated newspaper article of November 12, 1990, quoted him about the philosophical differences between the Japanese and American approach to innovation and success in world markets. Morita is convinced America is making the mistake of giving up on manufacturing and becoming committed to a service-based economy.

> The future of any nation, Morita noted, will be shaped not by those who can manipulate and exploit paper assets, but by the ability of that nation to manufacture good products. . . . Nothing is more fundamental to any nation or economy than the ability to produce real goods. (Marlowe, 1990)

Educator and writer Warren Bennis says, "Leadership requires persuasion, not giving orders." Akio Morita has this ability and has become a persuasive global salesman who changed the world of sound. This preeminent salesman used his talents to better the world and any aspiring innovator should attempt to emulate his persuasive talents.

Akio Morita
born January 26, 1921
Nagoya, Japan

Dominant Personality Characteristic: Persuasive—a preeminent salesman
Mottos: "Develop a product where there is *no* market—then create one." "Sony does what others don't; we lead, others follow."
Nickname: "Super Salesman of the World"
Firm Name: Sony (from *sonus* for "sound" in Latin)
Location: Tokyo, Japan
First Innovation/Date: Pocket-sized transistor radio, 1955
Products: Trinitron TV, Betamax, Walkman, Watchman, 8mm video
Initial Investment: $500 from founders Morita, Ibuka, and Maeda. Borrowed from Morita Sr. to keep the company afloat in early days
Second Innovation/Date: First transistor TV (1959), video tape recorder (1961), Trinitron TV (1968), Betamax VCR (1976), Walkman (1979), etc., etc.

Sibling Status: First son. Two younger brothers and a sister
Personality Profile: Extroverted Intuitive Thinking Judger (ENTJ)
Parents' Occupation: Fifteen generations of sake makers. Wealthy
Childhood Data: Very sound family life. Inquisitive. Built two-way radios
Family Socio-economic Status: Upper class. Own tennis court. Servants
Formal Education: Osaka Imperial University, physics
Age, First Business Venture: 25 when Sony founded, 1946
Age, Big Hit: 34
Hobbies/Activities: Pilots own heliocopter, tennis, golf, skiing at age 60

Marital Status: Married
Children: Two sons and one daughter
Religion: Raised Buddhist, not religious
Public Offering Date: January 1958, Tokyo Stock Exchange
Revenues or Units of Big Hit: 20 million Walkmans sold in 75 models
Revenues of Firm: $29 billion revenue in 1992. 100,000 employees
Estimated Net Worth: Huge homes in Tokyo and New York
Age Became Millionaire: At birth. Finally made it big at Sony in his mid-fifties
Heroes: Wagner, Brahms, Mozart
Honors: "Sony is the most well-known Japanese brand name in America . . . and . . . Akio Morita is the most well-known Japanese businessman."

17

Arthur Jones—Rebellious

*Rebellion is often the single most revealing trait of the creative and innova-
tive personality. Research into the gifted indicates that they rebel at a very
early age. They are intolerant of useless conformity even in school. They refuse
to be put into the box of mediocrity, which schools are wont to do. Innovative personalities are notorious for not conforming to the bureaucratic worship
of the "status quo." They refuse to operate by the book. They write their
own "book" and are defiant in their rejection of traditional values. They violate
conventional wisdom in the tradition of Schumpeter's "creative destruction."*

Albert Camus in The Rebel *said, "The spirit of rebellion can exist only
in a society whose theoretical equality conceals great factual inequalities."
Entrepreneurs, creators, and innovators strive to destroy those sacred dogmas
or "factual inequalities" and rebel in order to create the new and different.
They listen to their own counsel in a heuristic style that is based on an intuitive
belief in themselves. They are intolerant of bureaucracies and most authority.
They defy protocol, which has earned them not-so-endearing reputations of
mad, disruptive, wacky, ruthless, unconventional, maniacal, intense, eccentric,
bizarre, crazy, maverick, and obstructive. They are iconoclasts who are seen
as megalomaniacs on a mission.*

*Arthur Jones is the consummate rebel. His misanthropic approach to life
and business is legend. The media portrayed him as the quintessential rebel
with these quotes during the 1980s:*

Wall Street Journal (March 1981)	"Eccentric promoter"
Time (June 1985)	"More extraordinary than his machine"
Forbes (September 1983)	"Outrageous"
Newsweek (August 1983)	"Pugnacious, cocky, and swashbuckling"
Echelon (June 1986)	"Part lunatic, part genius"

Sportswise (February 1983)	"The Wild Man of Lake Helen"
Town & Country (October 1980)	"Misanthropic sadist at best and outright maniac at worst," "eccentric genius"
Money (1983)	"Stranger than remarkable"

The Promethean temperament is fundamental to the creative process because it searches for truth and breaks rules. George Gilder gave credence to this iconoclastic spirit saying, "Entrepreneurship entails breaking the looking glass of established ideas—even the gleaming mirrors of executive suites—and stepping into the often greasy and fetid bins of creation." Sam Walton's business philosophy was to break the rules. He said his Wal-Mart success was based on a philosophy of "Break all the rules. Swim upstream. Go the other way. Ignore the conventional wisdom." So did Jones.

> And whoever wants to be a creator in good and evil, must first be an annihilator and break values. Thus the highest evil belongs to the greatest goodness: but this is—being creative.
>
> Friedrich Nietzsche, *Thus Spake Zarathustra*

"Younger women, faster planes, and larger crocodiles" is the philosophy and motto of a misanthropic eccentric rebel named Arthur Jones. The above maxim has been the driving force of Jones's life since he was a teenager. It is what he has compulsively pursued on three continents. Women, airplanes, and wild animals somehow satiate Jones's unconscious psychological insecurities. He spent years obsessively pursuing ever-younger women, mastering ever-bigger and ever-faster airplanes, and capturing the world's largest crocodiles. These trophies nourished his starving ego and drove Jones with an intensity not seen in many people. Jones was evidently striving to exorcise ghosts of his youth and used these adult conquests to overcome some unrequited loves of childhood. His credo became the title for a talk show he attempted to produce with Gordon Liddy. His bizarre catchphrase about women, planes, and crocodiles is testimony to a hedonistic lifestyle, obsessive search for happiness, and a rebellious nature that led to the creation of the Nautilus empire.

Arthur created Nautilus in 1971. It was the variable-resistance principle (intensified work on the muscles at every point in the movement) that effectively "automated the barbell." This innovation revolutionized fitness training and spawned the "fitness generation" of the 1970s and 1980s. The narcissistic "me generation" worshiped physical prowess and fitness. Its fast-food mentality demanded a quickie workout with superior results and the Nautilus machine made that possible like no other equipment before it. Arthur Jones's timing was impeccable because he created a machine that gave an intensive workout in a very short time with superb results. He developed thirty-nine different exercise machines between 1971 and 1985, each designed to meet the various needs of specific muscle groups. The Nautilus equipment was the right product for the right time and was accepted as the panacea for fitness to such a degree that Nautilus became the "Kleenex" of the fitness revolution.

The original idea for the Nautilus design was spawned in the late 1940s, when Jones was looking for a more "logical" or "rational" approach to optimum exercise. He built the original Nautilus prototype while living and exercising in a Tulsa YMCA in 1948. He left it there for posterity as he did with thousands of other prototypes he was to build around the world. During the twenty-two years between this first attempt at automating exercise and his 1971 product introduction, Arthur Jones told countless people how to automate the barbell. He preached the gospel of negative/intensive workouts as being preferable to the explosive workouts used by weightlifters. According to Jones a machine could be built to perform to the needs of the weakest link of the body. In other words, the weakest link should not be the limiting factor in how much a muscle could be worked. A machine could neutralize the weakest link and allow the exerciser to maximize the workout. This is the magic of the Nautilus design. No one listened.

Jones continued to build prototypes of the Nautilus machine and left them in gyms all over the United States and from Central America to Africa. None of the other equipment manufacturers bought Arthur's reasoning or believed in an automated barbell. This marketing myopia was identical to Marcel Bich's experience with the ballpoint pen creation. The industry leaders were complacent and left the market opportunity available for Arthur Jones to pursue in 1969 when he returned from Rhodesia. He was broke, depressed, unemployed, and discouraged with life. He was in desperate need of some passion to pursue and it became Nautilus, whose time had finally come.

When asked by the *Wall Street Journal* in 1981 why he was able to accomplish what other industry leaders were not, he responded, "Before I came along, my field was dominated by myth, superstition, deceit, and outright fraud. I overcame it by the simple application of logical thinking." This logical thinking was his way of describing his right-brained intuitive approach to solving the design problems inherent in automated exercise machines.

Arthur's variable-resistance principle was the concept that made the "logical barbell" innovation a reality. His Nautilus machine allowed a person to uniformly "work" the entire range of motion of the muscle groups. This principle overcame the deficiency caused by the body's weakest links. The intensity of the workout was maximized while the workout time was minimized. This combination appealed to the fast-food generation of fitness-crazed baby boomers.

Jones's competition (York Barbells and Universal Gym Equipment) and exercise professionals repeatedly told Jones that he was attempting an impossible task and would fail. Jones's response to the advice of these experts typifies his rebellious attitude:

> If I listened to the advice of experts I would not have gone into this business. They said I could not sell painted machines, that they had to be chrome; they said I did not have the capability to make my machines; they said only multiple machines, not single-station machines would sell. As always, the experts are wrong. If they even think they are right, I am suspicious. People have opinions and beliefs, they don't think. *(Nation's Business,* July 1985)

The irascible Jones will expound on any subject and has had a long love/hate relationship with the media. When asked by a fitness magazine why he was able to do what others had not, he said that the establishment tends to "ignore, ridicule, attack, copy, steal. If you go back through the history of science you'll find that every idea of any benefit went through these steps, Einstein, the Wright brothers, Madame Curie, Edison, Pasteur." (Kornbluth, 1983) This emotional response gives testimony to the strong feelings of rebellion that Jones believes are the only way to operate and survive in a competitive and risk-averse world.

Personal History

Arthur Jones was born in rural Arkansas in 1923 and moved with his family to Tulsa, Oklahoma, shortly after his birth. He obstinately refuses to divulge any data on his age, his early childhood in Oklahoma, or allow any discussion of his mother. Arthur was sent to live with a German family in Tulsa just after his birth. This was probably a traumatic experience for him and the reason he has avoided any discussion on the subject in the hundreds of interviews he has held with the media. Even his ex-wives admit to not knowing his age or any specific details of his early life.

Arthur was born into a family of doctors. His grandfather, both parents, an uncle, and two brothers were all medical doctors. His daughter, Eva, is an obstetrician in New York City. His mother enrolled in medical school just after his birth and left Arthur to be raised by the German family and others. When queried about his childhood he speaks reverently of his father. He says, "He was a saint." He vociferously resists any discussion of his mother. This resistance is some indication of a lonely childhood, feelings of rejection and lack of love, early insecurities, and possibly a dysfunctional childhood.

Arthur was not interested in formal education. He dropped out in the ninth grade and therefore never made it to high school. When questioned about his lack of formal education, Arthur told *USA Today* in 1983, "I had done more reading at age ten than most people in their lifetime. I read my father's medical library and the whole damn public library at least three times." Jones's voracious reading included Voltaire, Mark Twain, Jonathan Swift, and Edgar Allan Poe. He claims to have read *Les Miserables* in the third grade.

Jones's retreat into the world of books and dreams led him into a fantasy reality that has a strong parallel in history to the lives of other great innovators, leaders, and inventors. Lincoln, Roosevelt, and other great world leaders were mesmerized by the lives of the great. Bill Lear, Ted Turner, Tom Monaghan, Fred Smith, Bill Gates, and other innovators described here were voracious readers with an interest in larger-than-life characters. These individuals escaped from the realities of an unhappy childhood by fantasizing about a happy and successful world. Jones's reading habits have matured and now include more adult indulgences such as Attila the Hun and the Marquis de Sade. His Jumbo Lair home in Lake Helen, Florida, has a library of 15,000 volumes (Bill Gates has 25,000 volumes in his new home in Washington).

As a child Jones had a passionate interest in flying, snakes, traveling, and girls. These interests evolved into an adult obsession with "younger women, faster planes, and larger crocodiles." Arthur was unhappy and precocious enough to begin searching for his niche in the world at a very early age. At the age of eight he first ran away from home in a search for truth, love, and adventure. This early rebellion was based on a search for companionship in a fantasy world of his dreams. It also confirms the temperament of the gifted, who typically rebel against what they feel is useless conformity. He continually ran away until he finally quit school in the ninth grade. He then took to the road and the rails to make his way in the world. (A fourteen-year-old on the rails during the middle of the Depression is not the normal training ground for the executive suite). Jones said. "I washed dishes, cooked, dug ditches, and cleaned cesspools." This was his formal education for survival in a dynamic world. At nineteen, he joined the Navy, learned to fly, and experienced the world in a more structured way (reminiscent of Lear, Turner, and Monaghan, who did the same at the same age).

Business and Personal Survival

Arthur Jones worked on his automated barbell theory throughout his life, even during his barnstorming, wingwalking, and African soirees. He built the first prototype in Tulsa in 1948 but had visions of greater conquests and relegated the exercise project to a lesser role in his life. Regardless of where he went, the problem of "automated exercise" continued to torment his psyche. He had a passionate interest in developing a better exercise tool for *himself.*

He had *no* interest in making money from the concept or in creating a new business opportunity.

Arthur continued building prototype models of his dream machine and finally settled on a "cam" design to make the machine optimally interact with the body. The "cam" looks much like the marine mollusk shell, thus the name Nautilus. This cam is the critical part in the Nautilus design, making it 92 percent efficient in working the muscles, in contrast to 6 percent for the classic barbell.

Jones had contemplated the "cam" design for years and had built numerous versions of it for use in his hundreds of prototypes. He awoke one night in Africa with the solution. This was during his "Wild Cargo" *National Geographic* filming days. The "Eureka" intuitive flash of insight hit him. He immediately started building the device in the middle of the night. His description of this episode is typical of most great creations. "I installed it and it did not work. It was a total absolute, abysmal failure. But it failed so obviously that for the first time I understood why. I knew how to modify and rebuild it immediately. . . . I stayed with it night and day and slowly solved the problems one after the other (Kalbacker, 1983).

The Nautilus machine would still never have been built had the Rhodesian government not confiscated his assets and run him out of the country. Arthur Jones was forty-five at the time (1968). The government seized $1.6 million worth of Jones's assets, including seven vehicles, two planes, a new helicopter, five million feet of film, and two complete video studios. They stole his livelihood and almost broke his spirit. Suddenly Jones found himself in Florida, unemployed, broke, and with no visible means of income.

Jones still had the designs for his new cam in his head. He borrowed $2,500 from his sister, sold a wildlife film, and rebuilt the prototype. An expired credit card helped him get the prototype to a Los Angeles weightlifting equipment show in 1970. Arthur still had no plans to market the unit or produce the machine in volume. He assumed some major manufacturer would see it, like the concept, and buy the manufacturing rights. He was wrong. In the age-old tradition of great innovators, he was trying to solve a problem and show the experts the "way." In the tradition of the experts, they were not interested in anything new or untried. However, many of the owners of health clubs were interested and gave him orders for his machine. This was unexpected. He was dumbfounded by their excitement for his new machine. Even though he was not prepared to build it, he took orders anyway, as it was a matter of survival. To finance the company, he asked for and received cash in advance for these first machines. They had never been beta-tested (put through a live statistical analysis of performance), built in volume, or proven to work in a commercial environment, but Jones was not concerned with such trivial matters.

It turned out that Jones's promotional skill and ingenuity in the Nautilus innovation exceeded his creative abilities. When deciding on a distribution strategy it occurred to him that the institutional—specifically the professional—sports market would accept a new concept for their fitness needs faster than more traditional markets. He was convinced that the traditional weightlifting aficionados and fitness experts would resist anything new. The experts had already told him the concept was not viable. He decided to avoid these traditionalists and to concentrate on educating a whole new generation on his system. He created a whole new market niche on the Nautilus way and became the leader in exercise equipment by destroying the old ways of exercise.

Millions in Free Testimonials

With this strategy in mind, Arthur delivered the first Nautilus products to the Kansas City Chiefs and the Boston Red Sox. Within a short period, twenty-two of the twenty-eight NFL football teams and all but one of the major league baseball teams purchased complete sets (twenty-four units) of the Nautilus equipment. This strategy had a two-sided advantage. It produced cash sales to high-profile customers who had an important need for speedy fitness. The spectacular physiological results created millions of dollars in free testimonials from professional athletes. One example was Fred Lynn's unsolicited testimonial on Nautilus's proficiency for muscle building. He gave Nautilus the credit for his 1978 batting title. Soon after, many additional testimonies surfaced from such notables as George Hamilton, Bo Derek, Victoria Principal, and Billie Jean King. The Nautilus products proliferated and soon dominated all institutional markets for exercise, including hospitals, high school and college gyms, racquetball clubs, tennis clubs, and corporate health centers. The unsolicited testimonials were worth millions in free promotion and brand recognition. Jones had managed to create this image by devising a unique form of distribution that created a whole new market niche. He had destroyed the old by creating the new.

Millions in Free Advertising

Arthur's distribution coup was even more responsible for the Nautilus success than the testimonials. This marketing stroke of genius was based on Arthur's total distrust of the legal community. He hated lawyers with a passion and thereby indelibly imprinted the name "Nautilus" on every exercise club and created a brand-name recognition that was second to none. He was able to identify the Nautilus name with optimum fitness by allowing the name

"Nautilus Center" or "Nautilus Club" to be used in every club without paying a franchise fee. This strategy made the Nautilus name synonymous with fitness.

To the casual observer it appears that Nautilus is a franchised system. Not so. Arthur so distrusted the legal profession that he refused to franchise the concept and actually gave away the use of the name "Nautilus" (and the Nautilus logo) to any club that agreed to purchase a complete set (twenty-four units) of his equipment. Hence, Nautilus centers sprang up everywhere. This strategy gave Jones instantaneous and universal brand-name recognition not normally possible for a fledgling private company. The promotional value was equivalent to a multimillion-dollar national advertising campaign. This strategy promoted the sale of Nautilus equipment, eliminated the need for large advertising expenditures, and made the Nautilus name as generic as Xerox and Kleenex. Nautilus became a ubiquitous commodity product and the catalyst for the fitness revolution.

A Fast-Food Unisexual Workout

Another factor in the Nautilus mystique and success was the speed and effectiveness of the product's benefits. Jones's innovation had created an instant workout that was compatible with the 1970s' fast-food generation of yuppies. Besides the speed of the workout, its intensity created superior results—far superior to the "explosive" workouts so popular with the gym freaks and the barbell crowd. Jones believes a workout of forty-five minutes each three days a week is preferable to longer workouts practiced by the gym freaks. He went even further by prescribing a twice-a-week workout for advanced trainees. The idea of a trim/fit body in a short time with minimal torture certainly fit the mentality of the fast-food generation. The Nautilus revolution allowed women to work out in carpeted, mirrored spas and not be intimidated by the muscle-bound crowd dropping weights on their toes in a sweaty gym.

By the mid-1980s, the Nautilus system included thirty-six machines, cost $40,000, and was found in 90 percent of the fitness centers in the United States. Ten thousand clubs had Nautilus equipment installed and many used the Nautilus logo as their own. Nautilus revenues reached $400 million by 1985, with more than 100,000 Nautilus units in use. Nautilus dominated the exercise equipment field, revolutionized exercise, and made it unisexual.

Personal Behavior Characteristics

One of Jones's five ex-wives gave some insight into his individualism and rebellious personality. She described Arthur as having a very lonely youth.

She said, "He wasn't raised, he just grew (*Time,* 1985). This insecure background helped mold Jones into the consummate iconoclast, eccentric, and rebel. He ignored all establishment rules, was intensely driven, and a nonconformist. He sacrificed personal wants, health, appearance, and money for the ego-gratifying goals demanded by an insecure youth.

Jones is a workaholic. He works eighteen-hour days. He says that he has slept only four hours per night for over thirty years. Nautilus employees say that he has to be reminded to have lunch. They describe 2 a.m. meetings, but ironically speak of him with reverence. They characterize him as an eccentric genius.

Arthur Jones seeks his own counsel on most matters, in the tradition of the introvert personality. He perceives the world in the macro way—he sees the forest not the trees—as his gut and intuitive skills are his forte. Arthur resolves problems and makes decisions through a rational thinking process. In other words he is insensitive to the personal feelings of others or himself while pursuing creativity or innovation. He is very structured and demands closure on virtually everything. Arthur Jones's personality can be summed up as an introverted-intuitive-thinking-judger type of personality, which is very consistent with the entrepreneurs and innovators of the world, according to Carl Jung.

One reporter characterized Jones as "a self-made man with a chip on his shoulder, but with considerable complexity and acute intelligence." This same reporter portrayed Jones as an "antisocial adolescent" and "one of the angriest men I had ever met." Another interviewer said that Jones had a "deliberate unconcern for anything but utility." Jones himself has described his antisocial and rebellious character: "By the time I was fourteen I associated exclusively with people in their late thirties and forties. I was, and still am, totally disinterested in my contemporaries" (Bilgore, 1980).

Another media person described Jones as a "human dynamo at sixty" and characterized him as a cross between a "cracker snake-oil salesman and a Midwestern evangelist." Jones himself has admitted that his political ideology is about 64,000 miles to the right of Attila the Hun. He says he does not socialize much, as he prefers the safe company of his animals. They are his refuge, as confirmed by this unbelievably irreverent statement to the press in 1983, "I've killed seventy-three men and six hundred elephants, and I felt worse about the elephants" (Roberts, 1985). This reporter characterized Jones as a "misanthropic sadist at best and an outright maniac at worst." Jones married five times; each wife was a teenager at the time of the marriage and under thirty by the time they divorced. It appears that Jones has some unconscious desire to satisfy his need for female love and companionship, as well as maintain a personal sense of youthfulness through continual conquests of young women. In any case, he has satiated his ego needs in a manner not normally seen outside of Hollywood. Jones obviously has some deep-seated, unconscious need to overcome a childhood deprived of intimacy, affection, and love by an absent mother figure.

Paranoia is exhibited in much of Arthur Jones's behavior. He carries a Colt .45 at all times because "most people believe in a benevolent Providence, I believe in a practical Hartford" (home of Colt Industries). He describes his management philosophy in the vernacular of Teddy Roosevelt, with an ironic twist: "Sneak around and carry a Thompson machine gun." This behavior is exemplified in the surveillance system at Jumbo Lair, which monitors all activities of his employees twenty-four hours a day. Ever suspicious of the species, Arthur's rebellion is made apparent by his oft-quoted label of mankind, "Homo lunaticus, Homo maniacus, and Homo berserkus."

Additional Innovation

Arthur Jones was an inveterate innovator and gambler who continued to create and innovate long after he needed to. He used the Nautilus success and monies to pursue some of his other childhood dreams. He reinvested most of the Nautilus profits in a $90 million video production facility at Jumbo Lair during the mid-1980s. In 1985 he told the media that it was the largest video production facility in the world. In his irreverent words, "It makes NBC's look like a shithouse." During this time he started his own TV production operation, Nautilus Television Network, to produce video documentaries and talk shows. He also began development of a Nautilus machine aimed at the mass home market, and another unit designed for back problems.

Rebellious Success

It takes a rebel to violate traditional dogmas and create true innovative breakthroughs. Arthur Jones is the personification of that personality type. We are told that we must be free to indulge our childhood fantasies if we are to be truly creative and innovative. Arthur Jones has always indulged in satiating his childhood fantasies. An example of this defiant and rebellious behavior is his adult toys. He personally owns and flies two Boeing 707 jets and a Cessna Citation. His six-hundred-acre ranch in Florida, Jumbo Lair, is a menagerie of wild animals, including ninety elephants, three rhinos, a gorilla, three hundred alligators, four hundred crocodiles, and numerous rattlesnakes, turtles, tarantulas, and scorpions. This is the setting for Nautilus's headquarters and business offices. It's not the typical corporate headquarters where one would invite the local banking community for tea.

Arthur Jones is not typical and not necessarily the model for anyone's idealized lifestyle or personality type. He has demonstrated an ability to innovate and create beyond the norm in society. Much of this creativity has been attributed to a rebellious attitude that allowed him to change the way the world exercises. This ability to ignore the experts and use the principle of "creative destruction" is the one part of Arthur Jones's behavior that is worth mimicking. It is this rebellious behavior that has made Arthur Jones a consummate innovative genius.

Arthur Jones
born 1923, Arkansas
raised in Tulsa, Oklahoma

Dominant Personality Characteristic: Rebellious
Motto: "Younger women, faster planes, and larger crocodiles"
Nickname: "Wild Man of Lake Helen," "Madcap Muscle Magnate"
Firm Name: Nautilus Sports Medical Industries
Location: St. Helen, Florida
First Innovation/Date: National Geographic syndicated series, "Wild Cargo," the first filming of live crocodile capture, 1960s
Products: Nautilus exercise machines, "the automated or rational barbell"
Initial Investment: $2,500 loan from his sister in 1968
Second Innovation/Date: First Nautilus prototype in Los Angeles, California, 1970

Sibling Status: First son. Two brothers and a sister
Personality Profile: Introverted Intuitive Thinking Judger (INTJ)
Parents' Occupation: Mother and father both doctors, as were grandfather, uncle, two brothers, and daughter
Childhood Data: Mother started medical school right after his birth. Arthur raised by German family. Ran away at 8 and 13
Family Socio-Economic Status: Upper middle class. No peers as friends, only adults
Formal Education: Ninth grade. Pilot at 18. Voracious reader
Age, First Business Venture: 25, began importing animals
Age, Big Hit: 47
Hobbies/Activities: Flying, big game hunting, working out, swimming

---

Marital Status: Five marriages to teenagers. Divorced all in their twenties
Children: Two sons, Gary and Edgar; one daughter, Eva
Religion: Vacillates between atheistic and agnostic
Public Offering Date: Privately held by Jones, sold in late 1990
Revenues or Units of Big Hit: 100,000 units in 1985. Product found in 9 of 10 of America's 10,000 fitness centers
Revenues of Firm: Over $400 million annually during the mid-1980s
Estimated Net Worth: $300 million, *Forbes* 1989 richest list
Age Became Millionaire: 49 (1972)
Heroes: Marquis de Sade, Voltaire, Mark Twain, Attila the Hun
Honors: None he would accept. Personal interviews by *Time, Playboy, Money, Wall Street Journal,* "Good Morning America," *People, Forbes,* etc.

18

Ted Turner—Risk-taking

All risk is a function of dealing with uncertainty. Those people who feel comfortable with uncertainty are usually self-confident individuals who have been blessed with high self-esteem. They feel safe in foreign environments. Children who were raised by overprotective parents do not enjoy risky activities. They fear the unknown. Similarly, employees who have never been allowed to fail will not be effective in the highly risky field of innovation and entrepreneurship.

College textbooks define entrepreneurship as synonymous with risk-taking. This is confirmed by recent research, which also depicts risk-takers as eminently successful individuals: "They are the most successful people. They tend to be effective on the job, leaders in their field, and highest in management ranks. They also attain higher income and profit levels while experiencing the least stress" (Peele 1982). This should not come as a surprise, since nothing is ever accomplished in life or business without a serious departure from consensual thinking. A backyard walk is not very stimulating, although it is safe. Skydiving and mountain climbing are far more exciting but the risk quotient is significantly greater.

Ted Turner epitomizes the consummate risk-taker in business. In 1970 he risked his billboard advertising business to acquire a failing UHF TV station, WTBS. He then risked the station to acquire the Atlanta Braves and the Atlanta Hawks. Next he risked the total $100 million organization to create CNN. Then he risked everything in an attempt to acquire CBS and nearly lost it all in his successful acquisition of MGM. These were significant risks to most of his employees, the media, and his family. To Ted they were not inordinate risks, as he believed that doing nothing was the greater risk. In his words, "You have to take chances and leverage yourself because you don't have fifty or a hundred years to build up a capital base like Time or CBS." A family friend, Irwin Mayo, gave this characterization of Turner: "Ted will *always throw the dice bigger, bigger, bigger. Even as a youngster he often pushed himself beyond prudent limits."*

Helen Keller said, "Life is either a daily adventure or nothing." Thrill-seeking psychological researcher Frank Farley found that "Big T thrill-seekers high in testosterone are risk-takers and adventurers who seek excitement and stimulation wherever they can find or create it." Innovators always opt for the "leap before you look" mentality. They see risks as rational and calculated opportunities while others see them as highly speculative and dangerous undertakings. Risk, therefore, is a function of the individual's perspective. Research has shown the adventurer who climbs the Matterhorn faces far less anxiety than the average pedestrian in Manhattan. The climber rationalizes and analyzes all potential risks and potentials for disaster and has devised a carefully planned course of action. The Manhattan pedestrian has no such plan and is dependent on the vagaries of the environment—taxi drivers, buses, muggers, and wayward bicycles. The innate skills of ill-trained pedestrians are not sufficient to ensure their safety, as are the skills of the mountain climber, who has a plan for every potential risk.

Entrepreneurs and innovators are positively inclined to embark on what the risk-averse would call "risky" opportunities. A 1984 study by Psychological Motivations demonstrated that successful entrepreneurs "tend to be excitement junkies. They have gambler's blood. . . . A fear of failure does not paralyze entrepreneurs as it does other types of people." Ted Turner has a gambler mentality, as did Bill Lear, Bill Gates, and most of the other personalities in this book. Turner lives on the edge. When asked why, he responded, "The best advice is never to do anything. You'll never get in trouble if you never do anything. But you'll never get anywhere, either. 'Faint heart ne'er won fair lady' " (Whittemore, 1990).

> The investor who never acts until statistics affirm his choice, the athlete or politician who fails to make his move until too late, the businessman who waits until the market is proven—all are doomed to mediocrity by their trust in a spurious rationality and their failures of faith.
> —George Gilder, *Wealth and Poverty*

"Lead, follow, or get out of the way." This has been Ted Turner's credo in both his personal and business life. It was also the title for his biography, written by Christian Williams in 1981. Williams's insights into the Turner psyche came as a crew member on the *Tenacious* during the tragic Fastnet Race won by Turner in 1979. Turner violated common sense and jeopardized the lives of himself and his crew by maintaining full sail into the heart of gale winds. Two-thirds of the boats were lost. He refused to succumb to the elements and headed full bore toward the finish line despite the life-threatening winds, which killed fifteen. However, to Ted Turner, the greater risk was in being tentative and not aggressively pursuing the corrrect goal.

Turner changed the face of television through his motto of "Lead, follow, or get out of the way." This was never more apparent than his ultimatum to cable operators who were vacillating about joining him in the dark days prior to the CNN launch. Turner ended up proceeding without the cable operators because his impatience and impetuousness could not tolerate their indecisiveness. They considered CNN a huge risk. Turner considered it just one more chess move calculated to dominate the broadcast media. Time has proven Ted's risky style correct. In only fifteen years Ted has become a media mogul, motivating *Time* to name him "Man of the Year" for 1991.

Should Ted Turner have been the father of the first satellite cable TV station broadcasts, or of the first twenty-four-hour cable news network? No way! He was a small operator with relatively few resources in this huge-stakes game and had absolutely no operating experience in the broadcast news industry. However, Turner didn't know that he couldn't do it, so he did it. He didn't know enough to be scared and wasn't about to bow to the dire predictions by the experts. He changed an insolvent UHF station in Atlanta into the Superstation, the "Chicken Noodle Network" (CNN) into the fourth most respected brand name in the United States, and a defunct MGM library of tapes into a mid-week viewing sensation for his Turner Network Television cable station.

The irony of Turner's spectacular success in TV is that he admits to having hated television—he had not watched a hundred hours of it prior to the launch of the Superstation. The major networks—ABC, CBS, and NBC—in those days had annual operating budgets of $100 million to $150 million for producing one thirty-minute news broadcast six days a week. Turner's total net worth was $100 million at the time, including the Atlanta Braves, Atlanta Hawks, a Charlotte TV station, an Atlanta radio station, and the Superstation. At the time of the CNN launch the networks were one hundred times his size. Within ten years they were only twice his size. He predicts that he will pass them by the turn of the century.

Turner was convinced he could *not* compete with the networks in the long run due to his immense resource disadvantage. This factor became the motivating force behind his acquisition mania during the early days. He was attempting to acquire unique programming material and air time to compete with the top dogs. His employees, the industry leaders, and his advisors all said he was crazy. They didn't believe he could compete at all. Hank Whittemore wrote of the CNN launch in *CNN—The Inside Story*, "To many of his employees the move was sheer madness, the act of a crazy man." His closest associates implored him to forget it. Terry McGuirk, one of his vice presidents, relates a moment of personal introspection by Turner just prior to the CNN launch, "Am I crazy? Why am I doing this? To make a go of it I'll have to commit $100 million! Have I totally lost my mind?"

Turner didn't bother to heed his own advice and charged ahead in the inimitable style of the consummate entrepreneurial visionary on a passionate mission. He created one of the great innovations in the broadcast industry, which had not been overly innovative since the advent of television. He succeeded, to the shock and dismay of the industry experts. They had repeatedly predicted his demise, which hurt his ability to hire people or attract large advertising dollars during the early days of CNN. J. Christopher Burns of the *Washington Post* was one of his major critics. He predicted CNN's early collapse because he believed news was the exclusive province of the networks:

> The reason that Ted Turner decided to go ahead with it in the form he's doing may be that he doesn't understand the problem. He's not paying attention. The cable industry doubts that Ted Turner knows his ass from a hole in the ground about news. (Whittemore, 1990)

Ted was so incensed by Burns's article that he decided to send Burns a dead crow and a fork as a present after the June 1, 1980, launch. However, his confidants persuaded Ted to relish his victory passively, which was not easy for the combative Turner.

The launching of the SATCOM I satellite by RCA in 1975 was the technological breakthrough that precipitated most of Turner's moves for the next fifteen years. Ted had the vision to see the vast opportunity in broadcasting TV programming via this new transmission medium. These opportunities were lost on even the most seasoned television executives, or they were too risk-averse to jump into the fray of innovation. Ted's vision of dominating regional programming was at the root of his purchases of the baseball and basketball teams, and later the MGM film library. Turner was looking far ahead in his innovative-visionary style while the experts were mired in the past and present. He was envisioning a greater future while they were protecting the safer present.

Turner's first innovation, the creation of the Superstation, was designed to reach the rural markets for programming, which were often ignored by the networks. This strategy started a volatile and controversial career in the broadcast industry. The broadcast establishment considered Turner a dangerous character to be watched, since he was violating sacred icons of their industry. He then infuriated the leaders in the other industries affected by the Superstation's broadcasts. Hollywood viewed him as a Robin Hood for stealing its movie customers and giving cable TV viewers "free" movies. The networks called him a traitor since he ignored the standard television licensing jurisdictions. He was invading their sacrosanct markets. The baseball and basketball franchisees felt he was intruding into their exclusive markets by telecasting the Braves into their cities. However, Ted was making a lot of consumer friends by providing a new, inexpensive entertainment product. His "creative destruction" was working to the betterment of society, even though Ted was creating legions of disgruntled enemies in the broadcast and entertainment industries.

Personal History

Ted Turner was born in Cincinnati, Ohio, on November 19, 1938. At age six he was left in a Cincinnati boarding school when his family left on a wartime assignment. According to his biographical account, this experience left him feeling rejected and insecure. His reflection indicates how indelibly it has been affixed on his psyche. Ted recently told David Frost of physical beatings by his father during his early years. One of these ended with Ted beating his father instead. Ted says this caused him to break down and cry. A love/ hate relationship grew between father and son, which became a major factor in the development of Ted's personality and drive.

The family moved to Savannah, Georgia, when Ted was nine. He spent most of his youth in two different military academies learning to survive in hostile environments where he was not accepted by the other children. Ironically, the students in these southern schools called the future "Mouth of the South" a Yankee and refused to accept him into their groups. His high school years were spent in McCallie, a Chattanooga military academy. He won the Tennessee debating championship at the school but was never happy. Judy Nye, Ted's first wife, said, "He hated it there."

Ted was never good in team sports or any physical activity dependent on eye/hand coordination. He rebelled against social interaction and became a voracious reader. He started reading the Greek classics at an early age; his heroes were Alexander the Great, Gen. George Patton, and Attila the Hun. Turner's and Fred Smith's early lives have remarkable parallels in private schooling, geographic setting, heroes, and education. Alexander became Turner's fantasy mentor of sorts. Alexander's death after winning a drinking contest with his men (six quarts of wine) left a memorable impression on young Ted. Turner emulated Alexander at Brown when he won a bet by downing a bottle of Chivas scotch in ten minutes. Alexander died from his victorious conquest. Turner lived to compete again.

Turner's father loved his son but believed insecurity would be a positive influence on Ted's development. According to Judy Nye, "He wanted Ted to be insecure, because he felt that insecurity builds greatness. If Ted was insecure, then he would be forced to compete" (Williams, 1981). It appears to have worked, as Ted told David Frost in October 1991, "You won't hardly ever find a super-achiever anywhere who isn't . . . motivated at least partially by a sense of insecurity."

Ted became a notorious, risk-taking sailboat racer as a youth. He earned the nicknames "Turnover Ted" and the "Capsize Kid" for constantly flipping his sailboat. His mother tells the story of his helicopter rescue when he was shipwrecked on an island. Ted's love of sailing made Annapolis his first choice for college. His father wanted him to attend an Ivy League school, so Ted decided on Harvard. Rejected by Harvard, he attended Brown and became the consummate playboy to avenge his previous rejections.

Ted's reading of the classics as a young boy prompted him to pursue a major in humanities at Brown. He switched to economics after his father wrote him a vile diatribe saying "you are rapidly becoming a jackass," and "you are in the hands of the Philistines" (Williams, 1981). Turner and classmate Peter Dames were lechers of the first order at Brown. Turner's only distraction from the pursuit of females was his election to captain of the sailing team. Otherwise he spent his collegiate days as a devoted party animal. He was suspended from school after a rowdy scene at a local women's college as a sophomore and enlisted in the Coast Guard during the six-month suspension. He re-enrolled at Brown but was thrown out for good after being caught with a woman in his room during his senior year.

Ted always had an irreverent approach towards authority and defied conformity and tradition. He was mischievous since childhood. This trait led to his expulsion from the Kappa Sigma fraternity. Steven Lieberman, a fraternity buddy, said, "He was just a crazy kid."

Business and Personal Survival—"Captain Courageous"

Ted Turner has proven that he is the consummate innovative visionary with few qualms about breaking the looking glass of tradition. He created two breakthrough innovations —the Superstation and CNN—with no moral support from his family, employees, media, or industry leaders. His most brilliant business success, however, is far less known but probably ranks as his greatest single business achievement. It was his first opportunity to assert himself in the business world and occurred as a result of the tragic death of his father in 1963.

Ted was twenty-four and working as a salesman for the family billboard business when his father committed suicide. His father willed the family business to Ted but in a twist of sadistic irony announced that he had sold the business to a competitor. Ted was distraught and desperately attempted to have the sale rescinded. The billboard business was Ted's only tie with his father and his only viable means of livelihood. The buyer, a large conglomerate, and competitor of Turner Billboards, adamantly refused to cancel the sale. Ted was dogged in his attempt to have the sale cancelled. He flew to Palm Springs to chase the vacationing chairman, to coerce him into canceling the sale. The chairman dismissed Ted as an inexperienced kid trying to get a few more bucks from the deal to go sailing. Ted was not considered a serious threat because of his naiveté in big business and his reputation as a wild playboy. This was destined to be an analysis of Ted Turner that was to be often repeated over the next twenty years, to the regret of those making it.

Ted was certainly a neophyte at the game of corporate business at the time. He was not steeped in corporate politics or finesse. He relied on his gut instincts and intuition, which impelled him to play the game of business as he would sail a race or engage in war. His competitive spirit took charge as he set out to employ the tactics he had read about as a kid and passionately believed. "Business is war" became his rallying cry and philosophy.

Ted implemented a bizarre corporate maneuver that would have done the CIA proud. Within twenty-four hours of his last rejection by the chairman, Ted secretly hired all of the employees of the leasing department of his father's company. As their boss, he instructed them to convert all of the billboard leases (the lifeblood of that business) to his new firm. He then gave the new owners an ultimatum. They had two weeks to cancel the sale of the business before he would *burn* all of their leases.

The Minneapolis-based firm decided that it was time to play hardball, as they were losing their patience with this precocious kid. Knowing that Ted had no money, they assembled a team of experienced lawyers and presented him a *fait accompli* in a counterproposal. They offered Ted $200,000 in a "take-it-or-leave-it" proposal. The agreement was for Ted to take the money and go sailing or to respond with a like offer to them for $200,000 and they would go away. Otherwise, the Minneapolis firm intended to enforce the contract to the full extent of the law. They then decided to give Ted a lesson in his own impetuousness by offering him thirty seconds to accept or refuse their offer.

The big guys made the same mistake that numerous others would make over the next twenty years. They assumed, wrongly, that he had only one option—to take the $200,000 and go sailing. Ted shocked them by doing the unexpected. He played offense when he seemed to be in a totally defensive position—a classic gutsy military maneuver. He told them, "I don't need your thirty seconds. I will pay your $200,000, now get out of my office." In shock and frustration these seasoned veterans of the corporate wars capitulated and accepted his offer. Afterwards he asked his financial advisor, "Where are we going to get the $200,000?" It turned out he was able to offer the company stock instead of cash. They were afraid of the capital gains on the transaction and their greed worked to Ted's advantage, as he ended up never having to pay off the debt.

This was Ted Turner's finest hour, and it was probably one of those character-building experiences that created an inviolable self-confidence in him, allowing him to make one colossal deal after another through sheer bravado. This experience gave him the confidence to make business deals over the next twenty years that other executives would not have attempted. He moved mountains due to an awesome self-confidence using positive, aggressive, and offensive tactics even when they were not expected. An omnipotent belief system was formed with this early success against a corporate giant. This win gave him an unshakable belief in himself and the courage of his own convictions. He would need the machismo developed and all the moxie, innuendos, and risk-taking maneuvers for his future fights with RCA, NBC, CBS, Time, Westinghouse, the Federal Communications Commission, cable operators, and the establishment, who all fought him on his march to success.

Victory for Captain Outrageous

Ted finally won a landmark lawsuit on March 3, 1980, that allowed CNN to link up with the SATCOM I satellite. The sheer bravado of this fight and win should be material for a Hollywood movie, as Turner was required to threaten, cajole, plead, and resort to the legal process to get launched. An eleventh-hour lawsuit against the FCC was the only way he could get on the air and if he had been unsuccessful Turner would have been bankrupt. He was finally granted a place on the satellite in the spring and aired his first CNN news broadcast on June 1, 1980. This signaled the beginning of the emergence of Ted Turner as a brilliant visionary in the broadcast industry and a party to be reckonded with.

Turner was asked how he was capable of creating CNN when virtually everyone in and out of the industry predicted his demise. He gave credit to his intuitive skills and a macro vision that was market driven. He accomplished the miracle with *no* market plan or documented evidence that he could succeed. When asked about his lack of market planning, Ted responded:

> There's never a reason for a study if your idea is conceptually sound. You have to have confidence in your own ideas. I never did a market study on Cable News Network, which is going to cost me every penny I've got. . . . I do my own marketing analysis. (Williams, 1981)

Ted Turner has proven to be a charismatic leader of gargantuan proportions. His power of persuasion and magnetism are legend in much the same way and degree as that of Fred Smith of Federal Express. George Babick of CNN's New York office said of Turner:

> If Ted predicted the sun will come up in the west tomorrow morning, you'd laugh and say he's full of it. But you'd still set the alarm. You wouldn't want to miss the miracle. (Whittemore, 1990)

Ted has always been an enigma to his friends, personnel, and ex-wife Janie. He preached one philosophy and would operate in another. He would say, "If you can't do something first class, don't do it at all." One would tend to believe him since he spent millions on sailing escapades and in various business ventures. His personal behavior was often diametrically opposite. He was unbelievably frugal, according to his wife and associates. He flew tourist everywhere and cut his own hair when his net worth was a $100 million. He personally cut his children's hair for many years, even after he had become super wealthy. His wife depicted him walking behind people and turning out the lights to save money and then moments later spending millions of dollars on a business whim.

Personal Behavior Characteristics

Turner's rebellious approach to sailing and business was unique. His iconclastic behavior began as a child, when he earned the reputation as "Terrible Ted." This image of nonconformity created an unconscious identity that he seemed driven to fulfill. He was a renegade teenager known as "Turnover Ted," an eccentric young adult—"Mouth of the South," a world-class sailboat racer— "Captain Courageous," and a nonconforming businessman—"Captain Outrageous." His maverick behavior culminated in 1977 when he fell off a chair in a drunken stupor while awaiting the presentation of the America's Cup trophy. This earned him the wrath of the sailing elite and the "straight-laced crowd." His rebellious behavior followed him to the business world and proved to be responsible for much of his success and for much of his misery.

Ted Turner is on the cusp of extroversion and introversion. He is energized by the external world of opportunities but also delights in the introspective world of reading. He is at one time sociable and at others very territorial— these are the two barometers of extroversion and introversion. He is infamous for partying and loquaciousness, both of which have caused him trouble with the media. His leadership style is visionary and intuitive, which causes him to perceive the world based on what "might be." He relies on his own hunches, insights, and intuition to drive him, which makes him an action-innovator type personality. He has a classic Promethean temperament symbolic of the innovator who seeks truth and knowledge and has a pioneering spirit. His motivation, drives, and energies are satiated by competing on a grand global scale and outsmarting the traditionalists who have predicted his demise. In his words, "I just love it when people say I can't do something. There's nothing that makes me feel better, because all my life people have said I wasn't going to make it" (Whittemore, 1990).

Christian Williams characterized Turner as relying on intuition in all major sailing and business decision-making. He would listen to his own counsel and he always makes thinking or rational rather than feeling type decisions. These decisions are made with an impetuousness that is unique. At CNN he never bothered to read contracts, even those calling for investing millions, much like Bill Lear. This judgmental or "closure" approach to business was evident in his personal and sports lives as well.

Procrastination was never tolerated because he wanted to get on with the program and was not comfortable with open-ended decision-makers. An example was his impatience with people who carried suitcases. He once told a friend traveling with him, "If you ever want to travel with me again, you leave that suitcase home." He felt the wait in the airport was a terrible waste of valuable time. This trait is what stress psychologists refer to as "rushing sickness." It is common among successful entrepreneurs and innovators.

Dan Schorr of CNN said of Turner, "He was a bundle of energy. He never stopped moving, almost with an animal quality, like a tiger, never not in motion" (Whittemore, 1990). Ted was also described as having the attention span of a gnat. CNN personnel have said, "Holding a conversation with him is like trying to talk to a radio." Whittemore, in *CNN—The Inside Story,* makes one poignant observation about Ted's unique psyche:

> It may be that the driving force behind Turner's inexhaustible need to accomplish more and more was an extreme form of insecurity and vulnerability. (Whittemore, 1990)

This insecurity, carefully bred in him by his father, apparently is what drove Turner to living on the edge in every facet of his life. Gerry Hogan, a CNN executive, said of his first meeting Ted that he had "unbelievable energy, like a hyperactive kid on Christmas Eve." This rushing-sickness mentality is the same as that of Type A overachievers and has been a key element of the Turner mystique. Ted also exudes a vital force of energy that envelops his personality. This vital force is the same aura or charismatic energy found in most of Turner's heroes—Alexander the Great, Napoleon, Gandhi, and Attila the Hun.

Ted has the enthusiasm of the consummate salesman. He is also extremely persevering, as attested to by this quote: "I never quit. I've got a bunch of flags on my boat, but there ain't no white flags. I don't surrender. That's the story of my life" (Whittemore, 1990). He is aggressive and combative. He believes "business is war" and uses the strategies and tactics of the great warriors in his business and personal relationships.

Turner's positive attitude would make Norman Vincent Peale proud. He takes negative comments by his dissenters and turns them into positive ones. This positive attitude proved to be contagious to his followers and employees. He was easy to follow because he knew where he was going. The ever-loquacious Turner said, " 'If we fail,' does not exist in my vocabulary." And, "Every time I tried to go as far as I could. When I climbed the hills, I saw the mountains. Then I started climbing the mountains." To sum up his demeanor and personality, Alvin Toffler, in personally autographing his book, *The Third Wave,* for Turner, said, "Ted Turner, I wanted to meet you. You *are* the Third Wave!" That is a real compliment from the expert on "societal change" in our era.

Risk-taking Proclivity

Ted Turner told Jane Fonda on meeting her, "I feel like I'm constantly at war, always fighting to survive, risking everything, putting all the cards on the table." Ever since his father's untimely suicide, Ted was on a nonstop emotional roller-coaster ride to win at all costs. Ted rescued his father's failing billboard business in 1963. Faced with a debt-ridden company Ted was required to sell off his father's plantation and risk his total inheritance in order to save the company. He faced constant crises but eventually turned the business around and then leveraged it to buy a radio station and the defunct UHF station WTCG. His board of directors fought him over these purchases and his father's longtime accountant resigned because he believed Ted was crazy and headed for disaster. Ted persevered and turned the virtually bankrupt TV station around, making it the cornerstone of his emerging empire.

Ted had the vision for a massive broadcasting empire long before he started implementing his plan to acquire satellite rights. He said, "I came up with the concept for Cable News Network even before the Superstation was up on satellite, because business is like a chess game and you have to look several moves ahead. Most people don't" (Whittemore, 1990). Those in the media and the industry viewed his moves as extremely risky. He did not, as he had a master plan in his mind calculated to achieve a long-term goal to dominate TV broadcasting.

Ted knew nothing about baseball but bought the Atlanta Braves baseball team in 1976 because he feared the team would be moved out of town. This was a part of his master plan. He couldn't afford the team but bought it with long-term debt and by leveraging the purchase with the team's own cash.

He had a motivated seller who wanted to unload a losing team, enabling Ted to buy the team with no cash. That has been his operating style ever since. The purchase of the ball team was not the realization of a childhood dream, as with Ray Kroc or Tom Monaghan. It was part of his macro-vision of dominating broadcast airtime with a popular event that had wide geographic appeal. The Braves had more dates to be broadcast than either football or basketball and therefore the team fit his macro-vision. The purchase worked so well he bought the Atlanta Hawks basketball team the same year and then the local soccer and hockey teams. His dream nearly paid off when the Braves finally made it to the World Series in 1991 and 1992, only to lose to the Minnesota Twins and then again to the Toronto Blue Jays. Ted and Jane were there cheering on their Braves.

A "Death Wish"/"Bet the Farm" Mentality

Turner has had a lifelong struggle against what he refers to as his "greatest fear"—the fear of death. *Time* quoted him, "If you can get yourself where you're not afraid of dying, then you can . . . move forward a lot faster." Turner was convinced that he would be murdered or otherwise meet an untimely death, which drove him to conquests at a pace alarming to his employees and considered idiotic to his friends and family. He came to terms with his obsessions in the 1980s and began using the drug lithium to overcome his manic-depressive states. This has helped in his constant battles with the "death obsession." Turner still lives on the edge as a consummate risk-taking entrepreneur but the lithium has mellowed him to the point of being more rational to those around him. He continues to maintain that the greater risk is doing nothing. This was the philosophy that drove him to perpetual flirtations with disaster during the mid-seventies and again in the mid-eighties.

Ted Turner's risk-taking proclivity reached its peak in one crazy period during 1976–77. The flamboyant Turner created the Superstation to broadcast the first TV station signals by satellite. He then purchased two professional ball teams and found time to win the America's Cup race all in one year. He was to outdo this flirtation with disaster ten years later with an even more dramatic demonstration of his risk-taking mentality. This fifteen-month period dwarfs any other entrepreneurial precocity seen in corporate America. His acquisition mania during 1986–87 included the $1.4 billion purchase of MGM, an unsuccessful $5.4 billion bid for CBS, $64 million paid for the Omni shopping mall/hotel complex in Atlanta, $500,000 donated to the Better World Society, a $26 million loss on the Goodwill Games, and a divorce settlement with his wife Janie of $40 million. Just the thought of this kind of risk-taking and acquisition mania would be frightening to the most daring of Wall Street tycoons and not even considered by most business executives.

Turner ignored all of the experts who said he was destined for calamity. The CNN risk was his greatest—a $100 million gamble according to his own estimate—and in accordance with the fundamental laws of risk and reward it proved to be his greatest win. He risked everything on his belief in a twenty-four-hour news concept and by 1990 had earned the richly deserved title, "the Godfather of Cable." Turner had dreamed of a twenty-four-hour news channel and was willing to bet the farm on his belief. Even his employees in mid-1978 had put a poster on his desk describing the confidence the world had in his innovative concept:

PLEASE, TED!
DON'T DO THIS TO US!
IF YOU COMMIT TO A VENTURE OF THIS SIZE
YOU'LL SINK THE WHOLE COMPANY!

Their logic was sound because the numbers could never have justified his decision to create a twenty-four-hour-a-day news network. He did not have the necessary capital to sustain such a venture. And the revenue projections based on collecting fifteen cents per cable customer per month would pay only 60 percent of CNN's monthly operating costs. Furthermore, these projections were contingent on attracting eight million cable subscribers. The Superstation had the only reliable data on cable customers at the time—a forty-five-state penetration that had attracted only two million subscribers—and it was supplying a proven product. Based on the Superstation data CNN would lose well over a million dollars per month.

Ted Turner had invested $35 million of his personal fortune by spring 1980 and was very close to bankruptcy when he sold his Charlotte station just prior to the CNN launch. In addition to the cash invested and debt, he had cashed in $7 million of his personal krugerands to cover the payroll in those dark days of 1980, just before the birth of CNN. He survived the launch date only to see CNN lose $2 million a month during its first year. Turner's financial obituary was written again and again during 1980 and 1981.

As soon as CNN became financially solvent Ted started making high-risk moves to assure his programming would remain competitive for all of his cable stations. In March 1986 he acquired MGM for $1.4 billion to gain access to its film library of 3,300 classics. He was called crazy once again, only more vociferously, but the experts were almost right this time. Turner came precariously close to bankruptcy due to the exorbitant debt created by his acquisition. He scrambled like never before and was bailed out by a $568 million infusion of cash by a consortium of cable operators. This cost him control of the Turner Broadcasting System (TBS). His 83 percent ownership was reduced to 43 percent.

Ted has since been vindicated in the MGM acquisition. Most industry experts who thought he had lost his mind have since labeled the move a mark of intuitive genius. They usually qualify their comments with the fact that he paid too much. Paul Marsh, a Bateman Eichler analyst, gave Ted his due with the following quote: "Now with the escalation in movie library prices, he [Turner] looks like a genius" (Cauchon, *USA Today,* March 19, 1990).

Ted Turner has had a romance with disaster his whole business career. His "living on the edge" reputation was always well earned in both his business and private lives. After the America's Cup win in 1977 he expounded on the tactics required for competing in sailing or business. His recommended tactics were "lightning strikes, sneak attacks, hit them before they know what's happening. . . . That's the only way a little guy can beat a big guy" (Williams, 1981).

Turner followed his own advice during the 1979 Fastnet race in Ireland, when he refused to reduce speed or lower sails during a gale that killed fifteen. Over 70 percent of the yachts never finished the race and twenty-five were lost in the disaster. Turner was intransigent in his focus on winning and ignored the life-threatening elements despite the risks. The *Tenacious* won the race, a tribute to Turner's skill, intuition, tenacity, competitiveness, fearlessness, and proclivity for risk-taking.

Risky Success

William James, considered the greatest American psychologist-educator, gave an elegant testimonial to the importance of risk-taking in life and business:

> It is only by risking our persons from one hour to another that we live at all. And often enough our faith beforehand in an uncertified result is the only thing that makes the result come true.

A 1989 quote from an article in the *Economist* sums up Turner's risk-taking career: "He has recovered so often from seemingly suicidal financial escapades that many Atlanta businessmen are by now convinced he is indestructible." The irony is that Ted Turner has now acquired a social consciousness that preaches the preservation of the planet and species and decries the use of risky behavior. He feels the planet is dying a not-so-slow death and wants everyone to help correct the direction of the decline.

Turner's business success was based on a risk-taking mentality that was lost on everyone from the establishment. The Monday morning quarterbacks now acknowledge Ted Turner's brilliance. His CNN operation began to make inroads into the networks' stranglehold on broadcast news during the 1980s and reached its peak during the Desert Storm war. When Pope Paul II was shot in Rome in 1981 CNN was the first to report it. In 1982 *Time*—a potential competitor—put Turner on its cover and dubbed CNN one of the "Big Four":

> By any measure, CNN is in the big leagues of news . . . Until recently the offices of news executives at the Big Three networks each contained three monitors tuned to ABC, NBC, and CBS. Now in many others there is a fourth, tuned to CNN. (Whittemore, 1990)

Newsweek then gave Turner his due by saying, "In an age of play-it-safe corporate bureaucracy, bold spirits like Ted Turner have become precious commodities." *Time* magazine, a long-time competitor and recently an investor in Turner's enterprises, gave Turner the ultimate tribute by naming him "Man of the Year" and placing him on its January 6, 1992, cover and calling him "the Prince of the Global Village."

CNN reached its peak in visibility and stature when in early 1991 during the Desert Storm war both President Bush and Saddam Hussein watched CNN exclusively. CNN by 1991 had extended its broadcast signal to eighty-five countries besides supplying programming to the rural markets of the West and Third World nations. Turner's dream of communicating to the whole world has come close to fruition with the spectacular success of CNN after just ten years of operation.

With WTBS, Headline News, CNN, and TNT, Turner's stations accounted for over 30 percent of all cable viewing in the United States in 1991. CNN had become the number two cable channel behind ESPN and was considered Turner's most important network. As of 1991 it had sixty million subscribers and was more influential in the creation of Marshall McCluhan's prediction of a "global village" than any other single societal factor. Turner Broadcasting had reached $1.8 billion in revenues and the networks were suddenly less than twice the size of TBS. Just ten years earlier they had a hundred times the edge in size. Turner told David Frost in October 1991 that TBS would bypass the networks by the year 2000.

As a final tribute from the industry that fought him for so long, Ted Turner was given the prestigious Paul White Award in 1988 as "Broadcaster of the Year." He was the first entrepreneur to have ever received it. Turner's successes have not dissuaded him from risk-taking. Always the inveterate gambler, Ted sponsored the Seattle Goodwill Games in 1990 and sustained an estimated $26 million in losses. In October 1991 he purchased Hanna Barbera for $320 million to enhance his programming library. He is no longer able to make acquisitions unilaterally. He is now a minority stockholder of TBS and has to ask for permission to spend over $2 million.

Ted Turner has been the consummate innovative visionary and entrepreneur. Harry Reasoner said of Turner after an interview, "I like Ted Turner. I'd hate to have to keep up with him, and I'd hate to be that driven myself." In his new book *Power Shift* (1990), Alvin Toffler describes CNN as "perhaps the most influential broadcast news source in the United States." He also says:

> Turner is by far the most visionary of a dozen or so hard-driving media barons who are revolutionizing the media—and whose efforts over the long term will shift power in many countries.

Ted Turner's reputation as a risk-taking entrepreneur has been exceeded only by his high libidinal drive and loquacious verbosity. He has reaped the spoils of entrepreneurship with a $1.9 billion net worth, according to the 1992 *Forbes* list of richest Americans, where he is rated as the seventeenth richest man in America. He has been married twice and has five children, a number of whom work for TBS. He married Jane Fonda, another free spirit, on December 7, 1991, her fifty-fourth birthday, at his Florida plantation. She gave up making movies for Ted, as, in her words, "Ted is not a man that you leave to go on location. He needs you there all the time." They have become residents of Atlanta, Georgia, and are constant global companions. Whatever is said of Ted Turner, he had the vision for societal change and the risk-taking mentality to implement his dreams. The world is smaller and better informed because of Ted Turner, and he has brought the "global village" closer to a reality. His risk-taking propensity has broken many barriers within the establishment and the world is better for it.

**Robert E. (Ted) Turner
born November 19, 1938
Cincinnati, Ohio**

Dominant Personality Characteristic: Risk-taking behavior
Mottos: "Lead, follow, or get out of the way." "Never get discouraged and never quit. Because if you never quit, you're never beaten."
Nickname: "Turnover Turner" and "Terrible Ted" (youth), "Mouth of the South," "Captain Courageous," "Captain Outrageous," "Godfather of Cable"
Firm Name: Turner Broadcasting System
Location: Atlanta, Georgia
First Innovation/Date: WTCG (WTBS) satellite Superstation, December 17, 1976
Products: Superstation WTBS, CNN, Headline News, TNT, Sports South
Initial Investment: Leveraged personal net worth from inheritance
Second Innovation/Date: CNN, June 1, 1980, 24-hour news, a $100 million risk

---

Sibling Status: First child and only son. One sister died of lupus
Personality Profile: Extroverted Intuitive Thinking Judger (ENTJ)
Parents' Occupation: Billboard company executive—salesman
Childhood Data: Boarding schools and military school in formative years. Known as "Capsize Kid" due to risk-taking while sailing
Family Socio-Economic Status: Upper middle class
Formal Education: Military schools and 3.5 years at Brown University
Age, First Business Venture: 24, operated billboard company
Age, Big Hit: 38, WTCG
Hobbies/Activities: 1977 America's Cup, *Tenacious.* Fastnet Race, Ireland

---

Marital Status: Married three times: 2 years to a racing buff and 20 years to Jane Smith—$40 million settlement in 1986. Married Jane Fonda in December 1991
Children: Two children from his first marriage, three children from his second
Religion: Agnostic. Peace and ecology and social consciousness his forte
Public Stock: Turner owned 83 percent until 1986, 43 percent since, with 55 percent voting rights
Revenues or Units of Big Hit: CNN, 60 million subscribers. 5 cable stations
Revenues of Firm: TBS, $1.5 billion revenue in 1992
Estimated Net Worth: $1.9 billion, 1992 *Forbes* 400
Age Became Millionaire: 24 at inheritance in 1963. Billionaire 1990
Heroes: Alexander the Great, Attila the Hun, Gen. George Patton, Gandhi
Honors: Paul White Award for Broadcast Excellence, 1988, 300 racing trophies, including the America's Cup in 1977

19

Inno-visionary and Creative Behavior

> My feeling is that the concept of creativeness and the concept of the healthy,
> self-actualizing, fully human person seems to be coming closer and closer to-
> gether and may perhaps turn out to be the same thing. . . . This means a
> new type of human being. Heraclitian, you might call him. The society which
> can turn out such people will survive; the societies that cannot turn out such
> people will die.
>
> —Abraham Maslow, *Further Reaches of Human Nature*

Anyone can become creative, innovative, and entrepreneurial, if they are willing to pay the price. More times than not the price will be excessive. The
individuals in this book were willing to pay that price. Not everyone is. But
everyone with normal intelligence is blessed with the innate capability of being
creative and innovative. Mark Rosenzweig at Berkeley has recently shown that
intelligence and IQ scores—once thought to be genetically fixed at birth—
can be improved and modified right into old age. The personalities and the
resultant innovative behaviors described in this text have this same propensity.
Learning to be creative, according to Rosenzweig, is a function of environmental
influences. He demonstrated this with rats placed in "enriched environments."
Regardless of their hereditary background, "intelligence, creativity, and brain
size continued to increase even into extreme old age" in the test rats. Conversely, wasting creative and innovative talent by placing that talent in an
"impoverished environment" will stifle creativity every time.

This author believes that great inno-visionary accomplishments are based
on a Promethean-type personality, and at times on serendipity. It is critical
to be in the right place at the right time with the right mental and emotional
desire to change the world. Other factors that appear to be critical to the
innovative process are a powerful inner drive to overcome basic insecurities,
an optimal cultural setting, and an inviolable resolve to negate the natural

human tendencies for self-preservation (see fig. 18). These factors will now be reviewed as to their impact on innovation and creativity.

Promethean Personality

A Promethean personality is most critical for effective large-scale innovation, especially for an entrepreneurial leader who is attempting to change the world to accept his or her vision of reality. The thirteen inno-visionary whiz kids reviewed here personify the behavior and personality traits necessary for creating large-scale innovative breakthroughs. These traits, revisited, are: autocratic, charismatic, competitive, confident, driven, focused, impatient, intuitive, passionate, persistent, persuasive, rebellious, and risky.

Research has shown that great leaders can positively impact the culture, style, and character of an organization through the imprinting of their personality on the organization. Richard Bandler's and John Grinder's pioneering research with Bateson, Satir, and Erikson on mimicking positive behavior has demonstrated that mirroring behavior can enhance a student's behavior. My research has validated this, as has other research. Therefore, it appears that an individual or an organization should define the desired behavior and then pick out proper role models and attempt to mimic that behavior.

Since organizations have personalities and qualities similar to people, they should pursue the same path to excellence. Organizations are usually a mirror image of their key people, especially their leaders, which tends to validate the whole issue. As the leaders go so goes the organization relative to its ability to function in a dynamic society. Likewise, employees tend to emulate their leaders and often take on their mannerisms and philosophies, not unlike children who emulate the styles of their parents. These organizational cultures are born through a developmental process not dissimilar to the psychosexual stages of development championed by Freud or the identity concepts of Erikson and Piaget.

Therefore, personality traits and leadership behavior become extremely critical to any organization's ability to create and innovate. Personality traits become the panacea for growth and change for both the organization and the individual. Those individuals or organizations desirous of competing in dynamic global markets must emulate the positive success traits of the Promethean personality and seek excellence in body, mind, and spirit.

These traits arm a person with the vision to create, the temperament to implement, the energy to persevere, and the power to sell their dreams to others. The other elements of consequence in the creative visionary personality are talent, timing (luck), and a vital force or passionate drive. These will be discussed now as important complementing factors in the process of effective innovation.

Figure 18

Profiles of Male Creative Genius
Behavior and Personality Characteristics Found in Great Achievers

1. **Promethean temperament** (Carl Jung and MBTI)—INTJ, ENTJ, INTP, ENTP
   Intuitive—Perception of world (forest vs. trees/macro v. micro)
   Thinker—Decision-making process (thinking vs. feeling)

2. **Competitive to a Fault**
   Aggressive behavior where winning is more important than playing

3. **Innovator operating style** (Kirton's Style Inventory)
   Preference for "doing things differently" vs. "doing things excellently"

4. **Self-employed fathers—Early vision for achievement outside establishment**
   Fathers made their own way in the world as dentist, truckdriver, or lawyer

5. **Big "T" personalities** (high in testosterone, thrill seeking—enormous risk-takers)
   Big Ts—High in risk-taking. Preference for uncertainty, unpredictability, variety, intensity, novelty
   Little Ts—Low in risk-taking. Preference for certainty, predictability, simplicity, low intensity, familiarity

6. **Self-confidence/high self-esteem**—Built in early childhood—permissive parents
   Allowing error and building sense of self. Arrogant attitude preferable to submissive one for innovative pursuits

7. **"Type A" behavior** (Meyer Friedman and Ray Rosenman)—Impatient and impulsive
   Impatient to a fault, obsession with winning, short attention span, multitasking personality types

8. **Charismatic**—The consummate salesmen
   Enthusiastic, passionate, and inspirational leadership qualities

9. **Right-brain, qualitative "gut" decision-makers**—qualitative vs. quantitative
   They utilize macro vs. micro, long-term vs. short-term, qualitative vs. quantitative, analogue vs. digital, inductive vs. deductive, and subjective vs. objective operating styles

10. **Psychosexually driven**—Sublimated libidinal drives of insecurity and inferiority
    Intensely driven individuals with high sex drive and/or need to overcome innate fears of failure. Consummate overachievers

11. **First-born males** (Adler and Kevin Leman)—Mother the major influence
    Perfectionism, striving for superiority, and need to achive. Natural leaders (12 of 13 innovative geniuses studied were first-born males, as were all 7 of the Mercury astronauts)

12. **Personality focused and goal-oriented**—Edison's aphorism "persistence vs. inspiration"
    Persevering prevails in entrepreneurship. Individuals who never give up never lose!

13. **Transient childhoods**—Leading to consummate self-sufficiency
    Ability to cope in foreign environments learned early in life

Talent

Edison, Einstein, Picasso, and the thirteen innovative visionaries in this work had enormous talent. Some were blessed with more talent than others but they all were energetic, insightful, articulate, and equipped with an above-average IQ. They have shown that higher education, money, breeding, intact family, and other variables often identified with creative talent are not necessary for successful innovation. They also demonstrated that being in the right place at the right time was also important.

Timing/Opportunity

The window of opportunity stays open but a short time in most industries and in most creative endeavors. Those who focus on that window and get through it—as Turner did with TV satellite broadcasts in the 1970s—will reap enormous rewards for having had the vision and the guts to pursue their vision. Timing is critical to breakthrough-type innovations. Edison developed the phonograph but was unable to refine it until there were recording materials available to create the entertainment demand for the phonograph. The light bulb was useless until there were electric utilities to distribute power. Many aspiring innovators forget the fact that one must make it easy for a consumer to acquire a product. The great ones like Edison create the necessary elements to allow their products to gain worldwide acclaim.

Fred Smith's successes with overnight package delivery would have been for naught had he been just a few years later in his innovation. The same is true of the Apple Computer story, oversized tennis rackets, and the advent of video games. The window of opportunity closes quickly and the faint of heart never get the brass ring, which is why the Type A impulsive entrepreneurs are often eminently successful while the Type B "show me" types often fail. Fred Smith has often said that he would have failed miserably with the Federal Express innovation had he been three years early or late. This was also true for Apple Computer and Atari, whose innovations were totally dependent on the microprocessor invention in 1971. Five years earlier or later would have rendered these innovations impossible. Nautilus, CNN, Microsoft, and other innovations had the same timeline for success. Once the innovator starts through that window of opportunity there is no turning back. Only those with passionate drive or "vital force" tend to make it through the window. Without a psychopathic, driven need to pursue the unknown, the window of opportunity could stay open forever and no one would venture through.

Vital Force

Edison, Picasso, and Einstein all had a vital force about them. Picasso's biographer Huffington said of him, "He had an inexhaustible vitality . . . a volcanic lust." These visionaries had a passionate drive to succeed often compared to Nietzsche's "will to power" that made them all consummate "Supermen" of creative and innovative endeavors. They all became superachievers with prodigious amounts of creativity left in their wake. The thirteen whiz-kid inno-visionaries were also superachievers who exhibited this vital force of energy. It overwhelmed everything they touched. They not only achieved what Maslow referred to as a "self-actualized" state of need fulfillment, they often functioned in a transcendental state or zone that emulated the Nietzschean Superman persona. They were in a constant state of flow which Csikszentmihalyi (1990) describes as a highly focused state of relaxed concentration that optimizes the boredom and anxiety existing in any person. He says these people are "so involved in an activity that nothing else seems to matter; the experience itself is so enjoyable that people will do it even at great cost, for the sheer sake of doing it." This concept of "flow" pushed Edison, Einstein, and Picasso and the inno-visionaries into higher levels of performance and lead them to previously undreamed-of states of consciousness.

Many of their passionate drives for success appear to have been the byproduct of an overactive psychic drive to compensate for other deficiencies in their psyches and lives. Michael Hutchison, in *Sex and Power* (1990), makes this point: "Sex and Power are inextricably intertwined. . . . Sex cannot only undo power, it is power." He says that superachievers seek power because of a biologically induced high testosterone level. This theory was based on University of Wisconsin researcher Frank Farley's Big T personality label, which he gives to all passionate risk-taking creative personalities. Farley characterizes these personality types as "thrill-seeking" and high in "testosterone" thus the "T" designation.

> Big T's, as a group, tend to be more creative and more extroverted, take more risks, have more experimental artistic preferences and prefer more variety in their lives than do little t's. (Farley, 1986)

Does Insecurity Breed Greatness?

Research has shown that the passionate drives of great leaders often emanate from childhood insecurities or personality dysfunctions that drive these leaders to overcompensate for early feelings of rejection or loss of love. Picasso never got over his 5'3" stature and a childhood of rejection. Edison couldn't hear and ended up revolutionizing sound through the invention of the phonograph. Einstein was not even fluent by the age of nine yet at twenty-six wrote three papers that turned the scientific world upside down.

The insecurities of the thirteen inno-visionaries drove them to identify with their goals to such an extent that the goals obscured all other elements of their lives. Most of the subjects in this work became obsessive-compulsive about their products and concepts. They were often labeled "maniacs on a mission" by the media. However, without this passionate labor of love for their dreams these innovators would never have achieved such enormous successes.

Crisis—The Mother of Innovation?

World-renowned psychologist Erik Erickson stated, "Crisis resolutions are critical to the totally integrated personality." And David Mackinnon (1975), a researcher on the creative personality, made this observation: "Persons of the most extraordinary effectiveness had had life histories marked by severe frustrations, deprivations, and traumatic experiences." Research on these innovative visionaries uncovered a similar and unexpected finding that could be pertinent to creative, innovative, and entrepreneurial behavior. Virtually all of the thirteen individuals in this work had a traumatic experience just prior to their breakthroughs. Most of them also experienced traumatic and abnormal childhood experiences. These occurrences could have been a contributing factor in their obsessive and at times compulsive personalities. Figure 19 shows the various crises that seem to have contributed to launching these individuals into the creative stratosphere.

Dissipative Structures

> It is out of chaos, turmoil, and disorder that higher levels of order and wisdom emerge.
>
> —Ilya Prigogine

Ilya Prigogine won a Nobel Prize for his mathematical theory on how to deal with "dissipative structures." His theory offers a solution for the nihilistic belief, substantiated by our laws of thermodynamics, that maintains that all people and societies are in the process of "burn out" or dissipation. Prigogine maintained that any structure or system that is teetering on the edge of disorder and annihilation will either destroy itself or reorganize itself into a higher order and therefore become stronger than before. In other words, it will die or be reborn into something bigger and better. Prigogine maintained that as "the instability of systems become more untenable, the systems or people that survive the crisis become greater and stronger."

Prigogine's theories are plausible since experience tells us that surviving a terrible disease arms us with antibodies that protect us from further assaults from that particular disease. Societies or organizations surviving great trauma or war end up stronger from the experience. Note the reorganization of Japan and Germany after the devastation of World War II. Prigogine said, "Life emerges out of entropy [chaos] not despite it." He also gave credence to the crisis theory of innovation with his statement that, "Every artistic or scientific creation implies a transition from disorder to order."

Reimprinting—Timothy Leary

Another method for developing creative behavior could be the reimprinting concept of Timothy Leary. Leary believed that behavior could be changed, especially during or just after some major traumatic life event. Leary is best known for his LSD drug experiments during the turbulent sixties. It was this research that caused Leary to theorize that drugs or trauma could alter one's behavior and could change a "Mr. Peepers accountant type" into a "charismatic flamboyant creative genius type." He felt that this transition could occur instantaneously as the result of drugs or other trauma.

We now know that superlearning occurs best in the theta state (trancelike state), which is exactly the state experienced during traumatic events. Leary's "traumatic shock" theory postulates a total reimprinting of the unconscious personality, causing people to become different, some for better, others for worse. One example of this metamorphosis was Patty Hearst entering the trunk and closet of her captors as an upper-middle-class heterosexual and emerging as a rebellious bisexual. Such traumatic imprinting could very well have influenced the behaviors of the inno-visionary personalities, especially those who had incidents of extreme trauma just prior to their breakthroughs.

Are traumatic induced reimprints and crises the impetus for most creative and entrepreneurial behaviors? Or does creativity and innovative vision evolve out of chaos and disorder, as Prigogine theorizes? Could there be other variables involved? There is certainly considerable circumstantial evidence that crisis and insecurity were a driving force in the particular creations of these thirteen innovative geniuses. Michael Hutchison (1990) says that imprints while in a vulnerable state (like brainwashing methods during wartime) represent a remarkable type of learning. He demonstrates how new learning takes place when trauma occurs during a person's "exceedingly vulnerable, malleable, open, and receptive state." No matter what the cause, it appears that a crisis can become a motivational element for creativity. It is not always a totally negative experience, since it can drive people, organizations, and societies into greater performance and self-actualized states.

Other Variables

Many of the thirteen visionary geniuses in this work were manic and/or obsessive-compulsive personality types. They exceeded the norms as postulated by society. Turner admits to using a mind-altering drug—lithium—to control his manic and obsessive behavior and regular bouts with depression. Does a predisposition to dysfunctional behavior assist in the creative process? Or does the creative process create the trauma and anxiety that leads to these compulsions? No conclusive evidence exists to prove these hypotheses but it certainly is highly coincidental that these individuals had such consistent experiences of crisis and compulsions beyond the ordinary.

These subjects also had an abnormal propensity for risk-taking, far beyond that of the average individual or executive. Since life has always proven far cheaper in any society that faced devastation or potential loss of personal values, maybe the crises and other negative factors in the lives of these visionaries was causal to their creativity. When life is cheap, risk-taking is greater, a fact repeated over and over in history. These visionaries had little to lose, as most started at the bottom and their risk-taking was beyond what would have been expected or prudent. Figure 19 lists the crises faced by these individuals. Some faced loss of life, others loss of employment, some loss of a life's work. The Orientals (Morita and Honda) were faced with loss of ego, or "loss of face."

Leadership Power

Two contemporary business philosophers—George Gilder in *Microcosm* (1989) and Alvin Toffler in *Power Shift* (1990)—have made strong arguments for "power" as the driving force behind our changing society and organizations. Toffler draws a picture of inexorable and unpredictable shifts in power as the guiding principle behind all change. In *Power Shift,* Toffler sums up the three principles he believes to be critical to all change in any society: "For inside the world of business as in the larger world outside, *force, wealth,* and *knowledge,* like the ancient sword, jewel, and mirror . . . remain the primary tools of power."

Michael Hutchison in *The Anatomy of Sex and Power* makes an eloquent argument for the power of sex. He shows how men use power to get sex and how women use sex to get power. His research demonstrates the conditioning and imprintings that endow leaders with much of their power. Hutchison

Figure 19

Adult Crises of Inno-Visionaries

Individual	Crises
Marcel Bich	World War II disrupted Bich's career and created much trauma for him. After the war, he and a friend borrowed $1,000, bought a leaky shed in a Paris ghetto and set out to create a "throwaway culture" via disposable pens, lighters, and razors.
Nolan Bushnell	His Pong creation was rejected by Bally. He had quit his job and was faced with financial survival. He was forced to borrow $500 to start Atari to market Pong—the first video game.
William Gates	Dropped out of Harvard and bet his career on his dream of writing software for personal computers. The dream burst with the failure of MITS, producer of the Altair, in Albuquerque. He went home to Seattle and signed agreements with Apple and IBM for MS-DOS and turned lemon into lemonade.
Howard Head	Repeated firings and demotions caused him to quit his job as an engineer. He was inadequate as an employee so he became an entrepreneur. He couldn't ski so he responded by creating the first metal ski. He couldn't play tennis so he appeased his inadequacies by developing the revolutionary oversized tennis racket.
Soichiro Honda	His factory in Tokyo was bombed out during World War II and then destroyed by an earthquake in 1946. At middle age he was forced to start over against the Japanese establishment, which never accepted him, thought him a rebel, and attempted to destroy him.
Steven Jobs	An orphan who was uneducated, unemployed, unattached, and unloved as a teenager. He was part of the counter-culture and rebelled against the establishment. He took Wozniak's PC designs and started Apple Computer with sheer force of will, as it was his only identity and redemption in his search for enlightenment.
Arthur Jones	The Rhodesian government threw him out of Africa in middle age and confiscated his company. They took his equipment and assets—a lifetime's work, and left him broke. They also placed a contract on his life. This forced him to respond with the creation of the Nautilus exercise machine, which he had originally designed twenty years earlier in 1948 but left dormant until his tragedy.

William Lear

Mental flagellation by a dominant German mother influenced his overachievement. His Learjet idea was rejected by the Board of Directors of the company he founded. He had to sell the firm to fund his dream and he bet his life's work and net worth to bring his dream to reality.

Tom Monaghan

Domino's was bankrupt in 1970 after ten years of sixteen-hour, seven-day weeks by Monaghan. His firm was taken over by a bank but Monaghan was retained since no one else would work eighty-hour weeks for $200 a week. Domino's was returned to him when the bank decided it would be in liquidation within months. Monaghan regained control and built the firm into the dominant company in the industry.

Akio Morita

Japanese *keiretsu* leaders and MITI rejected Sony in the early days of the firm. Rejection by the establishment forced Morita to create and innovate, since his wealthy father had invested the family's money in Sony based on Morita's request. Morita had declined his role as leader of the family sake business (Akio was the first son and expected to succeed to head of firm). He had to succeed or die of disgrace.

Sol Price

Fired by Fed-Mart and walking the streets of San Diego with his unemployed sons gave him inspiration for the Price Club concept. He was in his late fifties at the time and needed to salve the firing, redeem his self-esteem, and provide employment for his sons.

Fred Smith

The Federal Reserve Board canceled a contract that called for Federal Express's exclusive transfer of Fed funds. Smith had already purchased three jets and gone deeply into debt, so he was forced to start Federal Express as a package delivery firm to offset an otherwise disastrous situation. He was born with a crippling disease, which he overcame to reach the heights of business success. He bet and would have lost his total inheritance ($8.5 million) if the Federal Express venture had not made it.

Ted Turner

His father groomed Ted to be insecure so he would overachieve. He traumatized Ted by selling the family business and committing suicide. This caused Ted to prove his father wrong by getting the firm back in a Herculean struggle. This move catapulted Turner into a feverish drive for power in everything he touched. He bet everything on every move in his drive for power in the broadcasting industry.

goes to great length explaining how power and passion are inextricably tied together in the psyches of leaders and innovators. He illustrates how leaders learn very early in life how to use their power to get sex, and how women obtain their own form of power through the denial of sex. The inno-visionary personalities in this text shows an unusual likeness to the profile drawn by Hutchison as they possessed an inordinately high sex drive and fabricated power as their tool for creativity and innovation. And most were driven to seduction as a means of identifying their power and satiating an overactive libido.

This author has found innovative geniuses to possess a magical power that seems to emanate from four distinct areas. Leaders exude power through the use of their own personal magnetism (charisma), they are *given power* from the authority bestowed on them by their position within an organization or group, many generate their own *personal power* from their peculiar knowledge or expertise, and many leaders have an *innate power* through a sort of osmosis coined by Nietzsche and Adler as a "will to power." Let's explore these.

Personal Magnetism

The charisma of any leader is critical to his becoming empowered by his followers (employees). Unless empowered they are just ordinary individuals. Their strength is in the magnetic appeal that electrifies their followers and attracts a cult following. The charismatic leader generates tremendous power through the sheer force of his personality. Great world leaders like Napoleon and Roosevelt had this faculty for drawing people to their sides. Hitler, in a more negative sense, had this same power, as did the infamous Rev. Jim Jones of Kool-Aid fame.

Edison, Picasso, and Einstein had unbelievable power to attract followers who followed them blindly into bizarre situations. Most of the inno-visionaries in this work had an excessive and dynamic appeal or charisma. Fred Smith, Steve Jobs, Nolan Bushnell, and Bill Lear were especially endowed with this talent. Charisma is not inherent, according to Laura Rose, an Atlanta researcher on charismatic leadership. She holds that anyone can learn to be charismatic and can gain significant amounts of power from their efforts. It appears that success somehow gives people enormous amounts of power and an eminence not available before their success. Therefore charisma is *earned,* not necessarily *given.* Einstein and Edison are prime examples of this occurrence as they earned their eminence through quiet and diligent work that made them unique and demanding of charismatic respect.

Authority

This power is based on the hierarchical position held by the leader within an organization. It is typically given by the owners, and what is given can be taken away. The leader's personal power is a function of the size and economic status of the organization and the financial control or lack of it held by the leader. This power is embodied in a leader's authority to hire and fire, give raises and promotions, and control the career and financial destiny of his workers. In entrepreneurial organizations this authoritative power is usually controlled by the founder and if his financial control or ownership position changes through dilution (raising capital for growth), his power base is diminished accordingly. Aspiring entrepreneurs desiring this type of power can get it only through the group or organization. This power is seldom held by entrepreneurs or creative visionaries as they virtually never work for others and their power is made, not given.

Special Skills, IQ, and Education

This source of power is based on a special expertise, skill, or unique qualifications. An example of the importance of this type of knowledge is a hypothetical professional baseball or football coach who never played the game. Motivating players to take direction and performing it your way could prove very difficult in such an organization, where first-hand knowledge is critical to success. This power associated with the knowledge or unique expertise of the leader is a more powerful force than authority but less powerful than personal magnetism. Entrepreneurs and innovators are typically well-endowed with knowledge power, if for no other reason than that they are typically operating in the netherland where others have little knowledge. Consider Einstein, who was the authority on the theory of relativity even to the most renowned scientists of the world, who had difficulty understanding this esoteric principle.

Innovative leaders are often imbued with the self-confidence to convince their followers of their expert knowledge, even when they are operating at the edge of their expertise (Steve Jobs did this constantly at Apple). Any entrepreneur can gain this source of power by creating an environment where only he is familiar with the terrain. He therefore becomes the captain of his own destiny and those along for the ride are prey to his every move.

The Will to Power

The power of many great leaders, including most of those in this work, was taken, not given. It is what Nietzsche called the "will to power," which is the ability of a leader to grab the power and become the leader when others are afraid or unsure of the terrain. Adler referred to this as the "self-actualizing factor" in man's natural, instinctive drive for superiority. The leader having this potential power is normally aggressive, with a Promethean-type personality. He creates his own power through the sheer force of his will by taking on responsibility relinquished by others. Many classic examples are found in traumatic combat scenes during war where a private takes charge while the officer in charge remains paralyzed.

This source of power is commonly referred to as "guts" or "moxie" and is illustrative of the power that Steve Jobs used during his tenure at Apple. Steve had no title at Apple during the early years but was the most powerful person in the company through his will to power. He assumed the power and it was given to him by omission by Wozniak and those too weak to challenge his overpowering personality. Edison used this power by personally financing what was to become Con Edison, the first utility company in America, when everyone else was frozen or afraid of this unknown concept in 1880. Edison was not afraid and therefore became the "Father of Modern Electronics" by his will to power.

The inno-visionary personality is especially proficient at obtaining this source of power because of his high self-esteem and self-confidence. These type leaders represent only about 2 to 5 percent of the population, yet they typically control a disproportionate amount of the power because of their ability to will power to themselves and away from others. Consequently, their employees often follow them blindly toward their causes and dreams. Steve Jobs and Bill Lear were the most noted for having this innate talent to take power when it was left for the taking.

Insecurity Breeds Innovative Success

People, organizations, and nations are all afflicted with varying degrees of insecurity. The insecure tend to try harder and those who are very secure hardly try at all and their complacency buries them. Fear of failure is not bad if not obsessive. "Fat and happy" attitudes are not conducive to success in business, sports, or life. Wealthy children, industrial giants, and all bureaucracies epitomize this too-secure attitude and therefore rarely venture into the unknown waters of creativity. Minorities and neophytes are never complacent enough to lose too badly, as they tend to overcome their insecurities through overachievement. It is these people and groups that lead the way in most new creative endeavors.

Those with little to lose try harder, those with a lot to lose don't try at all. Consider nineteenth-century America with her innovative geniuses Carnegie, Rockefeller, Vanderbilt, Edison, and Bell, all poor immigrants who were self-made and driven to create a new and better way. Examples of nations later in this century are Japan, Taiwan, Hong Kong, and Korea, who have demonstrated the same intensity and desire to overachieve. They have made enormous strides in areas where they were totally incapable of competing. Their striving for superiority was immersed in their basic insecurities (see more on Japan's compulsive insecurity in the next section).

Organizations like IBM, Xerox, Kodak, and Ford have evolved in an "insecure to secure" transition during their growth from neophyte start-up firms to "fat cat" industrial giants. They began as risk-taking, innovative firms and evolved into bureaucratic protectors of the status quo. The thirteen innovative visionaries in this book are classic examples of creative people who succeeded because of and in spite of enormous insecurities. Mimicking this behavior will undoubtedly produce the same results for those willing to subjugate their egos to a more subservient role in their pursuit of excellence.

East and West: Significant Cultural Distinctions

PHILOSOPHICAL DIFFERENCES

Identical organizations in Japan and America facing similar decisions will approach most decisions in dramatically different ways. The basis of all decision-making in traditional America is a function of job security. A self-preservation (security-based) principle permeates all organizations and their executives. It overrides all other negative factors in Western-based cultures (California is an exception). In Japan, job security is never an issue in creativity and innovative behavior, since the lifetime employment principle eliminates fear of job loss in the decision-making process. Eastern executives direct all of their energies toward the best long-term decision for the organization, in contrast to the short-term mentality of the Western organization. No short-term personal interests enter into the decision-making equation, as the Japanese always subjugate their personal egos to the higher interests of the organization.

Risk-taking by Japanese management is externalized to the organization and not internalized to the individual, as in many U.S. organizations, making for dramatic differences in the risk-taking propensity of the two societies. Japanese executives use a long-term, macro, risk-taking, impersonalized, and holistic methodology in their business decision-making. Sound familiar? This profile is identical to that of the Promethean temperament of the inno-visionary personality. America's industrial giants, many in Detroit, use a short-term, micro, risk-averse, personal, and left-brained approach to business decision-making. No wonder the Japanese own nearly all of the leading edge and high-technology consumer products industries in the world.

This difference between the two cultures has a major influence on innovation, creativity, and entrepreneurial activity. Left to their own devices American executives always opt for personal safety and not the organization's safety. In Japan, personal rewards and aggrandizement are either nonexistent or secondary to the well-being of the organization. In America, the individual is first and the organization second and while this meets many of the West's great cultural needs for freedom of the individual, it is counterproductive to the innovative process. A reevaluation of the cultural influence is in order if the West is to compete effectively with the East.

EGALITARIAN INFLUENCE

The egalitarian Pacific Rim countries (Japan, Korea, Hong Kong, Singapore, Taiwan) have had an enormous impact on the world's consumer electronic industries. These societies do not pay high salaries to their top management. The top-to-bottom salary range in Japan has an approximately 5:1 ratio (president at $100,000 with the lowest employee at $20,000), while the U.S. practice is closer to 100:1 (president at $1,000,000 with the lowest employee at $10,000). This wide disparity in wages between the two societies is central to the problem of motivation and risk-taking propensity and therefore to innovation.

The East pays little homage to personal successes or failures. The team is expected to perform to its ultimate potential and then it wins or loses depending on the fates. Not so in America, where failure classically results in loss of employment and success means vast power and wealth. Employee motivation in the East is aimed at making the company the supreme power and recipient of all the rewards and notoriety. In America, the individual is the focal point of rewards and successes. Executives jockey for media space and personal recognition so they may have a chance to succeed to the executive suite. The individual in Japan is a part of the whole and in America the individual is the whole.

INCENTIVE COMPENSATION—DETERRENT TO INNOVATION

Compensation incentive policies for management are dramatically different in the East and West. These differences have had a major impact on how the Western executive performs relative to his Far East counterparts. High-risk and long-term decisions in the West are usually made by executives who have a great deal riding on the outcome personally. Their bonus compensation is materially impacted by any potential gain or loss. Incentive compensations of this type are never allowed in the East. The majority of Western executives receive a bonus based on quarterly profits, the Eastern companies only tally their profits at year end and still would not think of compensating an operating executive on the near-term profits. They believe the organization, not the individual, is successful or unsuccessful, and success is not solely dependent on the success or failure of its management. The manager could do a good job and the company could do poorly but neither should reflect on the other. The American approach rewards successful performance with huge financial incentives and penalizes failure with termination. This system is not necessarily conducive to innovation. It makes American executives far less secure in high-risk and long-term decision-making than their Eastern counterparts.

BONUSES AND LIFETIME EMPLOYMENT

Ironically the concept of lifetime employment was introduced into Japan by the MacArthur occupation forces just after World War II. This employment policy is the major dichotomy between the work forces of the two nations. Most large U.S. firms motivate their management with bonuses based on ROI—return on investment. According to Drucker, this incentive policy "is a near-complete bar to innovation." The Japanese never give incentives to their executives. According to Akio Morita, "There are no management bonuses in Japan, only workers bonuses—no golden parachutes—a simple lifetime parachute of guaranteed employment" (Morita, 1986). Morita was in shock when he discovered that Americans laid off employees in a recession. His response was, "If management takes the risk and responsibility for hiring personnel, then it is management's ongoing responsibility to keep them employed" (Morita 1986). This top management philosophy in Japan creates a family orientation that is very reassuring to employees. It is especially effective in high-growth, volatile, and dynamic new markets that require high-risk decision-making from its executives.

THE NOT-INVENTED-HERE SYNDROME—NIH

A U.S. executive search firm would never consider contacting the personnel department of a corporation in order to do business. Why? Because they would never be given the time of day. An engineering consulting firm would never contact the chief engineering executive in order to pursue an engineering contract. Why? Because they too would be ignored, even if the concept is revolutionary. Experience has shown that in-house management will always react personally and not in the best interest of the organization. The above engineering example would produce comments such as, "We can design it better and cheaper. Just give us the resources, and the opportunity." The in-house engineers are correct. Anyone can do it better given enough time and resources. But time is money, and in breakthrough-type concepts time is of the essence. This NIH factor runs rampant in most American firms, where ego runs supreme. It is virtually nonexistent in the East, where egos are left at home.

Inexperienced top management and bureaucrats are extremely susceptible to the pitfalls of the NIH syndrome. Management in America is supersensitive to the egos of their internal operating personnel. The top dog evolved through the same hierarchy and can identify and empathize with the in-house argument. NIH is not a factor for the Japanese, since their cultural system has shielded them from this ego-based problem. They have consistently purchased technology from other cultures and used these technological purchases to dominate the mass consumer markets in those other countries. They exploit the inventions of other nations with aplomb. Do you think anyone at Sony cared that Bell Labs invented the transistor? Or that Ampex and RCA invented the VCR?

The transistor invention by Bell Labs led to Sony's total domination of the transistor radio industry and ultimately the consumer electronics industry. The video cassette recorder was invented by Ampex and refined by RCA. The Japanese took these inventions and exploited them and now have close to 100 percent market share in this industry. The TV went through the same evolution. Two decades ago U.S. firms produced nearly 100 percent of the home electronics bought in America. Today, they make less than 5 percent. The NIH factor was a major reason for Japan's enormous success and America's demise in these important markets.

A SERVICE VERSUS A MANUFACTURING ECONOMY

The United States is fast becoming a service-based economy because of its inability to compete in manufacturing. Japan by contrast has based its worldwide expansion on a manufacturing expertise that is unparalleled in history. Akio Morita has been extremely vocal with the press in attempting to direct America away from becoming a totally service-based economy. He told the press in 1991, "The future of any nation will be shaped not by those who can manipulate and exploit paper assets, but by the ability of that nation to manufacture good products. . . . Nothing is more fundamental to any nation or economy than the ability to produce real goods."

MARKET SHARE

The Far East executive asks, "What price is needed to optimize the market?" And then, "How many units will I have to build in order to achieve the necessary economies of scale to meet the necessary costs?" There is little thought about short-term profits. It is secondary. Western executives typically use the reverse logic in looking at any new market potential. He or she asks, "What price can I sell the product for in order to build the number of units the firm will need to optimize profits now?" One philosophy is long-term and market-driven, the other is short-term and self-preservation driven. One is inductive and aimed at satisfying customer and market needs, the other is deductive and aimed at placating personal fears and anxieties.

Dominating market share has been the driving force for industry leaders since the time of Henry Ford. Strangely, it appears that the concept was shipped off to the Orient along with all the manufacturing jobs. Price-setting is very critical to dominating market share and the Japanese risk-taking proclivity is far better at this art than America's. Long-term Japanese strategies have outperformed short-term American strategies. The Japanese set prices designed to optimize long-term profits and market share while American management sets prices to optimize its near-term best interests and job security. This fundamental difference in pricing philosophy has had an enormous impact on market share. Akio Morita gave a succinct characterization of this problem when asked why Japan has such dominance in certain markets: "Share of market is more important to Japanese companies than immediate profitability."

Pricing a product higher than necessary in order to "cream" the market is a short-term mentality that is consistent in self-preservationist organizations and societies. A long-term mentality should always be the operative strategy to assure customer satisfaction and optimal market share. An old Wall Street adage prevails: "Bulls make money and bears make money, but pigs never make money." Peter Drucker says, "The attempt to achieve a higher profit margin through a higher price is always self-defeating." Henry Ford was one of the first Americans to utilize this principle when he priced the Model T below his cost, to the chagrin of his accountants and stockholders, who predicted his demise. He understood better than they and it is time we start emulating Henry Ford once again in America.

MARKET AGGRESSIVENESS

The Japanese success in world markets is deeply rooted in a basic survival instinct that has made them inordinately competitive and aggressive. They attack most problems with a tenacity and ferocity unknown in the West. This is based on their basic insecurity, due to having been born and raised on an island that is daily faced with earthquakes, typhoons, and volcanoes, and which has virtually no natural resources. This early environmental influence has been indelibly imprinted on their psyches creating a basic insecurity and drive for superiority. This psychological profile is identical to that found in the personality of the creative geniuses.

A typical example of this insecurity is shown in the approach a Japanese salesman takes in selling automobiles in Tokyo. Contrast this with the American way. An American salesman waits in the showroom for customers and will venture out only on request. In Tokyo all salesman are expected to canvass door to door, day in day out, in the hopes of stumbling on a prospect in his home, store, or Japanese bath. They go house to house and work diligently to generate a personal relationship with hundreds of potential customers based on a long-term strategy. They research the needs and wants of all potential clients and are willing to wait for years to make one sale. This patience, perseverance, and aggressive behavior is critical to the pursuit of any objective. It is long-term driven and not short-term driven. How many American car salesman would last in that regimen? This same aggressive approach is what has made the Japanese so successful in dominating world consumer product markets.

Another example of the tenacity and long-term attitudes of Japanese employees is their ability to work on a new product concept that has no chance of success for years. The Japanese manager is content to wait for the rewards of his work even if it takes ten or even twenty years. They know they will be around to see the fruits of their labor and are not so concerned with immediate rewards. American executives would not only *not* think about a ten-year product cycle, they would probably be *fired* for suggesting such a strategy. The Western fixation on near-term earnings performance prejudices work habits and risk-taking propensity, especially in respect to Far Eastern competition.

SUCCESS VIA CONSTANT FAILURE

Between 1975 and 1985 Japan experienced twice as many business failures as the United States, but had three times the growth rate. The moral of this statistic is that thriving economies have consistently higher failure rates than failing economies. High risk always begets high rewards, which is true of people, companies, and societies. Knowing this, American organizations must decide what risks are within the confines of manageable risk. The risk *not* taken is often the greater risk in the long run. Said differently, the greater risk is often not risking. If one is to create the new and innovative, the heuristic (trial and error) approach is critical. The age-old experimentation approach of fail, fail, fail must be adhered to if progress is to be expected. The fairy-tale fable is as true for innovation as it is for romance—"One must kiss a thousand frogs to find a prince or princess."

The Self-Preservation Principle

There is an overwhelming need for self-preservation within the species. Unfortunately our business organizations have sanctified this fundamental weakness in man and magnified it to enormous proportions in the form of "survival of the fittest for the mediocre." The corporate executive who equates security with preservation of job first and preservation of the institution second is guilty of this principle, which is counterproductive to the innovative process. This need to preserve the self becomes more pronounced in all eras where change, complexity, and the unknown are rampant. The unknown is fearful to the human psyche but never has it been so prevalent as during the 1980s and 1990s in America. Dynamic change and the unknown have created a fear mentality in most organizations, causing seasoned executives and even boards of directors to freeze. This freezing causes inaction, not action. Nothing is ever accomplished in a state of nonaction. Elimination of risk also eliminates all potential opportunity, a fact lost on all bureaucrats.

This nonaction mentality can be far more devastating than action, as shown by psychiatrist/writer David Viscott in *Risking:* "The driver most likely to be killed is the one who hesitates, loses his nerve and can neither accelerate nor apply his brakes. He cannot follow through on a commitment to act." Managers in large institutions become experts at doing nothing when faced with complex situations that are unfamiliar. Not knowing what to do perpetuates inaction when fear of making errors exceeds potential for gain. Employees have learned well from their leaders and now take no risks unless personal reward (promotion or money) are significantly greater than potential punishment (termination or loss of money). It is imperative to learn how to fail gracefully and with dignity and learn from failure so that the next risk has a better chance of success. Self-preservationist mentalities do not provide that potential. It is a negative approach that pervades all actions and ultimately leads to chaos and failure. The demise of the Sears catalogue in 1993 and the decline of other valued institutions are due to the failure to risk innovation.

The self-preservation principle tends to rule supreme in traditional corporate environments. Until this mentality can be replaced or changed to coincide with the demands of a dynamic world (dynamic environments demands dynamic methods), traditional organizations will be destined to stagnate and ultimately perish. All growth and expansion in America is dependent on innovative leadership capable of adopting creative and risk-taking approaches to dealing with change. They must find a way to eliminate the self-destructive self-preservation mindset that stifles all large-scale innovation.

Ayn Rand's philosophy, objectivism, is of excellent use to enterprising new inno-visionaries. Rand's philosophy decried self-preservation. She preached the gospel of positive selfishness to achieve success. Her alter-ego, John Galt, in *Atlas Shrugged* predicted the present crises found in corporate America. Her philosophy dictates an offensive, capitalistic, risk-taking operating style, in contrast to a defensive, bureaucratic, risk-averse operating style. Successful innovation can only occur if the mentality of individuals, managers, organizations, and nations can shed the self-preservation mentality that has become their crutch. Self-preservation is defensive not offensive, born of fear not confidence, tentative not aggressive, stagnant not dynamic.

Quarterly Report Syndrome

Wall Street has become a monumental negative influence on innovation in organizations. Its adulation of the quarterly earnings report has made most organizations run on fear instead of opportunity. Its demands for quarterly profits married management to the god of earnings per share and caused self-preservation to proliferate. Management's natural inclination for self-preservation has only been reinforced by Wall Street's perpetual demands for better and better short-term performance. Consequently, management in America spends most of its time worrying over quarterly performance and little time on future opportunities.

Obeisance to the altar of the quarterly report—and ever-improving near-term performance—results in sacrificing the future for the present. The large American organization today lives and dies by stock price. This mentality is furthered through compensation programs for top management featuring stock options and other incentives to increase stock price. The incentives all favor a risk-averse mentality in order to make the present quarter look good. Therefore, executives opt for a quantitative and micro mentality instead of the more desirable qualitative, macro mentality.

Akio Morita has better insight on America than most since he has lived and worked here, yet has the perspective to see us from afar. His view is akin to watching a football game from the third deck, a much better perspective than on the field, especially for discovering strategic nuances. In 1986, Morita told the *Wall Street Journal,* "If I were made dictator of America tomorrow, the first thing I would do would be to eliminate the quarterly report." Someone had better think about Morita's comment, as it appears he has a better handle on America's problems than America. It certainly is preferable to erecting ludicrous new trade barriers for protecting inept industries and firms. Mortgaging the future for the present is a deadly behavior that has become entrenched in the Western mentality. Only long-run decisions have true integrity in any business.

Conclusions

Innovative visionaries have changed the world since time began. Edison, Einstein, and Picasso are examples of creative genius changing the world for the better in the first half of this century. The thirteen inno-visionaries studied in this book changed the world more than most during the last half of our century. They accomplished gigantic breakthroughs and did so with virtually no advantages over others who were operating during the same era. This author is suggesting that their success was based on unique behavior traits and a driven personality that is within the province of everyone. Powerful leadership styles are made, not born. The creative and innovative personality is sometimes evolutionary and sometimes revolutionary, but virtually never genetically induced. The outstanding effectiveness of these individuals was never biased or influenced by competitors, Wall Street, industry experts, unexpected crisis, or any other obstacle. Their successes were due to their unique dreams of reality and their internal drive to actualize these dreams.

Great leaders in coming generations will require education and training to refine the traits and behavioral nuances that engender creativity and innovative excellence. Most astute and dynamic leaders operating in a free society have the ability to achieve monumental feats of innovation. Business organizations and nations also have this same potential. They can all lead the way in creative thinking and behavior, but only if they are willing to mimic the behavior of the great innovators. They will need to change their past styles and get into the "flow" of the process. They can no longer protect the status quo, preserve the present and past ways, fear the unknown, or defend old dogmas. These attitudes will be the Achilles heel of organizations and nations alike. Organizations and nations must be leaders, not followers, and be willing to adopt the inquisitive and risk-taking natures of the great inno-visionaries.

The inno-visionary personality is necessary for the making of the consummate entrepreneur and change master. This personal style is available to anyone inclined to pursue it. These visionary leaders had it, which gave them an unusual ability to focus on goals and dreams, a macro vision to see their dreams through to fruition, and the passionate energy to persevere when all seemed lost. This magic appears to be the ingredient for success in any creative environment. Any person with these qualities and desires can reach enormous goals. As Rosenzweig at Berkeley has demonstrated by changing dull rats into creative rats merely by changing their environment, we can all change our creative bent by operating in enhanced environments. The "wizard" is within and until it is understood, controlled, and motivated, success cannot follow. When the wizard is turned loose, there are no unreachable goals. Make sure that you take control and do not allow any organization or person to negatively influence your wizard.

Bibliography

Creativity, Innovation, and Entrepreneurship

Adler, A. 1979. *Superiority and Social Interest.* New York: Norton.

Agor, W. March 1988. "Finding and Developing Intuitive Managers." *Training and Developmental Journal,* p. 68.

————. First Quarter, 1991. "How Intuition Can Be Used to Enhance Creativity in Organizations." *Journal of Creative Behavior,* p. 11.

Amabile, T. 1983. "The Social Psychology of Creativity." *Journal of Personality and Social Psychology,* p. 357

American Psychological Association. 1987. *Publication Manual.* Third ed. Washington, D.C.: APA.

Babbie, K. 1987. *Methods of Social Research.* New York: Macmillan.

Bandler, R. 1985. *Using Your Brain for a Change.* Moab, Utah: Real People Press.

Bartlett, C., and S. Ghashal. July/August 1990. "Matrix Management: Not a Structure, a Frame of Mind." *Harvard Business Review,* p. 138.

Barzun, J. Summer 1989. "The Paradoxes of Creativity." *The American Scholar,* pp. 337–51.

Bennis, W. 1989. *On Becoming a Leader.* New York: Addison Wesley.

Brasington, C. 1968. "Birth Order and Personality." *Encyclopedia of Psychology,* pp. 152–55.

Brodie, J. 1987. *The Creative Personality: A Rankian Analysis of Ernest Hemingway.* University of Colorado Dissertation. Order #DA 8716230. Ann Arbor, Mich: University Microfilms.

Brownsword, A. 1987. *It Takes All Types.* Palo Alto, Calif.: Baytree Publications.

Buffington, P. 1990. *Charisma: Power, Passion, and Purpose.* Buffalo, N.Y.: Bearly Limited Press.

Business Week. September 14, 1990. "Innovation—The Global Race." Special

Issue by McGraw-Hill.

Capra, F. 1982. *The Turning Point.* New York: Simon & Schuster.

Chancellor, J. 1990. *Peril and Promise.* New York: Harper & Row.

Cherian, V. 1990. "Birth Order and Academic Achievement of Children in Transhei." *Psychological Reports,* pp. 19–24.

Clark, R. 1971. *Einstein—The Life and Times.* New York: Avon.

Conger, J. 1989. *The Charismatic Leader—Behind the Mystique of Exceptional Leadership.* San Francisco: Jossey-Bass.

Corriere, R., and M. McGrady. 1986. *Life Zones.* New York: Ballantine Publishing.

Corsini, R. 1984. "Psychosexual Stages." *Encyclopedia of Psychology.* New York: Wiley & Sons, p. 179.

Csikszentmihalyi, M. 1990. *Flow—The Psychology of Optimal Experience.* New York: Harper-Collins.

Dahlback, O. 1990. "Personality and Risk-Taking." *Personality and Individual Differences* 11 (12): 1235–42.

Derian, J. 1990. *America's Struggle for Leadership in Technology.* Cambridge, Mass.: MIT Press.

Drucker, P. 1983. *The Changing World of the Executive.* New York: Times Book.

———. 1985. *Innovation and Entrepreneurship.* New York: Harper and Row.

Dyer, W. 1989. *You'll See It When You Believe It.* New York: Avon.

Economist. December 24, 1983. "The New Entrepreneurs."

———. February 6, 1988. "America's Next Jobless," p. 15.

Farrell, W. 1986. *Why Men Are the Way They Are.* New York: McGraw-Hill.

Feinberg, A. May 1984. "Inside the Entrepreneur." *Venture,* p. 83.

Ferguson, M. 1976. *The Aquarian Conspiracy.* Los Angeles: J. P. Tarcher.

Fetterman, M. February 8, 1991. "How the Myers-Briggs Personality Test Works." *USA Today,* p. B–2.

Foster, R. 1986. *Innovation.* New York: Summit.

Francis, B. 1988. *The Proposal Cookbook.* Minneapolis, Minn.: Microfutures Inc.

Frankl, V. 1959. *Man's Search for Meaning.* New York: Pocket.

Freedman, G. 1988. *The Pursuit of Innovation.* New York: American Management Association.

Gilder, G. 1989. *Microcosm.* New York: Simon & Schuster.

Giovannoni, L., L. Berens, and S. Cooper. 1988. *Introduction to Temperament.* Huntington Beach, Calif.: Telo Publications.

Goldsmith, R. January 1985. "Personality and Adaptive-Innovative Problem Solving." *Journal of Social Behavior and Personality* 1: 95–106.

———. Spring 1986. "Convergent Validity of Four Innovativeness Scales." *Educational and Psychological Measurement* 46: 81–87.

Goodman, P., and Associates. 1982. *Change in Organizations.* San Francisco: Jossey-Bass.

Goodman, P., L. Sproull, and Associates. 1990. *Technology and Organizations.* San Franscisco: Jossey-Bass.

Gould, R. 1978. *Transformations.* New York: Simon & Schuster.

Harmon, F., and G. Jacobs. 1985. *The Vital Difference.* New York: McGraw-Hill.

Hersey, P., and K. Blanchard. 1988. *Management of Organizational Behavior.* Englewood Cliffs, N.J.: Prentice-Hall.

Herzberg, F. 1984. "Where's the Relish?" Buffalo, N.Y.: Creative Education Foundation.

Hill, N. 1960. *Think and Grow Rich.* New York: Random House.

Hirsh, S., and J. Kummerow. 1987. "Introduction to Type in Organizational Settings." Palo Alto, Calif.: Consulting Psychologist Press.

Huffington, A. S. 1988. *Picasso—Creator and Destroyer.* New York: Avon

Hutchison, M. 1990. *The Anatomy of Sex and Power.* New York: Morrow.

Ijiri, Y., and R. Kuhn. 1988. *New Directions in Creative and Innovative Management.* Cambridge, Mass.: Ballinger.

Inc. August 1988. "The Entrepreneurial Personality," p. 18.

International Encyclopedia of the Social Sciences. 1968. "History of Innovation, Entrepreneurship, Creativity, and Biographical Data on Say, Schumpeter, Toynbee." London: McMillan.

Jet. June 16, 1986. "First Borns Score Higher on IQ Tests, Study Shows," p. 31

Josephson, M. 1959. *Edison.* New York: John Wiley and Sons.

Jung, C. 1976. "The Stages of Life." *The Portable Jung.* New York: Penguin.

Kanter, R. 1983. *The Change Masters.* New York: Simon & Schuster.

Keirsey, D. 1987. *Portraits of Temperament.* Del Mar, Calif.: Prometheus Nemesis Press.

Keirsey, D., and M. Bates. 1984. *Please Understand Me: Character and Temperament Styles.* Del Mar, Calif.: Prometheus Nemesis Press.

Kets DeVries, M. 1977. "The Entrepreneurial Personality." *Journal of Management Studies* 14: 25–36.

Kirton, M. 1976. "Adaptors and Innovators." *Journal of Applied Psychology* 61: 639–49.

Klein, B. 1977. *Dynamic Economics.* Boston: Harvard Press.

Kuhn, A. 1982. *The Logic of Organizations.* San Francisco: Jossey-Bass.

Laszlo, E. 1972. *The Systems View of the World.* New York: George Braziller.

Leman, K. 1985. *The Birth-Order Book.* New York: Dell.

Levitt, Jr., A. J., and J. Albertine. August 29, 1983. "The Successfull Entrepreneur: A Personality Profile." *Wall Street Journal,* p. 83.

MacKinnon, D. 1965. "Personality and the Realization of Creative Potential."

American Psychologist, pp. 273–81.

Marzollo, J. December 1990. "What Birth-Order Means." *Parents,* p. 84.

Maslow, A. H. 1971. *Further Reaches of Human Nature.* New York: Viking.

McAleer, N. 1989. "Creativity." *Omni* 11: 44.

Meadows, D. H., D. L. Meadows, J. Randers, and W. Behrens. 1972. *The Limits to Growth.* New York: Signet.

Melrose, L. W. 1987. *The Creative Personality and the Creative Process: A Qualitative Perspective.* University of Georgia Dissertation #DA 8724638. Ann Arbor, Mich.: University Microfilms

Miraca, U. M. Gross. May 1989. "The Pursuit of Excellence or the Search for Intimacy." *Roeper Review* 11: 189.

Moore, T. March 30, 1987. "Personality Tests Are Back." *Fortune,* p. 74.

Morgan, G. 1986. *Images of Organization.* Newbury, Calif.: Sage Publications.

Myers, I. B., and M. H. McCaulley. 1985. *A Guide to the Development and Use of the Myers-Briggs Type Indicator.* Palo Alto, Calif.: Consulting Psychologists Press.

———. 1989. *Contributions of Type to Executive Success.* Gainesville, Fla.: Center for Applications of Psychological Type.

Naisbitt, J., and P. Aburdeen. 1990. *Megatrends—2000.* New York: Morrow.

Neven, T., G. Summe, and B. Uttal. May/June 1990. "What the Best Companies Do." *Harvard Business Review.*

Newsweek. October 2, 1989. "The Innovators—Americans' Creativity." 114: 34–35.

Piesl, A. September/October 1990. "Can a Keiretsu Work in America?" *Harvard Business Review,* p. 180.

Peters, T. 1987. *Thriving on Chaos.* New York: Harper and Row.

Peters, T., and R. Waterman. 1982. *In Search of Excellence.* New York: Harper and Row.

Petrof, J. October 1989. "Entrepreneurial Profile: A Discriminant Analysis." *Journal of Small Business Management,* pp. 13–17.

Quinn, J. May/June 1985. "Managing Innovation: Controlled Chaos." *Harvard Business Review,* pp. 73–84.

Rand, A. 1957. *Atlas Shrugged.* New York: Signet.

Robbins, A. 1986. *Unlimited Power.* New York: Ballantine.

Rogers, T. January/February 1990. "Debating George Gilder's Microcosm." *Harvard Business Review.*

Rose, L. H. January 1984. *Charisma—A Study of Personality Characteristics of Charismatic Leaders.* Athens, Ga.: University of Georgia Dissertation.

Schrage, M. November/December 1989. "Innovation and Applied Failure." *Harvard Business Review,* p. 42.

Shallcross, D., and D. Sisk. 1989. *Intuition—An Inner Way of Knowing.* Buffalo, N.Y.: Bearly Limited Press.

Skousen, M. August 19, 1991. "Roaches Outlive Elephants" (interview with Peter Drucker). *Forbes,* p. 72

Smith, S. 1983. *Ideas of the Great Psychologists.* New York: Harper & Row.

Springer, S., and G. Deutsch. 1989. *Left Brain, Right Brain.* New York: W. H. Freeman.

Stark, E. August 1985. "Birth-Order Bias." *Psychology Today* 19: 13.

Stone, I. 1980. *The Origin.* New York: Doubleday.

Taylor, I. and J. Getzels. 1975. *Perspectives in Creativity.* Chicago: Aldine.

Taylor, W. March/April 1990. "The Business of Innovation." *Harvard Business Review,* p. 97.

Toffler, A. 1981. *The Third Wave.* New York: Morrow.

———. 1990. *Power Shift.* New York: Bantam.

Torrance, E. Winter 1977. "Your Style of Learning." *Gifted Child Quarterly.*

Viscott, D. 1979. *Risking.* New York: Pocket.

Waitley, D. 1987. *Being the Best.* New York: Pocket.

Waitley, D., and R. Tucker. 1986. *Winning the Innovation Game.* New York: Berkeley.

Webb. J., E. Meckstroth, and S. Tolan. 1982. *Guiding the Gifted Child.* Columbus, Ohio: Ohio Psychological Publishing.

Weldawsky, A., and K. Dake. Fall 1990. "Risk in Business Decision Making." *Daedelus* 119 (4): 41.

Whiting, B., and G. Solomon. 1989. *Key Issues in Creativity, Innovation and Entrepreneurship.* Buffalo, N.Y.: Bearly Limited Press.

Wilson, R. 1983. *Prometheus Rising.* Phoenix, Ariz.: Falcon Press.

Yin, R. 1984. *Case Study Research and Design Methods.* Beverly Hills, Calif.: Sage Publications.

Inno-visionary Subjects

In addition to the following references, I have also consulted annual reports, 10Q's, case studies, press releases, and other corporate brochures and founders' biographical profiles, and have personally corresponded with a number of the individuals.

Bernstein, P. July 27, 1981. "Atari and the Video-Game Explosion." *Fortune,* pp. 40–46.

Bilgore, E. 1984. "Nautilus Madcap Muscle Magnate." *Town and Country,* p. 24.

Boyne, W. 1987. *The Smithsonian Book of Flight.* Washington, D.C.: Smithsonian Books.

Bragaw, R. Spring 1990. "The Price Club." *Californian,* p. 23.

Business Week. May, 5, 1986. "Business—The Ultimate Game" (Bushnell article), p. 31.

———. February 13, 1989. "Mr. Smith Goes Global," p. 66.

Butcher, L. 1990. *Accidental Millionaire.* New York: Knightsbridge.

Chposky, J., and T. Leonsis. 1988. *Blue Magic: The People, Power, and Politics Behind the IBM Personal Computer.* New York: Facts on File Publications.

Cohen, S. 1984. *Zap—The Rise and Fall of Atari.* New York: McGraw-Hill.

Conger, J. 1989. *The Charismatic Leader—Behind the Mystique of Exceptional Leadership.* San Francisco: Jossey-Bass.

Corr, C. July 14, 1991. "For Bachelor Software Billionaire, Home Is Where the Gadgetry Is." *The Washington Post,* p. A3.

Current Biography. "Lear, William." 1966, pp. 238–40.

Dewhurst, P. Spring 1981. "Bich-Bic." *Made in France International,* p. 38.

Dodge, J. December 18, 1961. "All the Ski World Loves a Cheater." *Sports Illustrated,* p. 48.

Drucker, P. 1985. *Innovation and Entrepreneurship.* New York: Harper and Row.

Dworken, A. January 3, 1984. "9th Grade Dropout Invented Nautilus Exerciser." *National Enquirer,* p. 11.

Farnsworth, C. December 29, 1972. "Cheap Bic Pen Made Baron Bich Wealthy." *New York Times,*

Forbes. March 1, 1977. "King Lear," p. 74.

———. June 1, 1977. "Howard Head Strikes Again," p. 76.

———. October 22, 1990. "400 Richest People in America," p. 116.

———. November 12, 1990. "200 Best Small Companies in America," p. 212.

Fortune 500. April 22, 1990. "The Largest U.S. Industrial Corporations," p. 338.

Foust, D., and R. King. November 29, 1987. "Why Federal Express Has Overnight Anxiety." *Business Week,* p. 62.

Fucini, J., and S. Fucini. 1985. *Entrepreneurs.* Boston: Hall and Co.

Garrison, P. September 1989. "Mr. Bill." *Flying,* p. 66.

Gentlemen's Quarterly. July 1989. "Tom Monaghan Kneads the Dough." 59: 136–41.

Gilder, G. 1984. *The Spirit of Enterprise.* New York: Simon & Schuster.

Guy, P. January 22, 1991. "CNN Coverage Sparks Demand for Cable." *USA Today,* p. B-1.

Harrigan, C. June 1986. "Arthur Jones Profile." *Echelon.*

Hillkirk, J., and G. Jacobson. 1990. *Grit, Guts, and Genius.* Boston: Houghton-Mifflin.

Hoover, G., and P. Campbell. 1990. *Hoover's Handbook.* Emeryville, Calif.: Publishers Group West.

Inc. October 1986. "Federal Express's Fred Smith," pp. 35–50.

Inc. 500. December 1990. "America's Fastest Growing Private Companies."

Jakobson, C. December 4, 1988. "They Get It for You Wholesale." *New York Times Magazine,* p. 24.

Kahn, J. April 1984. "Steven Jobs of Apple Computer: The Missionary of Micros." *Inc.,* p. 83.

Kahlbacher, W. 1984. "Playboy Interview—Arthur Jones." *Playboy.*

Keller, J., and J. Wilson. October 13, 1986. "Why Zap Mail Finally Got Zapped." *Business Week,* p. 48.

Kennedy, R. September 29, 1980. "I'm Giving Up the Thing World Howard Head." *Sports Illustrated,* p. 60.

Koepp, S. June 10, 1985. "Muscle Man." *Time,* p. 61.

Kroc, R. 1977. *Grinding It Out.* Chicago: Regenery.

Larson, G. December 1976. "Living Legends." *Flying,* pp. 53–57.

Levering, R., M. Katz, and M. Moskowitz. 1984. *The Computer Entrepreneurs.* New York: New American Library.

Levy, S. September 29, 1983. "The Wisdom of King Pong." *Rolling Stone,* p. 107.

Marbaci, W., and P. Abramson. November 15, 1982. "From Atari to Androbot." *Newsweek,* p. 123.

Marlowe, D. November 12, 1990. Akio Morita quote, *Las Vegas Revue,* p. 3D.

Marth, D. July, 1985. "A Driving Force Goes His Own Way" (Arthur Jones). *Nation's Business,* pp. 26–27.

Monaghan, T. 1986. *Pizza Tiger.* New York: Random House.

Morita, A. 1986. *Made in Japan.* New York: Penguin.

Mullich, J. May 1988. "The Price Club." *California Business,* p. 34.

Newsweek. July 14, 1969. "King of the Ballpoints" (Marcel Bich).

———. October 24, 1988. "Steve Jobs," p. 46.

———. June 11, 1990. "Ted's Global Village," p. 49.

Osborne, M. 1983. "Brains, Not Brawn Built Nautilus." *USA Today.*

Peters, T., and R. Waterman. 1982. *In Search of Excellence.* New York: Harper and Row.

Range, B. August 1982. "Morita Interview of Month." *Playboy,* p. 69.

Rashke, R. 1985. *Stormy Genius.* Boston. Houghton-Mifflin.

Rebello, K. January 16, 1991. "William H. Gates III—Playing Hardball in Software Business." *USA Today,* p. 5-B.

Rensin, D. September 1991. "Bill Gates Soft Icon." *Playboy,* p. 134.

Roberts, D. September 1985. "Citizen Jones." *Ultrasport,* pp. 49–55.

Sanders, S. 1975. *Honda, The Man and His Machine.* Boston: Little, Brown.

Schlender, B. October 9, 1989. "How Steve Jobs Linked Up with IBM." *Fortune,* p. 48.

———. June 18, 1990. "How Bill Gates Keeps the Magic Going." *Fortune.*

Shook, R. 1988. *Honda.* New York: Prentice-Hall.

Sigafoos, R. 1983. *Absolutely, Positively, Overnight!* Memphis, Tenn.: St. Lukes Press.

Silver, A. 1985. *Entrepreneurial Megabucks.* New York: John Wiley and Sons.

Smith, D., and R. Alexander. 1988. *Fumbling the Future.* New York: Morrow.

Smith, K. September 1983. "Nautilus Sports/Medical Industries." *Inside Business,* p. 29.

Stern, E. November 1989. *Runners World* (Monaghan), pp. 34–36.

Stevens, M. December 1990. "Revenge of the Nerd." *Inc-M,* p. 80.

Stevenson, H. 1967. "Head Ski Co. Inc." *Case Study for Harvard Business School.*

Strauss, G. December 7, 1990. "Warehouse Clubs Heat Up Retail Climate." *USA Today,* p. B-1.

Time. December 17, 1973. "Youth Will Be Served Honda," p. 100.

———. January 6, 1992. "Man of the Year—CNN's Ted Turner," "The Taming of Ted Turner," p. 34.

Tucker, R. October 1986. "Federal Express's Fred Smith." *Inc.,* pp. 35–50.

Uttal, B. September 1983. "The Lab that Ran Away from Xerox." *Fortune,* p. 97.

———. August 5, 1985. "Behind the Fall of Steve Jobs." *Fortune,* pp. 20–24.

———. October 14, 1985. "The Adventures of Steven Jobs." *Fortune,* pp. 119–21.

Vaughan, Roger. 1978. *The Man Behind the Mouth.* Boston: W. W. Norton.

Waitley, D. 1987. *Being the Best.* New York: Pocket.

Waitley, D., and Tucker, R. 1986. *Winning the Innovation Game.* New York: Berkeley.

Wall Street Journal. January 7, 1992. "Sony Is Turning More Cautious After Reverses," p. B-1.

Whittemore, H. 1990. *CNN—The Inside Story.* Boston: Little, Brown.

Wiegner, K. and J. Pitta. April 1, 1991. "Can Anyone Stop Bill Gates?" *Forbes,* pp. 108–114.

Williams, Christian. 1981. *Lead, Follow, or Get Out of the Way.* New York: Times Books.

Williams, G., and R. Moore. December 1984. "The Apple Story." *Byte,* pp. A67–71.

Young, J. 1988. *Steve Jobs.* Glenville, Ill.: Scott Foresman and Co.

Zachary, P. January 14, 1991. "Video Game Pioneer Tries to Blend Best of Computer, TV." *Wall Street Journal,* p. B-6.

Index